Brownfield Sites IV

Prevention, Assessment, Rehabilitation and Development of Brownfield Sites

WITPRESS

WIT Press publishes leading books in Science and Technology.
Visit our website for the current list of titles.
www.witpress.com

WITeLibrary

Home of the Transactions of the Wessex Institute.
Papers presented at Brownfields IV are archived in the WIT eLibrary in volume 107 of WIT Transactions on Ecology and the Environment (ISSN 1743-3541).
The WIT eLibrary provides the international scientific community with immediate and permanent access to individual papers presented at WIT conferences.
Visit the WIT eLibrary at www.witpress.com.

FOURTH INTERNATIONAL CONFERENCE ON PREVENTION, ASSESSMENT, REHABILITATION AND DEVELOPMENT OF BROWNFIELD SITES

Brownfields IV

Conference Chairmen

E Beriatos
University of Thessaly, Greece

C A Brebbia
Wessex Institute of Technology, UK

International Scientific Advisory Committee

Organised by
Wessex Institute of Technology, UK

Sponsored by
The International Journal of Sustainable Planning and Development

WIT Transactions

Transactions Editor

Carlos Brebbia
Wessex Institute of Technology
Ashurst Lodge, Ashurst
Southampton SO40 7AA, UK
Email: carlos@wessex.ac.uk

Editorial Board

Brownfield Sites IV

Prevention, Assessment, Rehabilitation and Development of Brownfield Sites

Editors

E. Beriatos
University of Thessaly, Greece

C.A. Brebbia
Wessex Institute of Technology, UK

WIT*PRESS* Southampton, Boston

Editors:

E. Beriatos
University of Thessaly, Greece

C.A. Brebbia
Wessex Institute of Technology, UK

Published by

WIT Press
Ashurst Lodge, Ashurst, Southampton, SO40 7AA, UK
Tel: 44 (0) 238 029 3223; Fax: 44 (0) 238 029 2853
E-Mail: witpress@witpress.com
http://www.witpress.com

For USA, Canada and Mexico

Computational Mechanics Inc
25 Bridge Street, Billerica, MA 01821, USA
Tel: 978 667 5841; Fax: 978 667 7582
E-Mail: infousa@witpress.com
http://www.witpress.com

British Library Cataloguing-in-Publication Data

A Catalogue record for this book is available
from the British Library

ISBN: 978-1-84564-105-4
ISSN: 1746-448X (print)
ISSN: 1743-3541 (online)

The texts of the papers in this volume were set individually by the authors or under their supervision. Only minor corrections to the text may have been carried out by the publisher.

Printed in Great Britain by Athenaeum Press Ltd.

Preface

The demand for development land has led to the reuse of properties that have been abandoned for a variety of reasons. Many of them are brownfields, ie sites which have deteriorated in different ways, including by contamination. These sites are usually a burden to government authorities in terms of economic losses and by contributing to the deterioration of the quality of life of entire neighbourhoods. They create enormous social problems in addition to severe land, soil and habitat degradation. The rehabilitation and redevelopment of brownfields and derelict lands in general is one of the first priorities of environmental and spatial planning. The main objective for these sites is to find appropriate new uses and activities, taking into account their economic and social acceptability.

Rehabilitation of brownfields, particularly those which are contaminated can be an expensive undertaking and requires not only technical solutions but the involvement of financial, regulatory and community stakeholders. Fundamental to this process is the analysis of the risks involved and the development of the appropriate strategies. Those need to be weighted against the economic and social benefits of brownfield development, to assess the general viability of the redevelopment. In most cases the demand for development land drives the process forward, while sometimes the rehabilitation is grounded on the wish to restore the landscape and the ecology of a region.

Brownfield development is in many cases essential to attract new business to the locality and for the creation of healthy communities. Therefore, there is a great need for deeper research and study of all aspects of the problem – technical, institutional, financial, social – and an exchange of ideas, know-how and experience among experts and scientists.

This book contains contributions from the participants at the 4th International Conference on Prevention, Assessment, Rehabilitation and Development of Brownfield Sites held on the Island of Cephalonia, Greece in 2008. It follows the success of three previous conferences in this series held in Cadiz (2002), Siena (2004) and Tallinn (2006). The meeting produced an international forum for discussing problems facing the governmental and private sectors in terms of brownfield land available for development. The conference brought together international information, experience and research to provide the knowledge to help revitalise affected communities as well as restore degraded landscapes.

The Editors are grateful to all authors for the excellent contributions published in this volume. They are particularly indebted to the members of the International Scientific Committee and other colleagues who helped in the selection of the papers.

The Editors

Cephalonia, Greece, 2008

Contents

Section 3: Remediation studies and technologies

Section 4: Case studies

Section 5: Risk assessment and management

Section 6: Community and public involvement

Section 1
Rehabilitation of brownfields

Integrating sustainable development and brownfields reuse – principles and practice

C. N. Brooks
President, Greenfield Environmental Trust Group, Inc. (GETG), Watertown, Massachusetts, USA
President, Resources for Responsible Site Management, Inc. (RRSM), Watertown, Massachusetts, USA

Abstract

Sustainable development practices began making their debut in the US at about the same time that brownfields reuse came of age, although both have traveled independent, disconnected paths. Indisputably, reusing brownfields advances the three inter-connected pillars of sustainable development: environment (by remediating threats to public health and the environment), economy (by creating jobs or revitalizing decayed, abandoned areas), and society (by enhancing community pride and security). Furthermore, most agree that recycling land—the fundamental premise of brownfields reuse—does, in fact, represent sustainable development. However, at present there are few meaningful resources or guidelines for the holistic integration of brownfields reuse and sustainable development. Notwithstanding the separation in the policy and practice of brownfields reuse and sustainable development, both areas share many overlapping, similar and recurring issues, strategies and key success factors. The purpose of this paper is to provide an overview of the best practices in brownfields reuse and sustainable development in order to demonstrate the multiple areas of commonality and overlap in both fields. Utilizing the separate lessons learned from brownfields reuse and sustainable development, this paper offers a set of practical, guiding principles and criteria that integrate the best practices of both fields. Ultimately, this paper seeks to place brownfields reuse and sustainable development on a unified, shared path so that brownfields can be redeveloped in a truly sustainable manner.

Keywords: brownfields, redevelopment, sustainable development, best practices, smart growth, LID, green building-development.

WIT Transactions on Ecology and the Environment, Vol 107, © 2008 WIT Press
www.witpress.com, ISSN 1743-3541 (on-line)
doi:10.2495/BF080011

1 Introduction

In the last decade, escalating demand to redevelop contaminated sites has been driven by diverse stakeholder agendas—new jobs, tax revenues, the protection of public health, environmental restoration, a paucity of well-situated sites in high growth markets, efforts to curb sprawl, and pressure to revitalize decayed, urban centers. Today these multi-stakeholder interests continue to dominate the drive to remediate and reuse brownfields, which are estimated to number between 500,000 and 1,000,000 in the United States alone, according to a 2004 report to the US Congress. In fact, the forces pushing brownfields into the limelight have spawned a host of economic and environmental policy programs and created a US market valued at $2 trillion in 2006. More recently, newly emerging values, priorities, markets and technologies have placed brownfields squarely at the center of broader efforts aimed at social, environmental and economic sustainability. The impetus to redevelop brownfields has assumed new urgency as communities, businesses and government grapple with rising energy costs, quality of life issues, societal and market demands for environmentally sustainable developments, and increasingly, global climate change. Brownfields reuse can and should be integrated into sustainable development initiatives, such as smart growth, low impact development (LID), transit-oriented, mixed use villages, infill redevelopment, renewable resource projects and the protection of ecological and rural lands.

That land itself is a renewable resource lies at the heart of brownfields reuse. That brownfields can and should be re-cycled in a holistic, sustainable fashion—satisfying the inter-connected needs of society, environmental and economic capacity—is the fundamental premise of this paper. Typically brownfields reuse is bifurcated, segregated or regulated separately from the techniques and practices of sustainable development. And too often sustainable, "green" developments are built on virgin, "greenfield" land, demanding new supporting infrastructure (even if less than conventional development) with its accompanying destruction of natural resources that might otherwise be preserved.

In the US, a raft of policy initiatives and government regulations either enable or encumber brownfields reuse, while sustainable development practices are either ignored, envisioned but rarely enacted, or pursued by only a handful of public and private interests. As redeveloping brownfields enters mainstream practice, and absent regulatory reform or meaningful institutionalization of a coherent process, it is incumbent on all stakeholders to ensure a sustainable approach to brownfields reuse. This paper presents a set of practical guidelines for the holistic integration of brownfields reuse and sustainable development. Based on prevailing principles, methodologies and key success factors governing both sustainable development and brownfields reuse, it identifies the areas of natural and logical overlap and commonality in the best practices for both fields. Finally, it recommends a set of multi-stakeholder principles for the sustainable redevelopment of brownfields.

2 Brownfields—the challenge and the opportunity

For more than a decade, brownfields have been blamed for countless multi-stakeholder issues: lost value, jobs and tax revenues; unmitigated threats to public health and the environment; and seemingly unlimited financial and societal liability. The four most significant barriers to reuse are: unknown, potentially unlimited liability for expensive clean-ups and lawsuits under US hazardous waste site clean-up laws; time-consuming and expensive remediation requirements under environmental regulations; market perceptions and "stigma" that de-value such sites and raise doubts about whether they can be safely re-used; and the complex transactional and development challenges to reusing such properties (as compared to virgin "greenfield" sites). Since the mid-1990's, when the ubiquitous nature of these sites was first recognized, a host of government initiatives, technologies and innovative financing and development tools have been created to address these barriers to reuse.

2.1 Unknown, unlimited liability

Unknown, unlimited liability has been a threshold issue since 1980 when the US Congress enacted the superfund (superfund refers to the Comprehensive Environmental Response, Compensation and Liability Act (CERCLA)) laws mandating clean-up of the country's most hazardous waste sites under a "polluter pays" principle. Under superfund's 'strict, joint and several' liability scheme, current and past owners, tenants, contractors, transporters and others are named Responsible Parties (RPs) and can be compelled by the US Environmental Protection Agency (EPA) (or its state government counterpart) to pay for and clean-up these sites regardless of how much it costs, how long it takes, or whether they actually contributed to contamination. This onerous liability scheme has had a chilling effect on US real estate: buyers shunned sites with real or perceived potential contamination to avoid RP status; owners chose to 'moth-ball' rather than sell properties for which they had no continuing use to avoid triggering potentially very expensive clean-up obligations if hazards were discovered; and communities were left with idle, polluted sites and their accompanying lost jobs, taxes, health threats and decay. Although many brownfields are not heavily contaminated, the risk of being named an RP made buying, selling or leasing these sites untenable. Sadly, liability concerns extended to very costly "third party" lawsuits where an RP could be sued for human health impacts attributed to contamination at a site (so called "toxic tort" claims) or lost property values due to the migration of contaminants onto nearby land. The result was property gridlock.

State governments responded to this gridlock by adopting "voluntary clean-up programs" (VCPs) whereby buyers and owners could choose to clean-up sites under defined clean-up standards. In exchange, environmental regulators granted assurance and closure that the VCP parties had resolved their liabilities at a site. To date all fifty states have adopted some form of a VCP although programs vary widely from state to state. For its part, in the mid-1990s the federal government, through EPA, launched several programs to address liability, including issuance of Covenants Not To Sue (CNTS) Agreements, later termed Prospective Purchaser Agreements (PPAs), to buyers who had not contributed to site contamination (i.e., "innocent landowners") and were willing to perform certain tasks (related to site remediation) in exchange for a CNTS or PPA. More significantly, after years of wrangling, in 2001 the US Congress passed the Small Business Liability Relief and Brownfields Revitalization Act (SBLR-BRA) which codified a process that relieved innocent landowners of liability under superfund, so long as they complied with specific requirements for property due diligence, known as All Appropriate Inquiry (AAI). During this timeframe, private insurers began developing new insurance products designed to protect purchasers from clean-up cost overruns, future regulator enforcement action and even third party (including toxic tort) claims.

Neither state VCPs nor federal reforms have been a panacea for US brownfields, in part, because they exclude heavily contaminated sites, third party claims, and, with few exceptions, parties that may have contributed to contamination. Also, there are still scenarios under which an entity could be named an RP and thus held liable for exorbitant clean-up costs, especially large corporations (the so-called "deep pockets" often targeted by government regulators) who still lack incentive to reuse idled sites and thus keep them moth-balled. Private insurance also has limitations, including costly premiums and limited 'terms' of coverage. The keys to successfully leveraging these liability protection mechanisms include: "micro-managing" the details before and during the transactional and implementation phases; utilizing the necessary technical and legal experts very early in the process; and partnering with government regulators to achieve a timely outcome.

2.2 Time-consuming, expensive clean-ups

Time-consuming, expensive clean-up requirements, with or without regulator enforcement, contribute to the gridlock keeping US brownfields idle and abandoned. To begin addressing these issues, many state VCPs feature complementary brownfield programs that provide financial, technical and other resources to help reduce the cost and complexity of reusing contaminated land. Financing programs include grants, low-interest loans and tax incentives (abatements, credits, refunds and tax increment financing). VCPs often include established schedules for regulatory approvals that better conform to development needs.

Numerous federal programs have been launched to help address the costs of assessment and clean-up of brownfields. Beginning in the mid-1990s, EPA began offering financial assistance to communities and non-governmental organizations (NGOs) seeking to revitalize brownfields. Passage of the SBLR-BRA increased EPA funding for these programs by up to $200 million per year, covering grants, revolving loans, direct clean-up costs and job training—most of which benefit communities or states seeking to remediate and redevelop brownfield sites. Similarly other federal agencies—US Department of Commerce (DOC), US Department of Housing and Urban Development (HUD),

US Department of Transportation (DOT), Department of Agriculture (DOA), and US Army Corps of Engineers (ACE)—have launched brownfields initiatives aimed at job creation, housing, transportation and infrastructure revitalization and the restoration of rural lands. All programs are designed to infuse critical "public capital" into brownfields to incentivize other stakeholders to participate in redevelopment (i.e., closing the financing gap between brownfield and greenfield sites).

Based on experience, key success factors in utilizing these programs include: (i) structuring multi-stakeholder public-private partnerships that leverage public capital to create value and save costs as an inducement for more risk-averse private investment; (ii) recognizing that those attributes which made a site attractive for use in the first place (infrastructure, access to labor and markets, etc.) often have not changed and leveraging such attributes as part of a site's reuse can save redevelopment costs and enhance eligibility for public funds; (iii) understanding that a community-based approach is critical, not only because land use is governed locally in the US, but also because communities are often the most eligible and preferred recipients of public capital that benefits the panoply of other stakeholders.

One of the most popular reforms for addressing clean-up cost and efficiency is Risk Based Corrective Action (RBCA)—a risk-based approach to managing site contamination. Under RBCA, the level of clean-up is governed by the future use of the property because the nature of such reuse drives the risk to human health and the environment. RBCA entails a scientific assessment of risk posed by specific, on-site contaminants and the likelihood and mechanism by which humans and the environment might be harmed by such contaminants now and in the future (a "risk assessment"). Clean-up goals are based on reducing risk to a level whereby contaminants no longer threaten public health and the environment. For example, a site reused for a playground requires a more stringent clean-up than one redeveloped for light industry. RBCA is often used when technological, practical or economic constraints preclude elimination of contaminants, which are then left on-site. At these sites, the risk-based approach may include an "engineered control" (such as a cap or a fence) to prevent contact with contaminants and an "institutional control" (such as a deed restriction, covenant, or zoning overlay) to provide the legal or administrative mechanism to ensure that the engineered control remains in place and is maintained in perpetuity. Proponents of RBCA argue that it promotes: more efficient clean-ups—focusing on the highest risk issues and avoiding unnecessary mitigation of low risks; greater flexibility in site remediation; consistency in clean-up levels across jurisdictions; and remediation and reuse of sites that might otherwise be ignored by limiting clean-up to the levels required for current and future use of the property. Opponents bemoan the contamination left in-place at many RBCA sites and the lack of reliable mechanisms to ensure that future site users will comply with "institutional controls".

Beyond RBCA, new technologies have also been developed to more effectively, efficiently remediate contamination such as: phytoremediation (remediating with plant systems); bioremediation (remediating with microorganisms or fungi); thermal treatments (using very high temperatures to destroy or facilitate extraction of contaminants); and soil vapor extraction.

Keys to success with RBCA or new remediation technologies include: (i) early identification of and community buy-in to the specific planned reuse in order to focus the risk-assessment on realistic anticipated risk (versus all potential risks for all types of uses—from residential to industrial); (ii) securing early end-user commitments to a site so they can participate in risk management and remediation decisions; (iii) integrating risk management tools and remedial action into the planned reuse for a property (e.g., siting and building parking facilities or building foundations to function as caps on contaminated soil); (iv) analyzing full lifecycle economics that fairly and accurately compare the costs of remediation to the total costs (to all stakeholders) of maintaining, monitoring and enforcing institutional controls; and (v) ensuring long-term preservation of the remedy through proactive community participation in designing clear, unambiguous, enforceable institutional controls because the community will be living with a site long after the other stakeholders have moved on.

2.3 Stigma

Stigma refers to market devaluation and fear of real or perceived contamination at brownfield sites and represents one of the most challenging barriers to site reuse. Stigma operates like a self-fulfilling prophesy in that fear of site's low value and unsafe conditions prevents remediation and reuse, furthering site stigma because unaddressed contamination can and does migrate to surrounding areas just as the decay of a stigmatized site spreads to nearby properties and neighborhoods. Stigma can endure long after a site has been remediated, especially if it posed a real or perceived threat to public health. Sites that have been the subject of extensive litigation, especially around human health issues (i.e., toxic tort), can be difficult to redevelop because the publicity and notoriety of lawsuits creates further stigma and doubt about whether they can indeed be safely reused. Nevertheless, redeveloping highly stigmatized sites can have far-reaching, multi-stakeholder benefits ranging from catalyzing areawide revitalization to creating new real estate value. Based on experience, stigma can be overcome through: multi-stakeholder collaboration on remediation and redevelopment, including goals, expectations and results; meaningful, inclusive stakeholder communications, outreach and education; and public-private partnerships to secure public investment in a stigmatized site that can help convince private investors that a site is safe to reuse and thus catalyze reuse.

2.4 Complex transactional and vertical development issues

Brownfields pose much more complex transactional and vertical development challenges than conventional real estate development. Nevertheless, these sites can be developed for the benefit of public and private interests by utilizing the tools, strategies and techniques outlined above. Several factors critical to successfully navigating these challenges include: vigilant, very detailed management of all phases of the transaction and development; and retention of the necessary technical, legal, financial and communications experts to address these issues in an integrated, multi-disciplinary fashion at the onset of a project.

3 The practice of sustainable development

As an idea, a goal and a mandate, sustainable development means many things to many people. The most common definition—"development that meets the needs of the present without compromising the ability of future generations to meet their own needs," [1]—fuses "environment" and "development". Many have capitalized on the ambiguity in this definition introducing broader or more constrained interpretations of what constitutes "environment" and "development"; thus, concepts like biodiversity, ecosystem renewal, conservation, poverty, justice, equity, and freedom have been added to the meaning of sustainable development. Notwithstanding different terminology and language, most agree that there are three fundamental pillars of sustainable development—economy, environment, and society. Many also can and do accept that sustainable development represents a "condition" or "state of being" (as compared to an outcome) whereby the oft-competing goals and needs of these three global spheres operate in harmony and equilibrium. Practitioners face the unresolved challenge of translating such esoteric concepts into useful, practical paradigms that answer the economic, environmental and societal goals and realities of their specific community in ways that honor their community's inter-dependence and inter-connection to all other communities. In the US, many programs and practices have been adopted in the last two decades to promote the principles of sustainable development. Some of the most evolved, widely known initiatives, their barriers to implementation and key success factors are described hereafter.

3.1 Smart Growth

Smart Growth might be termed a "movement" aimed at curbing suburban and exurban sprawl. It originates at a grass roots level and is legitimized by governmental and institutional programs. Smart Growth seeks to manage growth and its impacts on a particular community in a sustainable fashion. Its focus is on the revitalization of declining urban centers through creation of town-centered, transit- and pedestrian-oriented, mixed use developments with diverse residential, commercial and industrial uses and protected open space and ecological resources. The guiding principles of Smart Growth promote healthy, vibrant, diverse communities that include: mixed land uses; compact buildings; diverse housing options; walkable neighborhoods; distinctive, attractive communities with a strong sense of place; preserved open space, farmland and sensitive environmental areas; strengthened existing communities; transportation choices; predictable, fair, cost effective development decisions; and community and stakeholder collaboration [2]. Smart Growth plans are implemented, in part, by: new or revised local building codes; regulations and zoning laws to promote and incentivize high-density, mixed-used, transit-oriented developments; new approaches and technologies for walkable, compact town-centers and protected natural environments; and public-private partnerships. Smart Growth can be hampered by traditional zoning and local land use laws, which often segregate land uses (separating residential from commercial areas) and create large lots inconsistent with compact, walkable villages or a diverse housing stock. Conflicting, uncoordinated political jurisdictions also impede Smart Growth.

3.2 Green Building and Development

Used here, Green Building and Development (GB&D) refers to the technologies, practices and tools intended to reduce the impact of the built environment on the natural environment (in contrast to "conventional" building and development which is usually a source of new waste and adverse environmental impacts).

3.2.1 Overall goals of GB&D

GB&D is manifested by: principles that recognize the inherent connectivity between a building, its occupants and its environment; and practices set forth in five basic GB&D goals (discussed below): (i) to utilize efficient, renewable energy; (ii) to minimize environmental impacts; (iii) to conserve natural resources; (iv) to enhance indoor air quality; and (v) to engage the community.

3.2.1.1 Efficient/renewable energy resources This is a GB&D goal that seeks to minimize non-renewable and maximize renewable energy resources in the construction and operation of a building or development by: utilizing active, renewable energy technologies (wind, hydro, biomass and geothermal power); integrating passive resources (solar power, natural lighting and natural shading); leveraging prevailing climate and environmental conditions in design and operations; using energy-efficient equipment, appliances and fenestrations; and optimizing the siting, orientation and "envelope" of a building. Some of the government- and NGO-created programs that promote efficient, renewable energy resources in the US include: EPA and US Department of Energy (DOE) ENERGY STAR program which qualifies certain products, appliances and technologies as energy efficient; Sustainable Buildings Industry Council, an NGO dedicated to energy efficient buildings; and DOE's Million Solar Roofs Initiative. Successful application of efficient, renewable energy requires: (i) an integrated, iterative, multi-disciplinary design process; (ii) assembling a team with the requisite expertise committed to realizing a project's energy goals; (iii) analyzing full lifecycle costs (to balance and offset front-end costs with long-term savings); and (iv) multi-stakeholder commitment to and recognition of the value (economic, market, and goodwill) of alternative, renewable energy. Major barriers include: (i) higher initial investment; (ii) lack of organizational and cultural commitment to sustainable energy and awareness of options; (iii) some location and landscape impacts from siting certain facilities (e.g., solar panels, wind turbines) and the resultant NIMBY (Not In My Back Yard) response from host communities; and (iv) industry reluctance to use full-lifecycle costs (compared to traditional pro forma analyses) (NIMBY is the acronym for Not In My Back Yard. The NIMBY Principle refers to a community's response when it opposes the siting of unwanted facilities in their neighborhood, which are objectionable to the residents (such as an incinerator, an airport, a waste disposal facility, a power plant and/or a prison) but may provide needed public or commercial services).

3.2.1.2 Minimizing environmental impacts This is a GB&D objective that strives to minimize disturbance and preserve integrity of the natural environment through a holistic approach that integrates the built environment into its natural surroundings. One of the most widely practiced methods for minimizing environmental impacts is Low Impact Development (LID)—a technology-driven system that emphasizes the value of water resources by focusing on site hydrogeology and the costs of stormwater management. LID uses innovative techniques to store, filter, evaporate and detain run-off by "imitating" a site's natural (pre-development) conditions in order to minimize development stormwater run-off and preserve existing groundwater recharge patterns. LID maintains pre-development flow patterns by minimizing how new impervious surfaces can adversely impact the amount, frequency, and quality of stormwater runoff through small landscape features on individual lots (such as on-lot micro-storage, functional landscaping and grading, open drainage swales, disconnected flowpaths, and bio-retention and filtration areas [3]).

Another technique for minimizing environmental impacts is "natural" or "green" landscaping, which includes planting native species, drought-tolerant plants in arid regions, wind-tolerant plants in high wind areas of a development, and naturally occurring wetland plants in waterways and detention areas. (Examples of green landscaping include planting deciduous trees for summer shade and winter sun or evergreens for windbreaks in north-facing locations—to ensure solar benefits of south-facing areas (Smart Communities Network, www.smartcommunities.ncat.org).)

Some of the keys success factors for LID and/or green landscaping include: (i) an integrated, iterative, multi-functional site design process; (ii) a multi-disciplinary team approach; (iii) multi-stakeholder recognition of water as a resource and full lifecycle costs of stormwater (mis)management borne by direct stakeholders and society; and (iv) effective land use covenants to ensure proper system maintenance in perpetuity. The major barriers are: (i) a dearth of appreciation, recognition or valuation of water as a resource and the total price of stormwater management; (ii) an absence of knowledge or awareness of LID and green landscape techniques and technologies; and (iii) the lack of regulatory or legal incentives.

3.2.1.3 Conserving natural resources This is a fundamental goal of GB&D. It extends across the lifespan of a project (including construction and operations) and encompasses programs such as recycling, waste minimization, material reuse and water conservation. Green roofs (i.e., roofs with plant cover) help conserve natural resources (by lowering cooling costs and preventing heat islands) and minimize environmental impacts (by preventing stormwater runoff, increasing air quality and available habitat). Conservation initiatives represent one of the most cost effective strategies for minimizing operating costs and environmental damage from development. The success of such programs depends on early integration of conservation measures into design and widespread organizational buy-in to and adoption of conservation values. Conservation efforts are often hampered by: prevailing practices and inertia; a lack of financial and regulatory incentives; and misunderstanding as to the true benefits of natural resource conservation.

3.2.1.4 Enhanced indoor air quality This is a goal that is increasingly linked to the health and productivity of building occupants. Because energy-efficient buildings are airtight, they increase the risk of indoor air pollution. Practices adopted to maximize indoor quality, include: using materials and products with low chemical content; and mechanical systems to provide fresh air into buildings and indoor air exchange. The success of indoor air quality programs depends on: (i) early integration of products and systems into development design; (ii) explicit analysis of employee health and productivity gains (fewer sick days, greater productivity, etc.; and (iii) recognition of reduced liability benefits by avoiding "sick building" issues.

3.2.1.5 Community engagement This is a GB&D goal that seeks to integrate sustainable development into the surrounding environment by preserving and protecting community assets—cultural, historical and aesthetic—and incorporating beneficial public amenities (transportation services, pedestrian and bicycle paths, parks and open space). Successful community engagement requires: proactive, inclusive approaches to community participation; clear, early understanding of community goals, needs and expectations; and effective, honest multi-stakeholder dialogue as to how such goals and needs can (or cannot) be met. Barriers include: fear of community participation (and its perceived loss of control); and a lack of appreciation for the broad value of community participation (approvals, incentives and consent).

3.2.2 GB&D for practitioners

The above five GB&D objectives are embedded in broader strategies and programs aimed at promoting sustainable development pursued by various government agencies, NGOs and, to a lesser degree, private interests. Most US GB&D programs are voluntary initiatives designed to incentivize and promote sustainable development, although recently governmental entities have begun mandating GB&D practices in projects that utilize taxpayer funds.

One of the most widely recognized systems and standards for the voluntary pursuit of sustainable development is Leadership in Energy and Environmental Design (LEED) certification, which is administered by the non-profit US Green Building Counsel (USGBC). LEED certification measures the sustainability of a building in a four-level system (Certified, Silver, Gold and Platinum) depending on how many credits are earned in five LEED categories (sustainable sites; water efficiency; energy and atmosphere; materials and resources; and indoor environmental quality). LEED covers new commercial construction, renovation, interiors and building operations. Standards for commercial "core and shell" and new home construction, as well as neighborhood developments are planned.

Overall, successful GB&D practices require: (i) early marshalling of multi-disciplinary resources and expertise to optimize GB&D in an iterative process;

(ii) proactive, inclusive multi-stakeholder dialogue and community partnering; (iii) full lifecycle cost-to-benefit analyses (that ideally include costs to society and the environment); and (iv) organizational culture, priorities and leadership that recognizes the value of "going green" externally (by markets, shareholders and customers) and internally (by employees and host community). Barriers to GB&D include: (i) lack of knowledge and awareness of sustainable strategies; (ii) higher front-end costs; (iii) prevailing industry practices (inertia); (iv) a paucity of data documenting economic benefits (such as reduced operating costs or greater employee productivity); and (v) lack of meaningful regulatory incentives (or penalties) and reliance on voluntary participation.

4 Criteria and guidelines for sustainable brownfields reuse

Despite numerous recurring themes and patterns, brownfields reuse and sustainable development in the US are often pursued along separate, unrelated paths. Yet the processes, strategies and issues attendant to brownfields reuse should resonate with the sustainable development community and vice versa. Indeed the interests of efficiency alone should compel practitioners to consider the shared, overlapping and familiar best practices of both pursuits, despite their fragmented, piecemeal and diverse programs and laws. In fact, the larger quest for global harmony in economy, environment and society mandates explicit fusion of brownfields reuse and sustainable development into an integrated, holistic, mutually beneficial process.

Based on experience, the keys to success for both sustainable development and brownfields reuse include community-engagement and leadership, multi-stakeholder collaboration, public-private partnerships, and multi-disciplinary teams in a front-end loaded, bottom-up, detail-oriented, iterative, incremental process. Specifically, practitioners can begin merging brownfields reuse and sustainable development into a cohesive, integrated process by evaluating, adopting and incorporating the following critical success factors and strategies (not presented in recommended sequence or order of importance):

(1) Early mobilization of critical expertise and resources;
(2) Multi-disciplinary team approach to analysis and decision-making;
(3) Iterative, incremental process (detail orientation and value engineering);
(4) Multi-stakeholder alignments (more inclusive participation);
(5) Public-private partnerships (to leverage public resources for private participation and investment);
(6) Community alliance, collaboration and leadership;
(7) "Begin with the end" (end-use/-user and end goals for environment, economy and society);
(8) Integration of the natural, remediated and built environments;
(9) Full lifecycle economics (assessing long-term costs/benefits and the value of non-economic benefits); and
(10) "Smart Re-Growth" (leveraging location and original site assets for the future)

The above list does not constitute a comprehensive guide for integrating brownfields reuse and sustainable development. It is intended to provide a set of governing principles, best practices and practical strategies to help advance the long-term fusion of brownfields reuse and sustainable development. The issues, challenges, needs and goals are always specific to a particular site, community and the key stakeholders; thus the role, importance and process for application of these strategies must recognize the unique circumstance of each site.

5 Conclusions

Brownfields reuse clearly promotes harmony among the three inter-connected pillars of sustainable development: environment (by remediating threats to public health and the environment), economy (by creating jobs and revitalizing decayed, abandoned areas), and society (by enhancing community pride and security). Experience with the practice of brownfields reuse and sustainable development demonstrates broad commonality in their respective issues and challenges. Yet there are few meaningful resources or guidelines for the holistic integration of brownfields reuse and sustainable development. Faced with a continued absence of policy initiatives, reform programs or new laws that fuse the overlapping needs and goals of sustainable development and brownfields reuse, practitioners can and should begin making brownfields reuse more sustainable by the lessons learned from each field. The best practices outlined here represent a point of entry—a place for practitioners to begin merging brownfields reuse and sustainable development into a shared, cohesive set of principles and best practices—for the mutual benefit of both endeavors. Over the long-term, comprehensive policies, guidelines, programs and regulations will be required to render brownfields redevelopment truly sustainable. Only with such long-term solutions will there be significant, meaningful progress toward the global mandate for true harmony amongst the competing needs of a stable economy, a healthy environment, long-term quality of life and genuine social progress for all communities and stakeholders.

Acknowledgement

Resources for Responsible Site Management, Inc. is the named US Federal District Court Trustee for the Industri-plex Superfund Site Custodial Trust.

References

[1] United Nations World Commission on Environmental and Development, WCED, *Our Common Future,* Oxford University Press, 1987, p. 40. (1987 UN Brundtland Commission)

[2] *Smart Growth Principles,* United States Office of the EPA 231-F-01-001A, Environmental Protection Administrator April 2001, 1EPA Agency (MC 1808), www.epa.gov.

[3] *Low-Impact Development Design Strategies: An Integrated Design Approach,* Prince George's County, Maryland, Department of Environmental Resources, Programs and Planning Division, June 1999.

Brownfield site rehabilitation: a Canadian perspective

K. H. Tiedemann
Applied Economics Consulting and Simon Fraser University, Canada

Abstract

Years of neglect have left a legacy of contaminated and underutilized brownfield sites in Canada, with attendant environmental, social and economic costs. Rehabilitation of brownfield sites has emerged as a major public issue in Canada over the past twenty years. This paper explores several dimensions of the brownfields issue in Canada: the size and nature of the brownfields situation by province; the role and extent of federal and provincial government regulatory activities and financing programs; and the cost effectiveness of brownfields site rehabilitation efforts.
Keywords: brownfield sites, environmental policy, cost effectiveness.

1 Introduction

Rehabilitation of brownfield sites has emerged as major public issue in Canada over the past twenty years. Years of neglect have left a legacy of contaminated and underutilized commercial and industrial brownfield sites. As indicated in the references, a number of studies have explored various aspects of the brownfields situation in Canada, but there have been few attempts to examine the environmental, policy and economic aspects of brownfields in Canada. This study attempts to help fill this gap by exploring the following related issues: (1) estimate the number of brownfield sites by province and characterize these sites; (2) review federal and provincial brownfields policies; and (3) undertake a cost effectiveness analysis of brownfield sites rehabilitation.

2 Canadian brownfields situation

The extent and nature of the brownfield sites situation varies considerably by province across Canada as shown in Table 1, but there are common features

WIT Transactions on Ecology and the Environment, Vol 107, © 2008 WIT Press
www.witpress.com, ISSN 1743-3541 (on-line)
doi:10.2495/BF080021

within each region. Table 1 provides the number of sites in each province, describes the locations and types of sites, and summarizes the causes for brownfield sites in the province.

British Columbia is estimated to have about 200 brownfield sites. The sites are concentrated in the major population centres of Vancouver, the remainder of the Lower Mainland and Victoria. The sites are related to historical poor environmental practices in the primary production industries of coal mining, metal mining, wood processing and pulp and paper production, which have been the historical basis of the economy.

The prairie provinces of Alberta, Saskatchewan and Manitoba together have about 95 brownfield sites. The sites are concentrated in Edmonton, Calgary, Regina, Saskatoon and Winnipeg, but Alberta has a number of significantly contaminated sites due to oil and natural gas production and processing in rural areas. The economies of the prairie provinces have undergone major transformations over the past fifty years, leading to relocation of economic activity away from downtown areas with their railway infrastructure and associated resource processing activities.

Ontario has about 1,500 brownfield sites. They are concentrated in the current and former manufacturing centres of Toronto, Hamilton, Kingston and Cornwall. Industrial development in Ontario occurred earlier than in Western Canada, at a time when little attention was paid to environmental issues. As large multi-story factories became uneconomic to operate, substantial urban areas were gradually abandoned, leaving become a trail of spills, piles of waste and illegal and casual dumping of toxic materials.

Quebec has perhaps 1,000 brownfield sites, second to only Ontario, but it probably has the largest area of brownfield sites. Many sites are along the St. Lawrence River in Quebec City, Trois Riveres, Shawinigan and Montreal. Quebec has suffered a significant decline in its industrial base since 1980, and this has led to a significant expansion in the number and total area of brownfield sites in the province. As is the case for Ontario, industrialization occurred early in Quebec at a time when environmental concerns were not on the public agenda.

The maritime provinces of New Brunswick, Prince Edward Island, Nova Scotia and Newfoundland have a total of perhaps 120 brownfield sites. There are major abandoned industrial operations in Halifax, St. John, St. John's and Fredericton. The Sydney Tar Ponds and Coke ovens may be the single most important toxic site in Canada, in terms of its long term impacts on the health of the surrounding population and the costs of clean up and rehabilitation. In May 2004, the Governments of Canada and Nova Scotia announced a joint ten-year, $400 million program for the ponds.

3 Federal and provincial policies and programs

The management and development of brownfield sites in Canada is affected by policies and programs at the federal, provincial and municipal levels. Table 2 provides information on federal and provincial policies including policies on contaminated sites, fuel tanks, waste generation and financing.

Table 1: Brownfield sites situation by province.

Province	No. of sites	Locations and types	Causes
British Columbia	200	Manufacturing and commercial in larger centres, smelters, wood processing, coal gasification, foundries, galvanizing operations in rural areas	Historical practices of site operators left soil and ground water contaminated, and re- development often requires costly remediation, potential legal liability of new owners
Alberta	50	Across the province, closed service stations, wood preserving facilities, oil and gas facilities	Financial costs of rehabilitation major cause of brownfield sites and population movement to urban areas
Saskatchewan	20	Exclusively urban, abandoned refineries, herbicide plants, scrap metal operations, landfills, National Defense sites	Population movement trends urban areas with consequent abandonment of sites, railway facilities closures
Manitoba	25	Generally urban, abandoned fuel service sites and industrial sites, rural service stations	Historical closure of facilities and environmental accidents with high potential site clean up costs
Ontario	1,500	Urban areas especially in Southern Ontario, coal gas plants, associated industries such as roofing materials, unique examples of steel mills, refining and petrochemical, metal refining	Early industrialization of province occurred at time when environmental sensitivity lacking, urban sprawl led to abandoned industrial and transportation sites, substantial rehabilitation costs to meet environmental legislation
Quebec	1,000	Major urban areas especially along the St. Lawrence River, including mainly abandoned transportation, distribution and industrial sites, including oil refineries, chemical plants and metal works	Historical factors similar to Ontario, decline of industrial activities since 1980 combined with population shifts from urban areas to suburban areas made redevelopment less attractive
New Brunswick	40	Urban areas including industry and service stations	Mainly site rehabilitation costs
Prince Edward Is.	0	No significant sites	No major issues
Nova Scotia	40	Urban areas including rail transportation, industry and service stations, also rural mining sites, Department of Defense sites	Mainly site rehabilitation costs
Newfound-land	40	Urban areas including industry and service stations	Decline of fisheries industrial base, but mainly site rehabilitation costs
Total	2,915		

Sources: NRTEE, Provincial Government Websites.

Table 2: Provincial and federal programs.

	Contaminated sites	**Fuel tanks**	**Waste generation**	**Financing**
British Columbia	Voluntary reporting, risk-based clean up guidelines	No registry	Mandatory registration and filing	Some financing, especially for infrastructure costs
Alberta	Reporting for spills, voluntary reporting others	Mandatory registration	Mandatory registration and filing	-
Saskatchewan	Voluntary reporting, risk-based clean up guidelines	Mandatory registration and filing	Mandatory registration	-
Manitoba	Voluntary reporting, risk based clean up guidelines	Mandatory registration	Mandatory registration and filing	-
Ontario	Voluntary reporting, spills mandatory, risk-based clean up guidelines	Mandatory registration	Mandatory registration and filing	Some financing, especially for infrastructure costs
Quebec	Mandatory registration, risk-based clean up guidelines	Mandatory registration for large tanks, small tanks exempt	Mandatory registration and filing	Quebec-Canada program for orphan sites and Revi-Sols program
New Brunswick	Mandatory reporting, risk-based clean up guidelines	Mandatory registration of tanks > 2000 L Mandatory registration of waste oil tanks	Mandatory registration and filing	-
Prince Edward Is.	Mandatory reporting, risk-based clean up guidelines	Mandatory reporting for underground tanks	Mandatory registration and filing	-
Nova Scotia	Mandatory reporting of pollutant release, risk-based clean up guidelines	Mandatory reporting for underground tanks > 2000L, above ground tanks > 4000 L	Mandatory registration and filing	Provincial funding for limited major sites
Newfoundland	Mandatory registration	Mandatory registration and filing	Mandatory registration	-
Government of Canada	Canadian Environmental Protection Act is primarily a registration and information mechanism	-	Canada Fisheries Act pertains to discharges to water bodies	$475 M through March 2008 for Federal Contaminated Sites, Green Municipal Funds

Sources: NRTEE, Provincial Government Websites.

The Government of Canada has encouraged public consultation at the federal level in the development of legislation and regulation. The Canadian Environmental Protection Act Environmental Registry provides a comprehensive source of information related to activities under the Act. Discharges into water bodies are regulated under the Fisheries Act, while emissions into the air are regulated under the Clean Air Act. Federal funding efforts are substantial, but they are largely limited to the management of federal contaminated sites. In the 2004 Federal Budget, $3.5 billion was committed for clean up of federal sites and $500 million was committed for shared liability sites. In the 2004 Federal Budget, $50 million was committed for the Green Municipal enabling fund (which provides grants for cost-shared feasibility studies, brownfields development plans and environmental site assessments) and $200 million was committed for the Green Municipal Investment Fund (which established a permanent revolving fund for innovative environmental infrastructure projects), with both funds administered by the Federation of Canadian Municipalities.

The provinces and municipalities have the prime governmental responsibility for the management and development of brownfield sites. These governments generally see their roles as primarily regulatory and advisory, and they usually hold the private sector financially and legally responsible for clean up and development. Private sector responsibilities typically entail: (1) assessment of soil and water quality; (2) undertaking remediation efforts in accordance with provincial criteria for the specific intended use; (3) making provision for future financial liabilities; and (4) financing and implementing the project. In some circumstances, provincial authorities will order private owners to assessment and remediation of a contaminated site. The provinces maintain various disclosure, reporting and filing requirements. Generally, these requirements include mandatory reporting for spills, toxic sites, fuel tanks and generation of wastes and contaminants. As Table 2 indicates, there is a patchwork quilt of regulatory and voluntary requirements across the provinces.

Provincial and municipal financial support for brownfields development is quite limited outside of the Province of Quebec. In 1998, the Government of Quebec established the Revi-Sols (Revitalize Soils) program to promote brownfields development. Phase I (1998-2003) provided $40 million to help finance study and rehabilitation of contaminated sites at Quebec City and Montreal, while Phase II provides $50 million for other municipalities in the province. The other provinces and some municipalities offer tax and financial support on case-by-case basis.

4 Site rehabilitation cost effectiveness

In this section, we examine the cost effectiveness of brownfields site rehabilitation using a case study approach. The sites were selected based on three criteria: first, rehabilitation and redevelopment work should be either completely or largely completed; second, there should be detailed information on the site, its pre-habilitation condition, the new uses of the site, rehabilitation costs and construction costs; and, third, the set of cases should cover the range of geographic areas, initial site conditions and final uses in Canada.

We apply a simplified cost-effectiveness framework in which site rehabilitation activities are undertaken to make it possible to use the site for residential, commercial, industrial or mixed uses. Investors wish to minimize the costs of rehabilitation while maximizing the commercial value of the site. It is natural then to compare the rehabilitation costs with other investment costs as a measure of the cost effectiveness of rehabilitation. We also attempt to estimate the impact of rehabilitation cost of the internal rate on return (IRR) on invested capital. A review of various company reports and the relevant literature suggest that the IRR is typically about 12% on commercial and industrial investments and about 8% on residential investments in Canada. Differences in the rates of return reflect the perception that commercial and industrial investments are riskier than residential investments and so require a risk premium in the form of a higher rate of return.

Table 3 summarizes some key dimensions of the ten brownfields rehabilitation cases. These dimensions include site description and new use of the site; former use of the site and its environmental condition before rehabilitation; site cleanup and rehabilitation costs; other investment costs including construction, services and project planning and management; and estimated IRR.

The sites range considerably in size from three acres to 9,000 acres, with an average size of 959 acres. Removing the very large Voisey's Bay site, the average size is just under 100 acres, which appears to be larger than the typical area for the typical case study reported in the literature, which is often in the less than 10 acre range. Average cleanup costs per site are $26 million, or about $20 million per site without the Voisey's Bay site. Average development costs, exclusive of the cleanup costs, are $809 million per site, or $565 million without Voisey's Bay. Cleanup costs are thus about 3.1% of the combined cleanup and development costs, but the range of cleanup costs to total costs varies from 1.2% for the Cobourg, Ontario site to 55.2% for the Shawinigan, Quebec site. Estimated rates of return inclusive of cleanup cost are generally fairly reasonable, above 7.5% for most residential projects and above 11.0% for most commercial/industrial projects. The two projects where cleanup costs have apparently significantly reduced the rate of return are the Shawinigan project and the first of the two Vancouver projects.

5 Conclusions

Years of neglect have left a legacy of contaminated and underutilized brownfield sites in Canada, with attendant environmental, social and economic costs. Rehabilitation of brownfield sites has emerged as a major public issue in Canada over the past twenty years. This paper has explored several dimensions of the brownfields issue in Canada: the size and nature of the brownfields situation by province; the role and extent of federal and provincial government regulatory activities and financing programs; and the cost effectiveness of brownfields site rehabilitation efforts.

Table 3: Site clean up and development costs, selected sites.

Site Description and New Site Use	Former Use and Initial Site Condition	Site Area	Cleanup Costs	Develop Costs	IRR
Moncton, New Brunswick Industrial and commercial park, some residential housing, recreational	CN Rail repair shops; numerous soil contaminants, including petroleum hydro-carbons and metals	285 acres	$15 M	$200 M	11.2%
Voisey's Bay, Newfoundland Nickel plant, and other industrial and commercial	Canadian Forces military base and ERCO Phosphorus Plant; multiple contaminants	9,000 acres	$81 M	$3,000 M	11.7%
Shawinigan, Quebec Shopping mall	ICI chlor-alkali, solvent plants; mercury, organo-chloride compounds	3 acres	$16 M	$13 M	5.4%
Montreal, Quebec Light industrial and commercial, residential dwellings, recreational	CP Rail shops; heavy metals, petroleum hydro-carbons, polycyclic aromatic hydrocarbons	309 acres	$12 M	$474 M	11.3%
Toronto, Ontario Commercial and mainly residential with up to 20 high rise buildings	CN Railways site; metals, heavy metals, petroleum hydro-carbons, and other contaminants	45 acres	$35 M	$1,500 M	7.8%
Hamilton, Ontario Commercial and mainly residential	Bertram Steel Foundry; creosote, foundry sand, PCBs, hydrocarbons	12 acres	$2 M	$94 M	7.8%
Cobourg, Ontario Residential and recreational	Cobourg Ore Port and petroleum storage; heavy metals and petroleum hydrocarbons	10 acres	$2 M	$162 M	7.9%
Cornwall, Ontario Commercial and mainly residential	Canada Cotton Mills complex with several multistory buildings; contaminated soil, oil in bunkers	12 acres	$0.5 M	$20 M	7.8%
Vancouver, British Columbia Commercial and mainly residential and recreational	Sawmilling, metal works, foundries, shipbuilding, salt distribution; metals, asbestos, old fuel	50 acres	$30 M	$123 M	6.4%
Vancouver, British Columbia Commercial and mainly residential	Harbour, railway, coal gasification; heavy metals, creosote, coal tar	163 acres	$70 M	$2,500 M	7.8%
Average	-	989 acres	$26 M	$809 M	8.5%

Sources: NRTEE, City of Vancouver, Voisey's Bay, Johnson.

The federal, provincial and municipal governments in Canada have been seeking ways to mitigate the environmental, social and economic impacts of these sites. However, compared to the United States and Western European countries, responsibilities for the regulation and development of brownfield sites in Canada are fragmented and dispersed. In particularly, the federal government has a strong fiscal position but limited responsibilities for brownfields cleanup and rehabilitation, while the provincial and municipal governments, with the exception of oil rich Alberta and British Columbia, have poor fiscal positions but carry the main responsibilities for brownfields rehabilitation and development. This has meant that some cities with strong real estate markets, such as Toronto and Vancouver, have been able to redevelop brownfield sites with relatively little government planning, regulatory or financial support, but this is not a universal situation for all Canadian cities.

Escaping from this dilemma will require phased and integrated action on several fronts. First, there is an urgent need to create a comprehensive and usable database for brownfield sites. Several cities have begun to apply a risk-based land-use approach to database development, and this needs to be implemented by those Canadian cities with major brownfield sites. This is a complicated task, and it might be useful to focus first on larger sites. Second, the main barriers limiting and constraining brownfields development need to be addressed. The most important of these barriers for most cities are financial and liability issues, and while Vancouver and Toronto have made major strides in rehabilitating prestige sites, the comprehensive collaborative management and financing approach pioneered by the Government of Quebec could serve as a useful model for other provinces. Third, the case studies indicate that cooperation between municipalities and private developers, with some support from higher levels of government, can lead to integrated and viable brownfields development. Genuine public consultation, integrated planning which builds on stakeholder needs, and realistic choices on land use which support required rates of return appear to be crucial elements in generating timely brownfields site redevelopment.

References

[1] De Sousa, C.A., 2006, "Urban brownfields redevelopment in Canada: the role of local government," The Canadian Geographer, 50(3).

[2] Bergman, B. and J. Dumont, 2002, "Fouling our cities," Maclean's Magazine.

[3] Bartsch, C., R. Deane and B. Dorfman, 2001, "Brownfield State of the States: An End-of-session Review of Initiatives and Program Impacts in the 50 States, Washington: Northeast-Midwest Institute.

[4] U. S. Environmental Protection Agency, 2002, Small Business Liability Relief and Brownfields Rehabilitation Act 2002, Public Law 107–118, H. R. 2869.

[5] National Round Table on the Environment and the Economy, 1998, State of the Debate: Greening Canada's Brownfield Sites, Ottawa: National Roundtable on the Environment and the Economy.

[6] Desousa, C., 2001, "Contaminated sites management: the Canadian situation in international context, Journal of Environmental Management, 62(2).
[7] Benazon, N., 1995, "Soil Remediation: a practical overview of Canadian cleanup strategies and commercially available technologies," Hazardous Materials Management, 7(5).
[8] National Round Table on the Environment and the Economy, 1996a, Contaminated Site Issues in Canada Ottawa: National Roundtable on the Environment and the Economy.
[9] National Round Table on the Environment and the Economy, 1996b, The Financial Services Sector and Brownfield Redevelopment, Ottawa: National Roundtable on the Environment and the Economy.
[10] National Round Table on the Environment and the Economy, 2003, Cleaning Up the Past, Building the Future, Ottawa: National Roundtable on the Environment and the Economy.
[11] Hara, D., 2003, Market Failures and the Optimal Use of Brownfield Redevelopment Policy Instruments, paper presented to the Canadian Economics Association 37th Annual Meeting.
[12] Government of Canada, 2005, Federal, Provincial and Territorial Framework for the Management of Contaminated Sites in Canada, accessed at www.ec.gc.ca/etad/cswg/pub/fed_frame/en/toc_e.htm.
[13] Ford, G., D. Macdonald and M. Winfield, 1994, "Who pays for past sins? Policy issues surrounding contaminated site remediation in Canada," Alternatives 20.
[14] Therrien, R., 1995, "Canadian contaminated land policy," Chemistry and Industry, 13.
[15] Villemaire, R., 2001, "An urban recyclable: brownfield redevelopment as smart growth," Economy & Technology Journal of Canada.
[16] City of Vancouver, 2006, Southeast False Creek Redevelopment: Property Development Fund Pro Forma Update, Administrative Report, A10.
[17] Voisey's Bay Nickel Company Ltd., 2007, Overview of the Long Harbour Nickel Processing Plant.
[18] Johnson, E., 2001, "Brownfields across Canada," CBC Marketplace, Accessed at www.cbc.ca/consumers/market/files/environ/brownfields.

Brownfields revitalization: it's all about choices

S. O'Malley
Director of Economic Development, City of Derby,
Vice Chairman, Regional Brownfields Partnership,
Chairman, Comprehensive Economic Development Strategy for the Lower Naugatuck Valley of Connecticut, USA

Abstract

It can be said of New England and specifically the towns and cities that make up the Lower Naugatuck Valley ("the Valley") that these communities have almost made a complete circle back to the rivers and sites along those rivers that once created and supported great wealth and thriving communities. The towns and cities that have seen decline in employment, lack of developable land and a reduction in population have experienced regression, in part, because of the decline in manufacturing jobs, the difficulties faced with redeveloping contaminated properties, and the enormous task of restoring the rivers and parcels of land along those rivers to usable sites for economic growth and prosperity.

When addressing brownfields issues, most municipalities face a steep learning curve. Part of the educational process is looking back on the history of these sites and understanding the role they played in forming thriving communities and the potential role they play today in economic development. How does a municipality, once again, realize potential and capitalize on the very sites that spurred economic growth in the 19th and early 20th centuries in the United States? To realize the benefits of revitalizing these areas, economic developers and municipal officials need to focus on the factors that contributed to past successes and appreciate how economies were driven by the factories and mills that dotted the Lower Naugatuck Valley in order to realize the benefits of revitalizing these areas. Taxpayers need to understand the critical role these industries played (and can play) in helping to increase the tax base. Allowing these sites to remain fallow will further contribute to the problems already facing these communities. Municipal officials need to feel comfortable in spending taxpayer dollars on sites that, at first glance, seem to offer little hope. Successful buy in from the elected officials leads to successful buy in from the community and, more often than not, will result in a very positive outcome. The charge for the professionals is to raise money, build partnerships, find skilled technicians and learn the basics of the environmental assessment process. We will explore methods of reviving brownfield sites through a summary of available direct and indirect funding options and creative solutions for municipalities. It is important to understand that the revitalization and restoration of these sites is cyclical and essential to the resurgence of a community's economic growth and prosperity.
Keywords: funding sources, redevelopment, creativity.

WIT Transactions on Ecology and the Environment, Vol 107, © 2008 WIT Press
www.witpress.com, ISSN 1743-3541 (on-line)
doi:10.2495/BF080031

1 Rivers: the lifeblood of the valley

The early settlers had both beauty and utility in mind when they settled in the Valley. The six communities that make up the Valley today are Ansonia, Derby, Oxford, Beacon Falls, Seymour and Shelton. Surrounded on three sides by gently rolling hills, the Valley is a place where businesses and industries thrived. Earning its reputation as an industry-rich area where the economy of towns and cities pivoted around several copper, brass, and rubber factories, heavy-machinery manufacturers, and metalworking plants. The smokestacks that jut up into the sky along the Housatonic and Naugatuck Rivers were a sign of the Valley's successful economy.

In the 1600s water power was essential for commerce and for industry. Derby, in particular was the hub at which the two largest rivers in the Lower Valley met. To the northwest was the 160 mile long Housatonic River, which leads up into western Massachusetts, and to the northeast is the Naugatuck River, which flows for 40 miles into the interior of Connecticut. The two rivers converge in Derby and cut a wide swath for 13 miles down to the Long Island Sound.

In the 1800s waterpower was used from the rivers for manufacturing and industrial communities that developed along the Naugatuck and Housatonic Rivers. Attracted by abundant waterpower, industrialists quickly built factories and the Lower Valley joined what was considered to be the Industrial Revolution. Between 1836 and 1891 businesses grew to accommodate industry and their growing number of employees. Communities that grew up along the rivers were designed to support industrial, commercial and residential buildings. Ansonia and Derby, in particular, were devoted primarily to the manufacturing of rolls and heavy machinery for five major industries, rubber, plastics, metals, cane sugar and paper. Factories grew at an almost geometric rate along the rivers. During the Industrial Age in America, every town or city that had water power to turn a factory wheel became a manufacturing community and their products were used for sale to foreign markets.

2 The remnants of the industrial age

The Lower Valley received the most serious insult from the commercial operations; the contamination/pollution of our rivers and waterways due to the disposal of industrial waste. By the late 1800s, smaller iron, brass, steel and copper factories that were prevalent throughout the Valley, gave way to larger, mass produced enterprises. The Lenox Glass Works (along the Housatonic River) was the largest factory in the world under one roof.

"Today, what is left of the big building is a flattened and filled foundation beside the railroad and the river.....What remains of its machinery is sometimes grotesquely visible in the river, where it was jettisoned." Smith [1]

Shortly thereafter, heavy industries that clung to the riverbanks where they originally obtained water power were dying out. In the Years after World War II, manufacturing employment declined nearly 9% in the Valley. Unemployment in the Valley rose well above 10% and remained that way, standing at 17% in the early 1980s.

The Valley continues to struggle with the after-effects of the early industrial activities as evidenced by the numerous, abandoned and underutilized sites along these waterways. Most communities in Connecticut and especially those in the Valley are small and every acre is of considerable economic value. The lack of space forces communities to focus attention on revitalization efforts. Economic development professionals in older urban areas struggle to rebuild their tax base with limited space. Abandoned or underused industrial and commercial facilities can provide additional space and an avenue towards a higher tax base if the obstacles involved in reusing abandoned sites can be overcome.

3 Rise from the rubble

The decline of the industrial age and the decline of manufacturing in New England led to an exodus of large manufacturers who created and then ultimately left environmental problems in their wake.

Robert LeFevre, a local historian wrote 'There are only two sources from which all the difficulties we face arise. There are difficulties caused by nature and there are difficulties caused by man' (Cawley et al [2]). The only sure way to eliminate the difficulties caused by man is for municipalities to begin to understand what got us to this point and to understand the choices available to reverse the contamination and redevelop these once prosperous and desirable locations.

3.1 How to navigate the solutions for redevelopment

The difficulties facing communities with multiple brownfields sites involve complex solutions and the fix often requires a demonstrated and well orchestrated commitment of public and private resources. It is critical that municipal developers understand federal, state and local support can provide a good portion of the necessary resources for cleanup funding. Just as the waterways defined, early on, our role in the economic climate, these waterways can also be potential sources of funding for the abandoned sites that were built up around them. According to a study done by the U.S. Housing and Urban Development (HUD) agency, the number one obstacle to redevelopment of brownfield sites are the cleanup costs (including assessment, remediation, and legal expenses) and their relationship to the total project costs. This dominates all other factors as an investment deterrent.

3.2 Where is the money?

For smaller communities, the sources of funding are as numerous as the problems created by brownfields. In 1994, the U. S. Environmental Protection Agency (EPA) made its first three federal grants with a pilot program called the Brownfields Economic Redevelopment Initiative designed to return idle or underused industrial and commercial facilities back to productive use, in situations where redevelopment had been complicated by potential environmental contamination. The brownfields program was intended to make old industrial sites more attractive to new industrial users and to overcome the reluctance of prospective developers to move in because of the fear of incurring future environmental liability, i.e., "buying into a problem." EPA's initial pilot was successful in that it motivated communities and developers to restore the sites, incorporating the efforts of lenders, regulators, and others. The cyclical revitalization of the sites along the river ways could once again begin to create jobs, improve the local economy, generate more tax income and stimulate property values.

In the Valley's older manufacturing towns and cities, most economic development effort centers on these abandoned sites, thereby creating the need for multiple alternative funding sources. Funding sources must be as abundant and diverse as the communities that are in need of assistance. In order to realize beneficial redevelopment of a brownfields site, municipalities and communities must realize the endless possibilities for direct and indirect assistance.

Support for EPA's efforts and the brownfields concept comes from a wide array of states and localities, environmental groups, business, developers, and community activists. Communities have the potential to leverage federal, state, and private funds to improve the environment by addressing low-level, low-risk contamination that might otherwise lay dormant. The brownfields program was established administratively EPA under the aegis of the Superfund program. Superfund is the federal government's principal program for cleaning up the nation's contaminated waste sites and protecting health and the environment from releases of hazardous substances. Since the inception of EPA's pilot program, the program has expanded to include brownfields assessment grants, revolving loan fund grants to help finance the actual cleanups, job training grants, technical and financial assistance from approximately 20 participating federal agencies Since EPA's initial program, many federal agencies have followed suit including, the U.S. Department of Defense, U.S. Health and Human Services, U.S. Small Business Administration, U.S. Department of Commerce, U.S. Department of Transportation, Economic Development Administration, U.S. Department of Education and coordination with state, local and non-governmental efforts.

Most states provide incentives for participating in voluntary cleanups through some form of liability release or third-party liability protection. Other incentives include a streamlined process, financial or tax incentives, and technical assistance. Voluntary clean up programs do not typically focus on redevelopment and they don't specifically target urban sites, however, they help get simple less contaminated sites remediated regardless of whether they are reused. Brownfields programs focus on redevelopment and can be part of a broader State or municipal strategy aimed at improving urban areas. The State of Connecticut has also demonstrated its commitment to the revitalization of brownfields by creating a task force that has improved and updated the state's brownfields legislation, creating increased flexibility, mirroring the innocent landowner legislation of the federal government and creating an Office of Brownfields

Remediation consisting of the Connecticut Department of Environmental Protection, Connecticut Development Authority, and the Connecticut Department of Economic and Community Development. Connecticut and other States use voluntary cleanup grants to capitalize a revolving loan fund, or to develop a risk sharing pool, an indemnity pool, or insurance mechanism for providing financing for response actions.

4 Downtown redevelopment in the valley: a variety of choices

At the end of an industrial era that once defined the Valley, every town and city along the Naugatuck and Housatonic Rivers is looking to recreate its downtown. The Valley's downtowns consists of older, abandoned, industrial buildings requiring environmental assessment money to determine the level and extent of contamination before any movement can be made.

In the case of the City of Shelton, situated on the Housatonic River with a population of approximately 40,000, a well-known developer leveraged private funds to acquire a former asphalt plant. The site acquisition and work associated with its environmental cleanup and demolition is roughly estimated at $6.6 million. This will make room for the creation of energy efficient green buildings that serve as upscale condominiums. This new population of condominium owners has generated new economic growth. Additionally, the City of Shelton was able to receive federal assistance from the U.S. Economic Development Administration (EDA) due to sudden and significant job loss, which then spurred on job growth in other areas of the City that had been abandoned due to contamination and the migration outward of a large company. The City rebuilt a portion of its downtown, creating a greenway and farmer's market, which in turn generated additional activity.

Beacon Falls, a small town on the Naugatuck River, was able to take a Transportation and Community Systems Preservation Program (TCSP) grant from the U.S. Department of Transportation and create a gateway into their downtown area. They have attracted visitors and have transformed a once desolate and contaminated area into a recreational area. A portion of Beacon Falls redevelopment funds were used to continue a walkway along the Naugatuck River that will attract more pedestrians to its commercial district on Main Street. Funding for Beacon Fall's river walk came from EPA and the Connecticut Department of Environmental Protection.

The City of Waterbury, the 5th largest City in Connecticut, located along utilized U.S. Department of Defense brownfield funding to clean up an abandoned military facility once used to make ammunition for the war efforts and transformed the site into a generous mall that has helped increase the grand list, employ hundreds and helped to alleviate the burden of high property taxes.

The City of Ansonia, located adjacent to Derby and the Naugatuck River received U.S. Federal Emergency Management Agency Funds to revitalize a contaminated site that had burned down. In Ansonia's downtown there is a brand new Target store, which generates hundreds of thousands of dollars in tax revenue for the City annually on the site of this former mattress manufacturing building.

The City of Derby will restore its downtown with transportation money from the U.S. Department of Transportation and the State Department of Transportation for two major road projects in the region. One of these projects (a portion of Route 34) is located on Main Street in Derby and is adjacent to the City's downtown redevelopment area. Connecting streets can be enhanced with additional street grid funding can be sought through discretionary money from the U.S. Department of Transportation, dovetailing on the major road improvement projects. Enhancements to this road make the downtown extremely desirable to the thousands of cars and trucks that pass by daily. The City will use its Small Cities money from the U.S. Department of Housing and Urban Development and the Connecticut Department of Economic and Community Development for façade improvements to the local businesses in the downtown area – some of the buildings are old and dilapidated and this money will help generate interest and attract customers, U.S. Economic Development Administration (EDA) funds will be used to open up access to a vacant lot owned by the City and create an industrial park near the downtown area, Clean Water funds will be used to repair and replace aging infrastructure and add new sewer and water lines and state urban act funds will be used to help knock down blighted buildings. Additionally, the City of Derby has a tax district. Special tax districts are created to resuscitate blighted areas, freeze the amount of property-tax money going to local governments and divert any new money to local redevelopment projects. The City of Derby also has an Enterprise Corridor Zone that provides additional tax incentives to the developers in the downtown area. Derby is also looking to clean up and create open space in a contaminated area that will serve as open space and a new boat dock that will attract new residential development. All of these creative ideas will help to recreate a thriving new downtown for Derby.

Once the level of contamination and the extent of contamination are determined and the proposed reuse decided upon, then a plan must be established to create a funding mechanism to help redevelop the site. Ideally, most cities and towns would like their downtowns to be thriving mixed use centers that draw people from all over. Depending on the plan for redevelopment, multiple funding sources exist and often there are numerous opportunities for creative uses of those funds. Many sites require major infrastructure improvements that will need a number of private, federal and state options. Utility costs in these sites can be reduced by working cooperatively with the local gas and electric companies to help defray the initial development expenses. Energy efficient projects and "green" buildings are additional sources of money saving techniques. Enterprise Zones and Enterprise Corridors established through the State of Connecticut offer tax rebates and abatements helping defer cost of development and serving as additional incentives. In many cases, road improvements must be made to accommodate increased traffic in sites where redevelopment is taking place. These road improvements will most likely be funded through State, federal and municipal programs and can be designed in such a way as to make economic development more affordable because it improves visibility, increases parking and makes improvements to existing property along the roadways. A community can also incorporate some of its pre-existing enhancements to complement brownfields redevelopment. A greenway, for example, draws visitors into the downtown area and increases awareness of a City's or Town's attractive characteristics.

5 Conclusions

5.1 New options on the horizon

New ways to address brownfields are continually being developed. For example, EDA will make brownfield sites eligible for certain grants and will establish a demonstration program for "brightfield sites" which are defined as brownfields redeveloped using solar technologies.

In addition to state, city and community representatives, EPA has developed cooperative relationships with other federal agencies and created the Interagency Working Group on Brownfields, with staff from more than 20 federal agencies and the Interagency Steering Committee to share knowledge on economic redevelopment, environmental principals, and to develop a comprehensive, coordinated federal approach to local communities. With EPA's efforts leading the way and other agencies following suit on both the federal and state levels, the possibilities for redevelopment are endless. There is renewed hope and interest in these once great manufacturing sites. There is cooperation, problem solving, and creative solutions that are returning these sites to productive reuse.

In short, there are many options available to municipal developers, including, but not limited to tax incentives, utility incentives and reductions depending on the size of the project, lead abatement funding, energy efficiency programs, and various other incentives and programs. These tools are available to assist the many cities and towns that are dealing with the economic stresses associated with living in post industrial communities, including aging infrastructure, failing bridges and roadways, high unemployment rates, crowded schools, blight and crime. It takes commitment, creativity and a desire to reinvent your community.

References

[1] Smith, Chard Powers, The Housatonic River, Rinehart & Company: New York, N.Y., p.366, 1946.

[2] Cawley, James and Margaret, Exploring the Housatonic River and Valley, A.S. Barnes, South Brunswick, N.J. p. 43, 1978.

Challenges for brownfield regeneration: a comparison of English and Japanese approaches

N. Otsuka[1] & H. Abe[2]
[1]*Department of Real Estate and Construction, School of the Built Environment, Oxford Brookes University, UK*
[2]*Department of Global Architecture, Graduate School of Engineering, Osaka University, Japan*

Abstract

This paper explores comparative implications for brownfield regeneration in Japan and England. Concern for brownfield regeneration in Japan has been developed with a strong emphasis on averting environmental risks from contaminated land, rather than on seeking beneficial reuse of brownfield. In contrast, the UK government strategically worked on mitigating such negative views on brownfields and UK urban policies have acted as a key driver for promoting brownfield as a development opportunity. The paper seeks to reveal the contextual differences in the ways of understanding the term 'brownfield' between Japan and England. Historically the Japanese government has a tendency to consult the UK government's planning policies for the purpose of establishing new policy frameworks for emerging urban issues. Thus, the key question to be addressed through this paper is to what extent the English approach is adaptable to the Japanese context.
Keywords: brownfield regeneration, urban policy, UK-Japan comparison.

1 Introduction

In the rapid movement towards deindustrialisation in Japan since the 1990s, the regeneration of the post-industrial brownfields has been gradually recognised as a key agenda by policy makers, developers and researchers. The term 'brownfield' has started to be used in Japan by referring to relevant research papers and government policy documents in countries such as the UK and the

WIT Transactions on Ecology and the Environment, Vol 107, © 2008 WIT Press
www.witpress.com, ISSN 1743-3541 (on-line)
doi:10.2495/BF080041

USA, which have longer experience in tackling brownfield sites. However, researchers who introduced the study of brownfield regeneration in the UK and the USA [1, 2] reported rather descriptive case evidence from these countries without a clarification of contextual differences between Japan and those countries. For the purpose of establishing new policy frameworks for emerging urban issues, few research papers have discussed extensively the contextual differences and commonalities between urban issues in Japan and the UK.

This paper explores comparative implications for brownfield regeneration in Japan and England. The key question to be addressed through this paper is to what extent the English approach is adaptable to the Japanese context. There appeared to be fundamental differences in the government policies and public perception regarding brownfield between the two countries. Concern for brownfield regeneration in Japan has been developed with a strong emphasis on averting environmental risks from contaminated land. The Japanese approach assumes a close link between brownfield and contamination, and hence results in conveying negative implication for the management of brownfield sites. In contrast, the UK government worked strategically on mitigating such negative views on brownfields, and UK urban policies have acted as a key driver for branding 'brownfield' as a development opportunity rather than as planning problems [3]. The UK's positive approach towards brownfield regeneration has been further fostered by a relatively buoyant property market and the growing demand for new houses, especially in southern England [4].

The rest of the paper identifies firstly definitions of brownfield in the two countries and then explains the evolution of government strategies and policies on brownfield agendas. Subsequently, key drivers and barriers for promoting brownfield regeneration are compared. The final section concludes and discusses future research issues.

2 Definition of 'brownfield'

In England, it is widely recognised that not all brownfield is contaminated. According to Alker *et al* [5], the term 'brownfield' emerged rather as the opposite of 'greenfield'. However, it was a fact that brownfield historically conveyed negative connotations and was often used interchangeably with the term 'contaminated land'. 'Contaminated land' is defined by the *UK Environmental Protection Act 1990* (Section 78Q (2) of Part II A), which was primarily concerned with health risks and thus with identifying any land considered to be in conditions where: (a) significant harm is being caused or there is a significant possibility of such harm being caused; or (b) pollution of controlled waters is being, or is likely to be, caused. While the 'contaminated land' was clearly defined for the purpose of regulating contamination and averting environmental risks through land remediation, there was a lack of a universally agreed or accepted definition of brownfield during the 1990s. This resulted in producing different interpretations of brownfield among not only various stakeholders, but also in government legislative documents, which led to misunderstanding and confusion [5].

Therefore it was extremely important for the UK government to stimulate brownfield development in the process of changing negative perceptions, rather than just tackling specific technical land contamination problems [6]. Over the last decade academics as well as government policy makers have debated the definition of brownfield; it is now recognised as land or premises which have been previously developed, whether contaminated or not [7]. The UK government has now defined brownfield as previously developed land (PDL), '*which is or was occupied by a permanent structure, including the curtilage of the developed land and any associated fixed surface infrastructure*' [8]. PDL has become the basis for the statistics collected for the NLUD (National Land Use Database), which was launched in 1998 to make assessment of important redevelopment opportunities for such land, particularly residential development potential [3]. In 2005, some 63,490 hectares of land in England were categorised as brownfield land, and it should be emphasised that the fact of contamination was not represented in this data. As Adams and De Sousa [3] maintained, UK policy emphasis was placed not on the reasons why land became vacant or derelict, but rather on the processes by which it might be put to beneficial uses.

In contrast, the concept of brownfield in Japan seems to have mostly evolved with a strong emphasis on identifying the causes for it being vacant or derelict, in other words, risk aversion has been the main concern. Unlike in England, brownfield is a relatively new concept among urban issues in Japan, which has been gradually brought to the fore since the introduction of the *Soil Contamination Countermeasures Act 2003* (SCCA). The Act was the first legislation to provide a set of indicators to measure soil contamination for the purpose of preventing adverse effects on public health, and was largely drawn from the USA's approach to contaminated land. Consequently, the focus was placed on ways of tackling the soil contamination rather than on proposing beneficial uses on brownfield sites. A recent publication by Japan's Ministry of the Environment (MoE) uses the definition of brownfield as '*lands which are unused or with extremely limited use compared to their intrinsic value because of existence or potential existence of soil contamination*' [9]. The report stated that a small number of lands had been turned into brownfield in Japan since the history of applying soil contamination countermeasures was relatively short [9]. According to Yasutaka [10], only 1 or 2 per cent of potentially contaminated sites had been investigated under the SCCA. However, the actual existence of such land was predicted to be substantially high, and the study carried out by MoE estimated that about 113,000 hectares of land assets had soil contamination, thus having the potential to turn into brownfield [9].

MoE's main concern was the negative effects caused by the increasing number of land investigations of potentially contaminated land under the SCCA [9]. Once land is revealed as brownfield, whether the land appears to be contaminated or not, the revelation has a negative influence on land sales and impedes appropriate management for future use. Furthermore, the process of 'turning into brownfield' inevitably forces stakeholders to confront hostile and unfamiliar environmental issues [9, 10]. Under such negative implications associated with brownfield, there seems to be not much room for promoting brownfield as an opportunity area for future redevelopment in the Japanese context. It has become clear that the ideas of brownfield in Japan and England are considerably different.

3 Government strategies and policy frameworks

There are a number of economic, environmental and social barriers intrinsic to brownfield, which would hinder the process of transforming brownfield to beneficial uses. Without government intervention, it seems likely that brownfield sites would not be competitive compared with greenfield [11]. This section starts by explaining the UK government's strategies for promoting brownfield regeneration. Then the current state of the Japanese government's approach to brownfield is discussed.

It can be said that the UK government strategically placed brownfield regeneration as a key delivery mechanism for a new urban renaissance. Since the New Labour government came to power in 1997, urban renaissance has been promoted as the core concept for disseminating the government's commitment to the revitalisation of British cities [12]. Like many other developed countries, the de-industrialisation of the 1980s and 1990s forced many cities to rapidly restructure their economic bases from heavy industry to the emerging, non-manufacturing, knowledge and service based sectors [13]. As a part of the government's response to this, the Urban Task Force (UTF) was established in the late 1990s to propose strategies for the regeneration of such post-industrial sites. The UTF recommended a fundamental urban renaissance in order to attract people back to urban centres through the promotion of urban living and working [14]. Subsequently, the UK government published planning guidance to local authorities, the *Planning Policy Statement 1: Delivering Sustainable Development* [15], which sets out core principles for the planning system to bring vacant and underused previously developed land and buildings back into beneficial uses [6]. Thus *brownfield was promoted as an ideal platform* on which to create sustainable environment and communities. For the regeneration of brownfield, the government encouraged adaptation of certain ideas of sustainable urban forms such as high density, mixed-use development, good urban design, and energy efficient buildings and infrastructure [16]. Along with the regeneration of sustainable urban fabrics, it was argued that brownfield-led regeneration would be effective in bringing a range of socio-economic groups together into the newly revitalised urban sites. [17].

The UK government's approach to brownfield regeneration has been further reinforced by recent housing policies. Considering the high demand for new houses in the UK, it is not surprising that there appeared to be a strong linkage in policy terms with the emphasis on brownfield regeneration and the need for new housing on such sites [18]. It was 1998 when the government firstly announced that 60% of new housing should be provided on PDL and through the conversion of existing buildings by 2008 [19]. A team from the Department of Communities and Local Government (DCLG) and English Partnerships prepared a discussion paper [20] to address the key policy issues and the rationale for prioritising the reuse of brownfield lands. Furthermore, the recent Housing Green Paper [21] re-emphasised plans for delivering a large number of new homes (2 million new homes by 2016 and 3 million new homes by 2020). According to ODPM's provisional estimate in 2006, 73% of new dwellings were built on PDL (including conversions) in 2005, compared with 56% in 1993 [19]. In England, negative implications of brownfield seem to have been largely diminished and the presence or potential existence of contamination in such sites has been treated as a secondary issue.

In comparison to the UK, Japan seems to be far behind in establishing government strategies and policies on the regeneration of brownfield sites. The Japanese government's approach to the revitalisation of urban areas officially started with the establishment of the Urban Renaissance Headquarters in 2001, which was led by the then Prime Minister, Mr. Koizumi. The *Urban Renaissance Special Measure Law* was launched in 2002, and the basic policies for urban renaissance were drawn up identifying the priority urban development areas for injecting extensive investment 'in order to implement the revitalisation of urban areas in a prioritised manner' [22]. In this way, responses to urban problems derived from the rapid changes in the socio-economic conditions (e.g. decline in birth rate and de-industrialisation) could be efficiently addressed since regeneration funding was planned to be concentrated on priority cities where population, industries and other activities had concentrated [23]. Additionally, use of Private Finance Initiatives (PFI) was proposed to encourage the private sector to lead urban regeneration projects in order to decrease the public sector's financial burden and to support the process of economic recovery from recession since the 1990s. These approaches appeared to be highly economy-driven and property-led regeneration, which seems to be a reflection of the Thatcher government's key strategies (e.g. Urban Development Corporations and PFI) in tackling urban decline and economic recessions during the 1980s.

The economic recovery was the key agenda for the Japanese government in the early 2000s. Although sustainability related issues such as negative effect of urban sprawl and traffic congestion in urban centres were briefly mentioned in the policies [22], sustainability agendas were not placed as the key player for urban renaissance in Japan. Brownfield or previously used land (PDL) would be considered to meet one of the designation standards for categorising the priority urban redevelopment areas – 'areas with heavy industries and others, which led the period of high economic growth, and have the potential for large-scale conversion in land usage' [22, 24]. Hence, it is possible to argue that brownfield has a potential to be promoted as a development asset. However, in realty, brownfield has been viewed as a planning problem due to potential high remediation costs, complications in the development process and post-remediation stigma. Despite the fact that the *Soil Contamination Countermeasures Act 2003* (SCCA) offered some degree of financial support for undertaking investigations and suggested economical ways of managing contaminants (e.g. containment), policies for risk management of brownfield in general, do not seem to be well established. Furthermore, unlike in England, the shortage of housing is not a critical problem in Japan, and there has been lack of evidence to persuade developers to explore appropriate land uses on brownfield sites. Unless the Japanese government commits to the promotion of brownfield sites with a strong emphasis on urban renaissance agendas, it is almost impossible for brownfield to compete with 'clean' land and greenfield.

4 Key drivers and barriers for brownfield regeneration

The previous sections identified the contextual differences in understanding brownfield as a term and a political agenda between England and Japan. This section summarises key drivers and barriers for brownfield regeneration in the two countries (Table 1).

Table 1: Key drivers and barriers in England and Japan.

	England	Japan
Drivers	• Government policies (sustainable development and housing) • Corporate Social Responsibility • Strong lobbies for protecting greenfield • A relatively buoyant property market	• Lack of drivers is the problem
Barriers	• Regional differences: more brownfield in North-West England • Physical constraints: complex ownership, contamination, lack of infrastructure • Shortage of expertise (lack of skills)	• Limited acceptance for remediation methods: expensive 'dig and dump' is the mainstream • Stigma associated with brownfield: difficulty in communicating risk management to local communities • Lower awareness of greenfield protection. • Recession for the last 10 years

4.1 Key drivers

In England, without doubt, the ultimate driver for brownfield regeneration is the government policies on creating sustainable communities and housing development on PDL. Research carried out by Dixon [18] suggested that the majority of developers in the UK have increased their output on brownfield over recent years and the main reasons for this were 'government policy' and 'availability of land'. This implies that the government policies worked effectively in bringing brownfield sites forward for smooth development. Furthermore, a relatively buoyant property market encouraged developers to view brownfield regeneration as an 'opportunity for profitable development' [18]. In addition to the government policies, Corporate Social Responsibility (CSR) appeared to be another driver for developers. In the rise of sustainability agendas in the UK, a number of investors and developers started launching their own environmental policies to demonstrate their commitment to addressing the development impacts on environment and society. Finally, it should be stressed that there have been strong lobbies for protecting greenfield. Traditionally the containment of urban expansion has been always in place [25], which acted as a strong driver for the reuse of brownfield. There has been a clear correlation between the government interest in brownfield redevelopment and the extent of public and political concern about environmental protection of the countryside [3]. For example, such environmental groups as Campaign to Protect Rural England (CPRE) [26] have a powerful influence on the evolution of national planning policies, which further pushed developers to turn to brownfield sites.

In contrast to those key drivers in England, there is lack of incentives for brownfield regeneration in Japan. Not only does the government not have comprehensive policies on brownfield, but also Japan seems to be short of other rationales to demonstrate immediate benefits of reusing PDL. Neither CSR nor protection for greenfields has been at the front line of debate over the future urban environment in Japan. Severe economic recession since the 1990s has been another cause for not exploring opportunities in the regeneration of difficult sites such as brownfield.

4.2 Key barriers

In England, a full body of literature exists discussing various constraints on bringing brownfield forward to beneficial use. Three main points are summarised here. Firstly, regional differences between north and south raise serious planning issues in England. Brownfield is disproportionately concentrated in northern regions where property markets are traditionally weak, whereas there is a lack of readily available brownfield sites in southern regions where shortage of new houses are critical [3]. The second element consists of physical constraints including complexity in land ownership, and time and cost implications for the remediation and lack of infrastructure. The third factor is shortage of appropriate professionals who will champion stakeholders of a brownfield project [3, 20]. Nevertheless, although brownfield regeneration is still perceived as adding complexity, over 10 years of experience have brought some degree of confidence for stakeholders in England.

On the other hand, in Japan, there are a number of obstacles in the process of brownfield regeneration. Firstly, due to fear of health risks associated with contamination, only 'dig and dump' has been widely accepted for the redevelopment of brownfield. The SCCA applied a multifunctional approach for decontamination to contaminated land, thus standards for remediation were set to satisfy all types of end uses. Unlike England, Japan is bound to a limited number of remediation methods, which are comparatively expensive and environmentally unfriendly. Furthermore, stigma associated with brownfield seems to be much more significant than in England. According to a questionnaire survey of 9,000 medium-large enterprises (response rate 41%), 65% of the respondents answered that they would not purchase the real estate if there were a history of contamination [9]. Developers and end-users both are unwilling to get involved in brownfield development. Finally, Japan's lower awareness of rural protection should be noted. Historically, urban sprawl happened without much planning control and effectively there are not many voluntary or charity organisations to protect rural sites from greenfield development.

5 Conclusions

This paper revealed the fundamental differences between England and Japan in understanding the term 'brownfield', in the government policy frameworks, and in incentives and obstacles for promoting the regeneration of brownfield.

The paper identifies a number of barriers for promoting brownfield regeneration in Japan. It may be practical for the Japanese government to learn from the UK government strategies that successfully reversed negative associations of brownfield by promoting it as a development asset by reforming planning policies. It is also not surprising to see a number of recent visitors from the public sectors in Japan to study English approaches to brownfield regeneration. Although there is urgent need for the Japanese government to establish a mechanism for re-branding brownfield as a development opportunity, there is a question to be addressed in advance – to what extent are the English approaches adaptable to the Japanese context? The present paper attempts to explore the possibilities of adaptability by discussing the contextual differences and commonalities between the two countries based on secondary sources and a series of discussions carried out by two English and Japanese academic institutions (Oxford Brookes and Osaka Universities). Yet, further research is required to answer the question including primary investigations.

For international comparison it is important to look at not only physical differences, but also at the cultural motivations and institutional frameworks of each county [3]. In our personal observation, Japanese people seem to be vulnerable to risks from health hazard caused by artificial disasters while they are comparatively resilient to natural disaster such as earthquakes. This kind of hypothesis can only be verified by using research methodologies based on not only the field of built environment, but also social anthropology. Brownfield is a subject that requires a wider range of knowledge integrated from various disciplines. In the UK and European contexts, multidisciplinary research consortia on brownfield issues such as SUBR: IM [27] and RESCUE [28] have been established. In Japan, there is a need to extend brownfield issues from narrowly defined environmental investigation (i.e. risk aversion and remediation) to wider socio-economic research agendas. As a final remark, it should be emphasised that there may be potential for English developers and consultancies to explore their business opportunities in Japan since brownfield regeneration is a relatively new and emerging policy agenda in Japan.

Acknowledgement

This paper is based on a research project that is funded by the Daiwa Anglo-Japanese Foundation and the Great Britain Sasakawa Foundation in the UK.

References

[1] Kurose, T. & Murayama, A., Strategy for brownfield redevelopment on local cities in the US. Case studies of cities in New England. *Summaries of technical papers of Annual Meeting Architectural Institute of Japan. F-1,*

Urban planning, building economics and housing problems, Vol.2006 (20060731), pp. 223–224, 2006.

[2] Miyagawa, T. & Nakayama, T., Comparison of national acts on treating land contamination in Japan, The Netherlands, Germany, and the UK: Study on approaches to treat land contamination and redevelopment of brownfields Part 1, *Journal of architecture, planning and environmental engineering. Transactions of Architectural Institute of Japan,* No.547, p.177–183, 2001.

[3] Adams, D. & De Sousa, C., Brownfield Development: A Comparison of North American and British Approaches. *European Urban Research Association Conf. 'The Vital City'*, University of Glasgow, 12–14 September 2007.

[4] Dixon, T., Pocock, Y. & Water, M. An analysis of the UK development industry's role in brownfield regeneration. *Journal of Property Investment and Finance*, 24(6), pp. 521–541, 2006.

[5] Alker, S., Joy, V., Roberts, P. & Smith, N., The definition of brownfield. *Journal of Environmental Planning and Management*, 43(1), pp. 49–69. 2000.

[6] Raco, M. and Henderson, S., Sustainable urban planning and the brownfield development process in the United Kingdom: Lessons from the Thames Gateway. *Local Environment*, 11(5), pp. 499–513, 2006.

[7] Ganser, R. & Williams, K., Brownfield Development: Are We Using the Right Targets? Evidence from England and Germany. *European Planning Studies*, 15(5), pp. 603–622, 2007.

[8] Department for Communities and Local Government (DCLG), *Planning Policy Statement 3 (PPS3): Housing*, HMSO: London, 2006.

[9] Ministry of Environment (MoE), *Current status of the Brownfield Issue in Japan, Interim Report*, MoE: Japan, 2007. http://www.env.go.jp/en/water/soil/brownfields/interin-rep0703.pdf

[10] Yasutaka, T., *Qualification of economical and social effects from the soil contamination and its solution*, unpublished PhD thesis, Yokohama National University: Japan, 2007.

[11] Thornton, G. & Nathanail, P., Are incentives for regenerating UK brownfield sites sustainable? *Land Contamination & Reclamation*, 13 (4), pp.327–338, 2005.

[12] Imrie, R. & Raco, M., *Urban Renaissance?* The Policy Press: Bristol, 2003.

[13] Department of Environment, Transport and Regions (DETR), *Our Towns and Cities - the Future: Delivering an Urban Renaissance*. London, The Stationery Office, 2000.

[14] Urban Task Force, *Towards an Urban Renaissance*, E&FN Spon: London, 1999.

[15] Office for Deputy Prime Minister (ODPM), *Planning Policy Statement 1: Delivering Sustainable Development,* HMSO: London, 2005.

[16] Dair, C. and Williams, K., Sustainable land reuse: the influence of different stakeholders in achieving sustainable brownfield developments in England. *Environment and Planning A*, 38, pp. 1345–1366, 2006.

[17] Raco, M., Henderson S. & Bowlby, S., Delivering Brownfield Regeneration: Sustainable Community-Building in London and Manchester (Chapter 6). *Sustainable Brownfield Regeneration*, ed. T. Dixon *et al*, Blackwell Publishing, Oxford, pp. 119–139, 2007.
[18] Dixon, T., Integrating sustainability into brownfield regeneration: rhetoric or reality? An analysis of the UK development industry. *Journal of Property Research*, 23(3), pp. 249–279, 2006.
[19] Dixon, T. & Adams, D., Housing Supply and Brownfield Regeneration in a post-Barker World: Is There Enough Brownfield Land in England and Scotland? *Urban Studies*, 45 (1), pp. 115–139, 2008.
[20] English Partnerships, *Brownfield Strategy, Policy Consultation Workshop*, Discussion paper: Policy issues and outline proposals, English Partnerships: London, UK, 2006.
[21] DCLG, Homes *for the future: more affordable, more sustainable*, The Stationery Office: London, 2007.
[22] Prime Minster of Japan and His Cabinet, *Basic Policies for Urban Renaissance*, 19 July, 2002, http://www.kantei.go.jp/foreign/policy/tosi/kettei/020719kihon_e.html
[23] Izumi, H. Urban Renaissance in Japan, Urban Renaissance in Japan. Paper presented at *Seminar on Urban Renaissance in the UK and Japan*, The Daiwa Anglo-Japan Foundation: London, 22 September 2004.
[24] Kenmochi, I. & Yamagata, S., *Issues of urban regeneration and land valuation for contaminated land*, 2003,http://www.earth-app.co.jp/files/200310AcademicConference.pdf
[25] Ward, S. V., *Planning and Urban Change*, 2nd Edition, Paul Chapman Publishing: London, 2004.
[26] CPRE (Campaign to Protect Rural England), http://www.cpre.org.uk
[27] SUBR:IM (Sustainable Urban Brownfield Regeneration: Integrated Management), http://www.subrim.org.uk/
[28] RESCUE (Regeneration of European Sites in Cities and Urban Environments), http://www.rescue-europe.com/html/project.html

Section 2
Development issues

Brownfield identification: different approaches for analysing data detected by means of remote sensing

V. Ferrara
Department of Electronic Engineering,
University of Rome "La Sapienza", Italy

Abstract

This paper aims to show different techniques for identifying brownfields and for monitoring based on remote sensing. If brownfields are associated with urban wastes such as the demolition of buildings, dangerous materials or contaminants will be involved with them. Hazard and health risks increase, so the administration policy needs to detect, at an early stage, dangerous materials or contaminants and to manage the cleaning and recovery of these land areas. A detailed classification of the land and the identification of these typologies of brownfields can be carried out by means of hyperspectral remote sensing using the airborne MIVIS (Multispectral Infrared and Visible Imaging Spectrometer) sensor of the Laboratory of CNR (LARA). Thanks to MIVIS, we can detect many different materials. The subsequent integration of data into GIS allows identification of brownfields through our specific software tools that determine the contours of objects and evaluate the statistical parameters of the processed images. Moreover, other GIS tools correlate data in order to evaluate the extent and derivative parameters of the same brownfields. When brownfields are associated with urban or sub-urban abandoned industrial properties or a land with neglected vegetation, i.e. with the evident characteristic of land abandoned or under-used; then the previous method is useless. These brownfields are missing specific hazardous substances or contaminants and buildings and are generally in good condition. For these last cases, an alternative process should be implemented. A higher geometric resolution than MIVIS should be used, putting in evidence small objects in the soil and so IKONOS or QuickBird satellite imagery are required. In this case, brownfield identification will be carried out by means of object-oriented algorithms and the mutual relationship between them.

Keywords: monitoring, multispectral sensors, MIVIS, IKONOS, QuickBird, GIS.

WIT Transactions on Ecology and the Environment, Vol 107, © 2008 WIT Press
www.witpress.com, ISSN 1743-3541 (on-line)
doi:10.2495/BF080051

1 Introduction

The identification and location of brownfield areas are essential processes to help authorities implement their environmental policies. The recovery of those urban and suburban zones actually abandoned or underused decreases health risks when brownfields include hazardous substances. The process of mapping the roofing material and the detection of hazardous substances represent the first step to assessing the risk level, which is related to the study area under examination. Furthermore, when disused structures such as parking lots, commercial or industrial buildings, industrial hangars, etc., are detected, their recovery can turn the planning of administrative resolutions into economical advantages. In effect, brownfields of urbanized sites, where the network of utility structures are already in place, can be restored to productive use both from an environmental and economic viewpoint, thanks to the lower soil use. On one hand, the investigation must be concerned with the detection of hazardous material, and on the other in the individuation of disused buildings (or land areas now abandoned). In order to detect each specific target, one should acquire different images. This depends on economical convenience and on technical aspects: the required spatial resolution, the elaboration techniques of data, data correlation and specific software algorithms.

In our previous work, Atturo *et al.* [1], we showed a method for hazardous substances detection. That is realized from the Laboratory LARA (Airborne Laboratory for Environmental Research) of the Italian National Research Council (CNR) by means of the airborne MIVIS (Multispectral Infrared and Visible Imaging Spectrometer) sensor. Results of this activity are combined with software post-elaborations delimiting brownfield areas of crumbling buildings and urban wastes. GIS (Geographic Information System) tools then correlate the relevant data in order to evaluate extension and derivative parameters of the same brownfields [10]. These parameters are important for the elaboration of indicators that can be used within the framework of sustainable planning and development.

A procedure that identifies different types of areas, such as abandoned car parks, uses satellite imagery to a high spatial resolution, such as Quickbird, IKONOS and SPOT. Typically, the procedure compares data collected by consecutive images that produce significant indicators, such as the status indicator of neglect. Obviously, both preventive location and boundaries individuation of the area under examination should be carried out. The tools of many GIS can resolve the last problem, often by the semi-automatic mode.

All processes based on remote sensing (included airborne sensors) have advantages when both periodic investigation of large areas and automatic or semi-automatic analysis are implemented. The cost of these images is comparatively high, but the multiuse of the applications in different scientific fields of environmental management can reduce their economic burden. Administrative authorities investigate different environmental aspects such as traffic, bus line networks, air pollution, planning, etc. On the other hand the evaluation of brownfield recovery needs the knowledge of correlated data.

Frequently the easiest means of detection of these is by remote sensing. So, a relevant image can be used for the evaluation of several parameters and indicators. Multispectral images with different resolutions must be elaborated before using them in classification and correlation techniques.

GIS adding further data for each specific location, identified by a pixel of the image, allowing multidimensional processes. If GIS is open to external tools, like Terrapack® [3–6], algorithms can be experimented to find new solutions for better identification of substances or structures in automatic/unsupervised mode.

The results of this work show progress in our procedure for finding sites. At first, we will present the procedure based on the classification of hazardous substances and brownfield detection. Later on, we will examine another process whose design lines are: structure detection, definition of category of everyday use, evaluation of usage continuity, brownfield identification according to its use degree.

2 Hyperspectral classification

Thanks to the collaboration of researchers of the Italian National Research Council (CNR), in our previous work [1] we presented the hyperspectral classification technique. We refer to that article for fuller details. This paper reviews only the essential parts.

MIVIS is an airborne platform system included in the LARA Project (Airborne Laboratory for Environmental Research) of CNR. It consists of a modular scanning system that operates with a high spectral and geometric resolution (for instance, precision at soil 4 m x 4 m from 2000 m of altitude). It uses four spectrometers and 102 spectral bands within the 0.43 μm and 12.7 μm wavelengths (from visible to thermal infrared spectrum). This large number of spectral bands allows analysis of both chemical and physical parameters of the Earth's surface. In effect the process bases itself on the spectral signature concept. So, relevant classification characterizes many ground features such as vegetation, bare soils, building structures, road paving, wastes and so on.

The retro-diffused energy coming from the atmosphere towards the sensor can be important; consequently these effects of atmosphere are corrected by using IRC (Internal Radiometric Calibration) [13].

Owing to the detection methods of a remote sensing system, which varies several observation parameters (frequency, polarization and incidence angle of the scenes), many and different effects must be decreased. Specifically, alignment problems, contrasts equalization and compensation of the effects of high frequency attenuation. Radiometric correction and data conversion are realized at ground level by means of the MIDAS (Multispectral Interactive Data Processing and Analysis System) station.

A supervised classification technique called Spectral Angle Mapper (SAM) allows us to optimize the similarities (in terms of "angle") existing between image spectra and reference spectra [7]. The latter can be defined either in the laboratory or in the field or extracted interactively from the imagery.

In order to classify the whole area, some training areas or reference spectra resulting from specific "Regions Of Interest" (ROIs) or spectral databank are fixed as inputs of the SAM algorithm.

Integration of the hyperspectral data in GIS is the last step of the process. It allows the superimposition of morphological, chemical and physical features on the geographical maps. This integration is fundamental for the data interpretation by means of interactive reading.

3 Brownfield: wear state of structures

When the brownfield consists of buildings in a state of wear, it is likely to require the identification of hazardous substances. They stand out owing to collapsed roofs and walls. Obviously the presence of hazardous substances isn't a peculiar characteristic of a collapse: in a lot of towns and cities there are buildings still inhabited with asbestos-cement for example. So, a different indicator should be evaluated, one linked to the geometrical aspect of area.

The presence and expansion of this brownfield can be risky involving environmental contamination; consequently the investigation on their location and identification should assume a higher priority in the administration policy.

Mapping of the roofing material and the detection of hazardous substances are the first steps to evaluate the risk level of the area under examination. Remote sensing classification techniques, such as hyperspectral classification, allow the identification of risk of large areas.

In order to provide a more accurate risk level assessment, interpretation of remotely sensed data must always be associated to in situ measurements. A calibration is often decisive in distinguishing among different kinds of situation.

After territorial classification by means of hyperspectral remote sensing detection, recognition of brownfield should ensue from a series of consecutive and derivative steps: discrimination between brownfield and habitable structures, extension evaluation, possible risk assessment, nearness evaluations and so on.

Imagery of airborne remote sensing is correlated to others providing a more detailed recognition and a lower uncertainty of the geometric features. These other images are normally originated from a different source and frequently have a different resolution, they are geo-referred as remote sensing images and so overlaid over the same area.

3.1 Brownfield identification

Collapsed buildings and waste lands show irregular contours of the structure together with discontinuities of the surface coverings. A remote sensing in the Visible spectrum allows us to evaluate these irregular geometrical features. Nowadays, three-dimensional maps [2,11] are available. They are the best inputs for software tools that show buildings pulled down. However, their use increases the cost. The process described in this paper makes use of two-dimensional maps only. They are more common and are already included in the midst of hyperspectal data. Sometimes a better resolution could be used and new geo-referred images acquired, but at a lower cost.

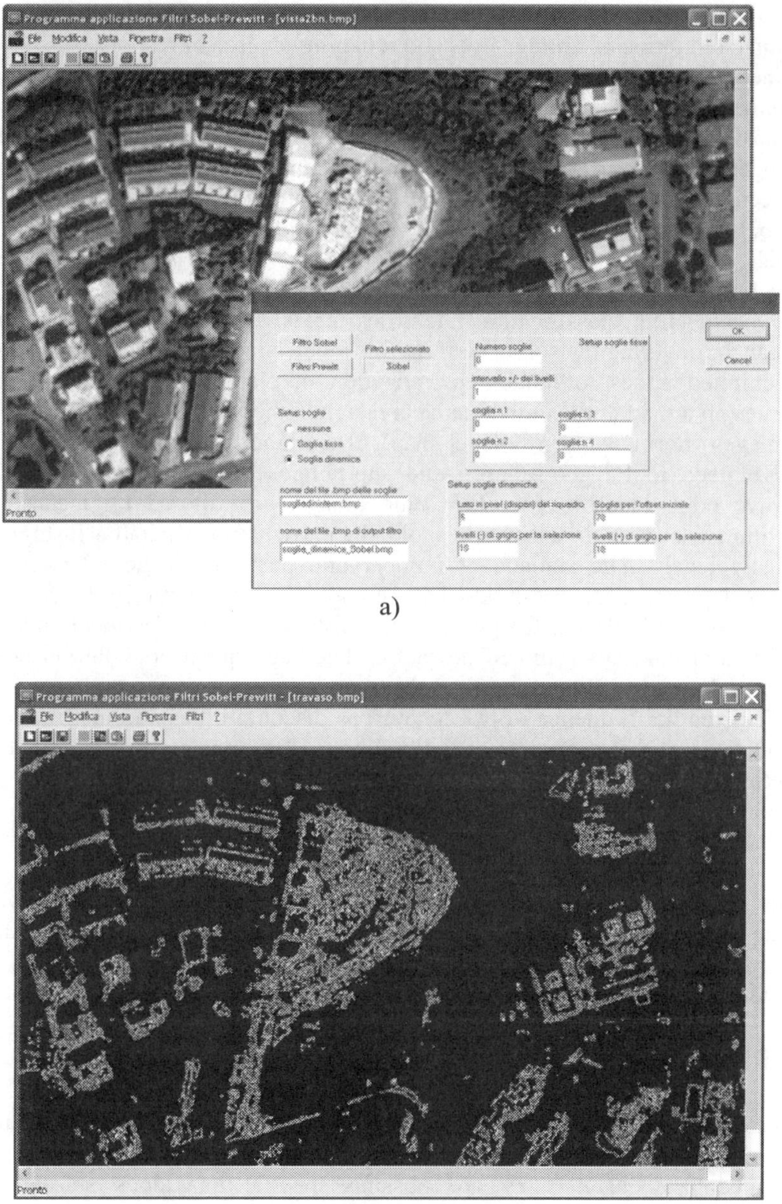

a)

b)

Figure 1: Extraction of contours by means of Prewitt's filter application. The figure shows input window (a) and the results of the first elaboration step (b) by using dynamical thresholds.

Obviously the evaluation method of irregular geometry will have been optimized in terms of timing, tools and reliability degree of response.

The software procedure uses two different investigations whose results can be combined to increase the degree of reliability of the identification. The first one emphasizes the building contours, whereas the second one evaluates the surface homogeneity. These are surely two indicators that can be used to distinguish between good conservation and the wear state of a building.

Contours are analyzed by means of classical filtering techniques that use kernels of Sobel or Previtt. Each kernel is a 3x3 matrix that must be used for convolution operation together with the matrix of the image [12,16].

Hyperspectral classification identifies areas where there are hazardous substances covering the soil or roof. In this mode contour analysis can be applied to delimited zones to obtain the reduction of elaboration cost. Convolution operates on a map in the individuated area and in the Visible spectrum [17].

Images (normally a grey-level map) of a higher resolution than data from MIVIS need to be geo-referred and superimposed on the map. In order to improve edge identification, the same images are filtered by means of an algorithm based on intensity threshold. In particular we get the histogram of intensity levels. The statistic of number and position of the intensity peaks defines the dynamical thresholds that we apply the filter with. In the case of the wear state of a building, the peaks of the histogram are not evident and spread with a high value of standard deviation. The subsequent convolution between kernel and images (filtered) outlines the boundaries.

The irregular sequence of the contour, as discontinuities and interruptions, is an indicator of the wear state of the building. Unfortunately different materials, covering the soil and roofs, could show the same grey-level intensity. If they are adjoining, anomalous discontinuities together with wrong lines appear as a result of the convolution. In order to reduce false responses, we intersect data of hyperspectral classification with a grey-level map. So, we separate pixels of the same grey-level but classified in a different way. Next, we generate the vectors of the contours. GIS tools can use both vector and raster data and identify brownfield by means of the evaluation of discontinuities, rate of variation in the area under examination (index of surface homogeneity) and standard deviation.

4 Brownfield: disused structures

Abandoned industrial properties and land with neglected vegetation are examples of lands abandoned or under-used, which are not identifiable by the procedure described previously. They are missing specific hazardous substances or contaminants and buildings are generally in a good state.

For these cases, an alternative process should be implemented. Literature proposed a methodological approach that satisfies the essential prerequisites allowing classification of complex objects and to use high quality data [9,15]. Following the essential lines of that method we implemented our process through which to extend the spectrum of identified cases.

Even if MIVIS shows high spatial resolution, e.g. four meters in the Visible spectrum, the specific brownfield sites identification and their location could require higher resolution data. The IKONOS satellite collects both multispectral and panchromatic images simultaneously. The geometrical resolution for soil is four meters and one meter respectively. If the acquisition is shot from nadir, the resolution improves at eighty centimetres for the panchromatic and thirty-two decimetres for the multispectral. In order to further improve to one meter the resolution of multispectral data, data fusion should be applied.

As well as IKONOS, QuickBird uses eleven bits for imagery enhancing radiometric resolution. QuickBird is a high resolution satellite operated by DigitalGlobe. It collects image data to sixty-one centimetres of resolution (from nadir, whereas it collects seventy-two centimetres from 25° off-nadir). The images are panchromatic with bands from 0.45 μm to 0.9 μm of wavelength: blue, green, red and near IR. The revisit time is one day for IKONOS and from one day to 3.5 days, depending on latitude, in the case of the QuickBird satellite. Unfortunately imagery of these satellites show highly textured data. This is due to a source of noise whose increase generates a decrease in accuracy of land use classification, based on a per-pixel method. However, urban brownfield sites must be defined suitably by the different elements of which they consist – buildings, roads and so on. In other words the interpretation of an image is not per-pixel, but by means of identification of the objects and by their reciprocal connections.

Classification is definable per-field; it needs a preventive delimitation of imagery characterized by homogenous patches of land. So, image segmentation sets up a phase of the procedure because it allows the division of suitable imagery into homogenous areas. In the case of multiresolution, the segmentation is realized in each band with the specific weight [14].

The process consists therefore of three phases: the multiresolution segmentation, the assignation of each segment to a class (realizing a supervised classification) and finally individuation of brownfield class. Obviously the optimal situation is to reduce to two the number of classes. MVIS data can help supervised classification adding more radiometric resolution bands.

In order to define typologies of brownfield classes, segments, such as industrial buildings and the state of parking and roads, are combined using fuzzy logic and the analysis of the hierarchical connection [8,18].

However, in this procedure, the characteristic "disuse" of a structure, such as an industrial building, is not deducible with certainty. It could be determined, for instance, by examining frequency of use of a parking lot. If it is empty, without a car, on a working day, it is likely it has fallen into disuse. Confirming the absence of cars in two or more weekdays by means of multitemporal imagery the reliability of brownfield detection improves.

5 Discussion

Remote sensing has been used to implement two different methods; each of which has its own advantages. Specifically, the object-oriented approach includes a higher level of interpretation activity, but it is complicated from numerous factors such as organization of test sites, timing acquisition and so on. For instance, time acquisition is important for the interpretation of an empty parking area, but it furthermore characterizes the aspect of the entire image in terms of the presence and extension of shadows. These are a noise source, particularly important in the correspondence of narrow streets.

Obviously, multitemporal acquisition, stereo-imagery (IKONOS supplies it), orthophotos or different thematic maps that are superimposed on the imagery under study can help to discriminate objects and to decrease erroneous interpretations (failures of the method).

When brownfield sites are identified, both the additional source data and the GIS tools are involved in a new step of "interpretation" with the aim of evaluating indicators of the brownfield state: all useful information for redevelopment and reuse of area. Each additional image is correlated to others, geo-referred as the first one, overlaid to the same geographical area, even if having a different resolution.

6 Conclusions and acknowledgments

More remote sensing techniques have been used, identifying different brownfield sites. Some brownfields are characterized by the presence in the area of hazardous materials, some are only a structure or land that is under-used or abandoned. In the first case, during monitoring of brownfield sites, MIVIS hyperspectral data together with GIS showed good results.

The use of MIVIS data allows identification of numerous and different materials by means of classification techniques. In order to locate brownfields, our algorithms intersect the data of classified imagery with data in the Visible spectrum. The procedure analyzes specifically the information associated to a single pixel. A different approach to investigation has been implemented to detect urban structures not-used or under-used. The last procedure, based on an object-oriented technique, solves the classification by means of both fuzzy logic and analysis of the hierarchical connection. The two methods are complementary. The second process is totally "supervised", and it denies itself the characteristic "automatic" of the first one. By assembling together the methods, the number of identifications has increased, adding a lot of different typologies of brownfields. Thus, classification of potential urban brownfields in the study zone produced promising results.

Further test areas will be examined in our next study on confirming reliability of each procedure and to verify more interaction between the two methods.

The author wishes to thank Dr Lorenza Fiumi and his team for support and contribution on MIVIS data. Moreover he thanks Professor Cesare M. Ottavi who coordinated the development of the GIS Terrapack®.

References

[1] Atturo, C., Cianfrone, C., Ferrara, V., Fiumi, L., Fontinovo, G. & Ottavi, C.M., Remote Sensing Detection Techniques for Brownfield Identification

and Monitoring by GIS Tools, *Proceedings of 3rd international Conference Brownfields III*, ed. Wit Press Southampton, Boston, pp. 241–250, 2006

[2] Richman, A., Hamilton, A., Arayici, Y., Counsell, J. & Tkhelidze, B., Remote Sensing, LIDAR, automated data capture and the VEPS project, *Proceedings of the Ninth International Conference on Information Visualisation (IV'05),* IEEE, 2005

[3] Ferrara, V., Gariazzo, C., Ottavi, C.M. & Poli, U., An Integrated approach to the pollution hazard analysis and management, *Proceedings of RISK ANALYSIS II*, ed. Brebbia, WIT Press, Southampton, pp. 23–32, 2000

[4] Ferrara, V. & Ottavi, C.M., Structures and organisation of an information tool dedicated to simulation and management of environmental risks, *Proceedings of RISK ANALYSIS III*, ed. Brebbia, WIT Press, Southampton, pp. 213–222, 2002

[5] Ferrara, V., Integrated data and utilities to support sustainable planning, *Proceedings of Sustainable Planning & Development*, Wit Press Southampton, Boston, pp. 375–382, 2003

[6] Ferrara, V. & Guerriero, M., Territorial Information System interoperability: a design improving interaction in an emergency, *Proceedings of Risk Analysis IV*, Wit Press Southampton, Boston, pp. 475–484, 2004

[7] Boardman, J. W. & Kruse, F. A., Automated spectral analysis: a geological example using AVIRIS data, North Grapevine Mountains, Nevada, *Proc. of the Tenth Thematic Conference on Geologic Remote Sensing, San Antonio Texas USA*, I, pp. 407–418, 1994.

[8] Shackelford, A. K., 2003. A Hierarchical fuzzy classification approach for high-resolution multi-spectral data over urban areas. IEEE Trans. Geosci. Rem. Sens, 41(9), pp. 1920–1932, 2003.

[9] Barnsley, M. & Barr, S. A graph-based structural pattern recognition system to infer land use from fine spatial resolution land cover data. Computers, Environment and Urban Systems, 21(1997), pp. 209–225.

[10] Thomas, M.R., A GIS-based decision support system for brownfield redevelopment, *Landscape and Urban Planning*, pp. 58:7–23, 2002.

[11] Gatti, M., Stereoscopia ottica ASTER ed interferometria differenziale SAR a confronto, *GEOmedia*, GEO4all, **1**, pp. 6–13, 2005.

[12] Gonzales, R. & Woods, R., *Digital Image Processing,* Addison Wesley Publishing Company, 1992.

[13] Ben-Dor, E., Kruse, F. A., Lefkoff, A. B. & Banin, A., Comparison of three calibration techniques for utilization of GER 63 channel aircraft scanner data of Makhtesh Raamon Negev, Israel, *PE&RS*, **60(11)**, pp.1339–1354, 1994.

[14] Johnsson, K., Segment-based land use classification from SPOT satellite data. Photogrammetric Engineering & Remote Sensing, Vol. 60, 1, pp.47–53, 1994

[15] Banzhaf, E., Hannemann, K., Martini, M., Grescho, V., Netzband, M., Monitoring the urban development with integrated system from RS

observation and GIS information, *Proceedings of Urban Remote Sensing Joint Event, IEEE,* 2007
[16] Haykin, S., *Adaptive Filter Theory*, Prentice-Hall, Inc., 1996.
[17] Parker, J. R., *Algorithms for Image Processing and Computer Vision*, John Wiley & Sons, Inc., New York, pp. 23–29, 1997.
[18] Klir, G. J. & Yuan, B: Fuzzy Sets and Fuzzy Logic. Theory and Applications. Prentice Hall, UpperSaddle River, N J, 1995.

GEMS: GIS and geo-statistics integrated in Brownfield remediation and redevelopment, applied in the Vilvoorde region

P. Schrooten & A. Van Alphen
Soresma NV, Antwerp, Belgium

Abstract

Belgium was one of the first European countries to become industrialised. The initial industrialisation has caused numerous soil and groundwater contaminations. Almost 70 years later, these contaminations became a major issue of concern for the redevelopment of former industrial areas. Real-estate developers are familiar with the costs for demolishing and redeveloping industrial areas, but less with the cost due to soil contamination. Two types of costs associated with the contamination can be identified: (1) the cost for the remediation (removing risks) and (2) the cost for treatment of the less contaminated soil during construction works (redevelopment). Due to these important cost factors, the need to assess them more reliably becomes more important.

To address this issue the GEMS (Geographic Environmental/Economical Management System) tool was developed. This GIS based programme allows the designation of different types of land use to different areas (e.g. housing, industry, roads, green areas…) of the redevelopment area. For each drawn land use specific parameters need to be added (depth of underground constructions, percentage of surface area excavated for underground lines…). The model then determines which volume of soil will need to be remediated based on the selected land use and parameters. This is automatically done for a risk-based and reference value remediation target. It also determines the remaining volume of soil that needs to be excavated based on the planned infrastructure and that which needs further treatment before it can be reused. For these volumes of soil a cost is calculated based upon the type of contamination and the contamination levels.

The basis of the model is a geo-statistical 3D contamination map for different types of contaminant groups (BTEX, TPH, PAH, heavy metals, cyanides…). These maps are calculated from site measurements. A first working example of the GEMS tool was developed for the Watersite Brownfield project (Novovil) in the city of Vilvoorde. In the past a large portion of Vilvoorde city was used for heavy industry. It also incorporated some major traffic lines, some scattered housing and a railway. The GEMS tool allowed the Watersite Brownfield developers to model different urban planning scenarios in order to determine the most ideal scenario for the future redevelopment.

Keywords: regional redevelopment, GIS, geo-statistics, soil contamination.

WIT Transactions on Ecology and the Environment, Vol 107, © 2008 WIT Press
www.witpress.com, ISSN 1743-3541 (on-line)
doi:10.2495/BF080061

1 Introduction

In the 19th century the industrial revolution created new kinds of work. Large manufactories were created along important waterways or close to city centres. In the beginning the industrial processes were very crude, and wastes were mostly dumped on-site. At the beginning of the 20th century the chemical industry became one of Belgium's most important industrial activities. Belgium was one of the five leading industrialised countries in the world. An important area at that time was situated north of Brussels in the Vilvoorde area (Figure 1), along the Brussels-Mechelen canal. Different types of industrial activities were present: foundries, coking plants, refineries, solvent treatment, paint production, basic chemical industrial activities, etc (Figure 1). From the 1970s onward the area became more and more derelict. At that time the industrial facilities had surrounded the housing areas and major traffic ways were constructed (railways and motorway). In the following decades more and more factories were closed.

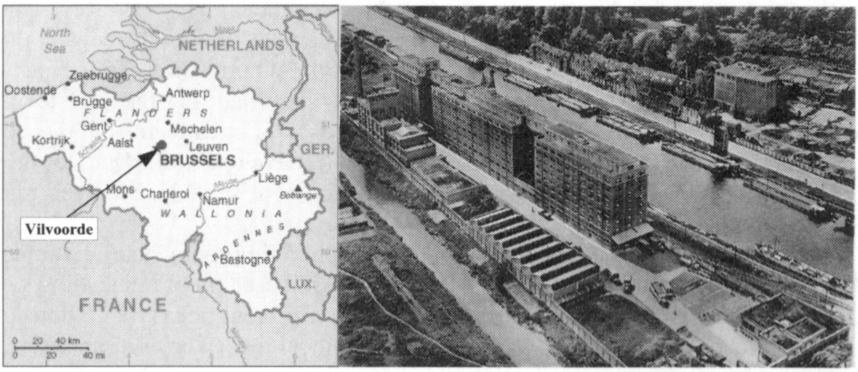

Figure 1: Vilvoorde location and industry in around 1930.

At the end of the 1990s the local authorities decided to start redevelopment of the area, to allow for new industrial activities and improve housing and mobility. The Brownfield redevelopment project "Watersite" was born. Ten years later only a few areas of the Watersite project were under redevelopment. One of the major obstacles in the redevelopment process was the unknown cost related to the remediation of the soil and groundwater contamination caused by the former industrial activities. Almost 20 years of soil and groundwater investigation in this area had shown numerous contaminant sources and types impacting several hundred thousands of m². Several areas are heavily contaminated and need urgent remediation or safety measures. Other areas where industrial reuse was possible, did not allow for residential redevelopment without remediation.

The Flemish soil decree regulates all issues concerning contaminated soil and groundwater. Strict remediation targets depending on the land use (residential, industrial, agriculture, etc) are defined in this legislation. In some cases, after BATNEEC evaluation, other, more risk based remedial targets are allowed. Another part of this law deals with soil that is only slightly contaminated, but when excavated, cannot be reused as soil due to the contamination present. This type of soil brings along extra costs for the redeveloper, as he needs to clean this soil before reuse. Soil that is not excavated can be left in place as long as it does not pose a risk for humans or the environment.

Confronted with the unknown costs related to the soil and groundwater contamination and the Flemish soil legislation, the Vilvoorde Brownfield manager (Novovil) commissioned Soresma to develop a working tool to determine the costs based on the remediation of the contaminations present for different redevelopment plans taking into account the soil legislation. The developed tool, called "GEMS" (Geographic Environmental/Economical Management System), is an application where 3D geo-statistics and GIS are combined to create a dynamic and flexible evaluation tool in Brownfield redevelopment.

2 Geo-statistics: the basis of GEMS

Geo-statistics were developed in exploration geology to determine ore volumes based on point measurements. Essentially, geo-statistics combine the numerical value of the measurement with its spatial location to determine the values of other points in the project area. Detailed information on the use of geo-statistics in environmental applications can be found in Goovaerts [1] and Sanchez-Villa [2]. The GEMS tool needed a 3D representation of the different contaminations to determine the soil volumes that need remediation or the quality of the soil that will be excavated for construction works. The principle of determining ore volumes by geo-statistics is similar to that of determining soil contamination volumes. Data is collected based on chemical analyses from point samples [3–6].

Therefore the first step in the geo-statistical evaluation was to collect site data measurements. This data was obtained from the Flemish waste agency (OVAM). This authority evaluates and collects all soil and groundwater investigations undertaken in the Flemish region of Belgium. This data is collected in a GIS linked database. The soil and groundwater analyses in this database are defined by unique XYZ-coordinates. A polygon of 240 ha overlapping more than the Watersite Brownfield area was defined. The OVAM then provided all soil and groundwater analyses in their database located in this polygon. In total 2230 sample points were obtained. The measurements at these sample points comprised analyses for heavy metals, PAH, BTEX, TPH, cyanides, VOCl and EOX.

The next step in the geo-statistical evaluation is the clean-up and statistical evaluation of the obtained data. Double analyses, sample points without measurements and monitoring data were removed from the dataset. These fake analyses can result in "phantom" effects in the final 3D maps. Monitoring results or double analyses can result in over or underestimations of the calculated concentrations.

To minimise computer time and limit model size, it was decided not to work with all analytical parameters (contaminant compounds). Therefore guide parameters were selected for each parameter group (PAH, heavy metals…). Table 1 presents the different guide parameters for each parameter group.

Table 1: Guide parameters.

Parameter group	Guide parameter	
	Soil	**Groundwater**
Heavy metals	cadmium chrome lead zinc	arsenic chrome mercury lead
PAH	benzo(a)pyrene naftalene	naftalene fluoranthene benzo(a)pyrene
BTEX	benzene toluene	benzene toluene xylene
TPH	TPH (total GCMS/IR)	TPH (total GCMS/IR)
VOCl	PCE TCE DCE VC	PCE TCE DCE VC
Cyanides	total cyanides free cyanides	Total cyanides

Table 2: Flemish remediation values.

Guide parameters	Flemish remediation values	
	Soil (mg/kg d.m.) *Housing (type III)*	**Groundwater (µg/l)**
arsenic		20
cadmium	4	
chrome	256	50
lead	614	20
mercury		1
zinc	802	
benzo(a)pyrene	1,44	0,7
naftalene	4	60
fluoranthene		
benzene	0,5	10
toluene		700
xylene		500
TPH	500	500
PCE	0,7	40
TCE	0,7	70
DCE	0,4	50
VC	0,01	5
total cyanides	12	70
free cyanides	5	

The available values of the sample points represent absolute soil or groundwater concentrations for a certain parameter. Absolute values cannot be used to make comparisons between different types of parameters representing different toxicological, physical or chemical properties or to compare the amount of contamination between different locations. To resolve this problem all concentrations were divided by the remediation values (Table 2) as defined in the Flemish legislation. These values are based on toxicological studies, so the resulting value of this division is a factor that gives an indication of the human toxicological impact of the contamination. These factors allow comparison between different parameters and give an overall indication of the impact of the different contaminant parameters at a certain location by adding the factors.

As presented above, different remediation values were developed for five different land use types. This means that for each land use type (housing, nature, agriculture, industry and recreation) different contamination factors need to be calculated. The impact of the contamination is therefore not only dependent on the physico-chemical and toxicological properties of the parameter but also on the land use of the contaminated area.

Taking into account the conceptual redevelopment plans for the Vilvoorde project area only three land-use types were selected: housing, recreation and industry. For each of these three types a geo-statistical evaluation was performed.

The calculated contamination factors were used in the geo-statistical evaluation to create 3D contamination maps. First a 3D grid was defined. The 3D grid represents the soil; each block of the grid is a soil volume for which a contamination factor is calculated. This grid comprises blocks with a surface of 5 x 5 m and a thickness of 0,5 m (a volume of 12,5 m^3). The geo-statistical evaluation based on the distribution of the available data calculates the "most likely" contamination factor.

Indicator Kriging methodology was used to calculate the contamination factors for the soil blocks. This methodology takes into account the distribution of dataset values in indicator classes, defined by threshold values, resulting in more smoothed volumes. The model parameters for the different steps (threshold indicator evaluation, semi-variogram analyses, post-processing) in Indicator Kriging were determined for each individual guide parameter. The calculations were performed with Vesper 1.6 and WinGslib 1.4 geo-statistical software. The geo-statistical evaluation resulted in 3D contamination maps for each of the guide parameters. Figure 2 shows a detail overview of the contamination of the Vilvoorde project area for PAH (the colours indicate the amount of contamination: darker areas: no contamination above the Flemish remediation values (FRV), lighter shaded areas: gradually exceeding the FRVs).

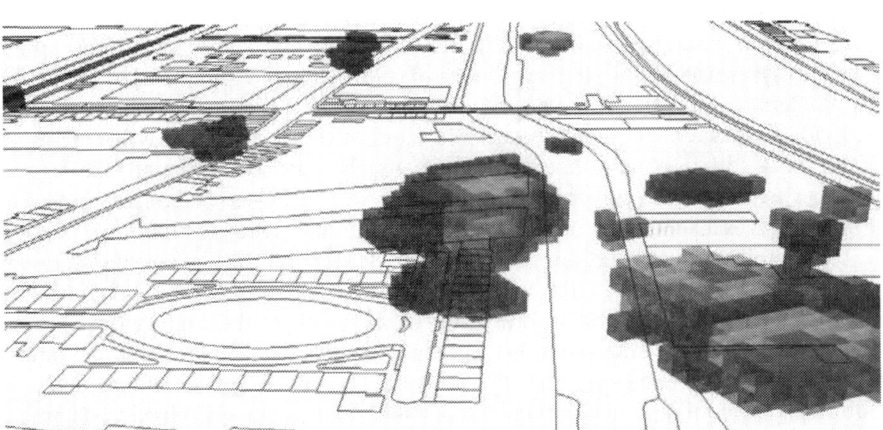

Figure 2: Detailed overview of the soil contaminations for PAH.

The soil contamination maps were only calculated to a depth of 4,5 m below ground level. The available data for the deeper soil was not sufficient to calculate reliable contamination volumes.

A similar evaluation was undertaken for the groundwater contamination. The Flemish remediation values used to calculate the contamination factors for groundwater are not land use dependent. So only one 3D geo-statistic evaluation was necessary. The same 3D grid size was applied for groundwater. The contamination factors were calculated for a depth interval from 2 m to 10 m below ground level. The overall groundwater table at the project location is present at approximately 2 to 3 m below ground level.

3 Cost module: theoretic model

The next step in the development is the integration of a cost assessment based on the soil contamination and the planned redevelopment areas. The cost we want to determine is dependent on (1) if or not the soil needs to be excavated due to contamination and/or construction works, (2) if or not this soil is contaminated and (3) how much it is contaminated. Non-contaminated soil will have normal excavation and transport costs. Slightly contaminated soil may have a higher cost due to the necessary treatment. Heavily contaminated soil may need extra measurements and treatment that bring along even more costs.

In order to determine if a soil at a certain plot needs to be excavated for a remediation, the planned land use needs to be determined. This is done by designating the plot with one of the three land use types (housing, industry or recreation). Then all 3D contamination maps for this land use are consulted to determine if soil blocks with contamination factors equal to or above 1 are present in the designated area. If this is the case than the soil contamination poses a risk to humans and needs to be remediated. For the blocks where the contamination factor is smaller than 1 excavation might be necessary due to planned construction works. In order to determine this construction input parameters for underground facilities (basement, foundations, service lines, sewage…) are added to the attributes of the evaluated plot. Based on these parameters a soil volume can be calculated. The quality of the soil (i.e. individual values of the contamination factors of the soil blocks) will determine if (or not) soil is contaminated and how much it is contaminated. This is in relation to the legal remediation values, the soil clean-up technique and cost. Figure 3 gives a schematic overview of the above mentioned evaluation.

By implementing the above described evaluation the exact volumes of excavated soil for remediation and for construction works can be calculated by adding up the soil blocks from the 3D grid. For each of these individual blocks the CFs and the contamination parameters will determine what treatment techniques can be used. To limit the potential options of soil treatment only the following technologies were considered: biological treatment, physico-chemical treatment (soil washing), thermal treatment and landfill. This allowed putting concrete unit costs per volume of soil into the evaluation model. A cost for the excavation and transport of clean soil was also added.

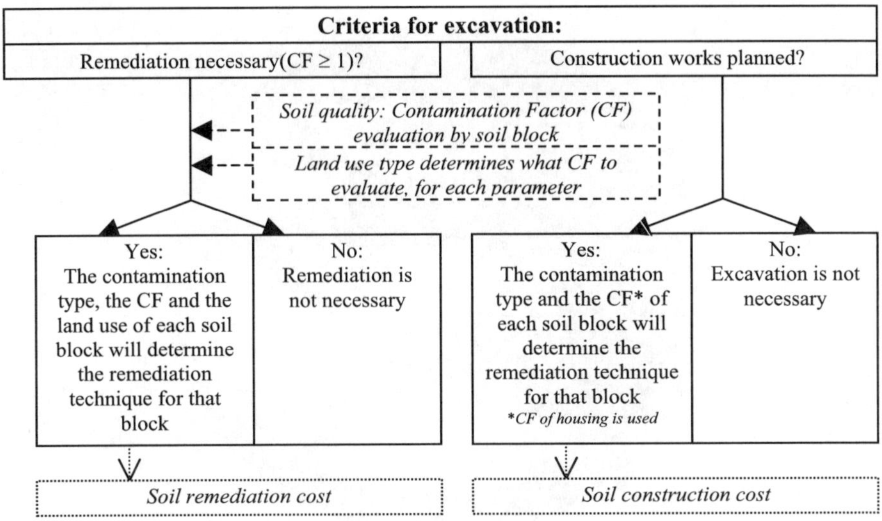

Figure 3: Evaluation diagram for excavation criteria.

4 GIS: integrating 3D maps, the cost module and spatial planning

A GIS application was developed in ArcView 9.2 to integrate the 3D contamination maps with the spatial planning scenarios and the cost module:

- The 3D contamination maps were transformed in 2D+ layers. This means that each 0,5 m thick soil layer became a flat data layer in the GIS application. Thickness was no longer a dimension but is represented by an individual attribute layer;
- A cadastral map is used as a background for the spatial planning layer. The cadastral map was selected to allow the user to draw development scenarios based on the current spatial planning layout on a cadastral parcel scale. The spatial planning layer is the only editable layer in the model. This is necessary so different planning scenarios can be evaluated. Spatial planning scenarios are entered in the model by drawing shapes in this layer and adding dimension and land use attributes to the shapes;
- The cost module is integrated as linear logical functions that use parameters from the spatial planning layer and the contamination layers. Cost parameters for different types of remediation or soil treatment techniques are also a part of the cost module. These parameters can be changed in the function of the site-specific criteria of the evaluated Brownfield project.

Figure 4 represents the schematic build-up of the integrated GIS application.

Several GIS Brownfield GIS applications have already been developed. Most of them focus on the identification of potential Brownfield sites or the evaluation of land-use and stakeholders [7, 8]. A flexible GIS application to evaluate the soil pollution and costs as presented above is not available.

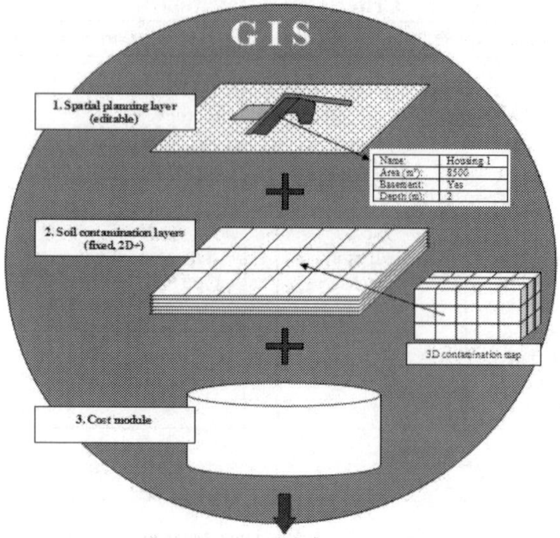

Cost estimation spatial planning: scenario 1

	Housing 1	Road 1	Industry 1	Park 1
Contaminants	TPH, BTEX	BTEX	PAH	--
Remediation cost	150.000 €	--	400.000 €	--
Soil removal cost (construction works)	20.000 €	105.000 €	--	--

Figure 4: Integrated GIS.

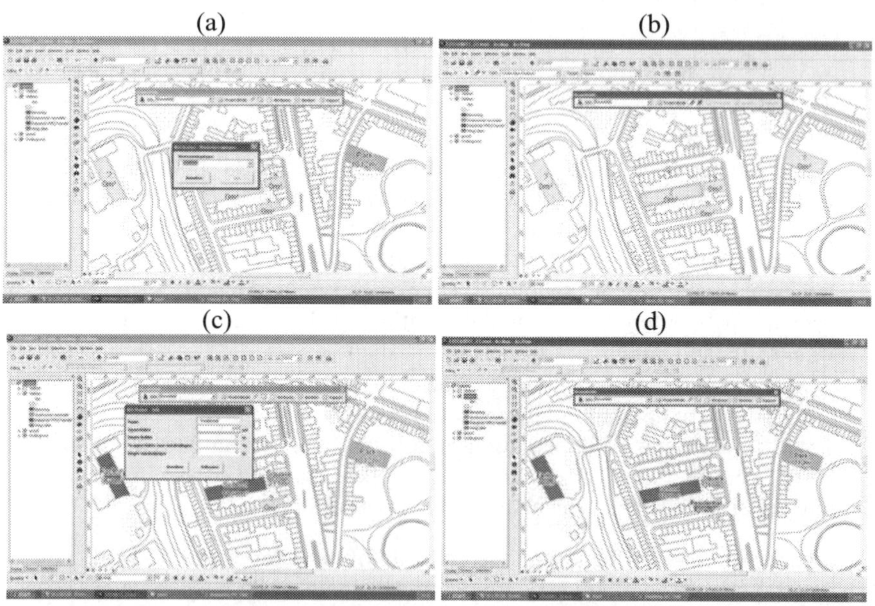

Figure 5: Screenshots of GEMS.

5 Case: Vilvoorde

The first fully working GEMS tool was developed for the Watersite Brownfield project in Vilvoorde city. It comprised a total area of 185 ha with a total of 94.500 m^3 of contaminated soil down to 4,5 m below ground level. Figure 5 shows several screenshots of the GIS application ((a) drawing zones, (b) designating land use, (c) adding attributes and (d) reporting).

6 Conclusion

The integration of 3D geo-statistics and GIS in the development of the GEMS Brownfield redevelopment tool resulted in a flexible instrument to minimise the remediation costs in the function of spatial planning. The developed methodology will aid in a better understanding of the influence of spatial planning on remediation costs. Real-estate calculation modules are under development and will be added to the GEMS tool to allow investment and profit evaluation.

References

[1] Goovaerts, P. Geostastics for Natural Resources; Oxford University Press, pp. 483, 1997

[2] Sanchez-Vila, X., Carrera, J. and Gómez-Hernández, J., geoENV IV - Geostatistics for Environmental Applications, pp. 560, 2004

[3] A. Facchinelli, E. Sacchi, and L. Mallen, Multivariate statistical and GIS-based approach to identify heavy metal sources in soils, Environmental Pollution Volume 114, issue 3, pp. 313–324, 2001

[4] Stein, A., Modelling spatial variability of soil pollution variables with geostatistics for environmental purposes, Proc. 1st Eur. Conf. Integrated research for soil and sediment protection and remediation (EUROSOL), Maastricht 1992. Integrated soil and sediment research: a basis for proper protection, H.J.P. Eijsacker, T. Hamers (eds.). Wageningen, pp. 431–434, 1993

[5] Fabbri, P. and Trevisani, S., A Geostatistical Simulation Approach to a Pollution Case in Northeastern Italy, Mathematical Geology, Springer Netherlands, pp. 569–586, 2005

[6] Malherbe, A., Designing a contaminated soil sampling strategy for human health risk assessment, Accreditation and Quality Assurance: Journal for Quality, Comparability and Reliability in Chemical Measurement, Springer Germany, pp. 189–194, 2004

[7] Boott, R., Haklay, M., Heppell, K. and Morley, J., The Use of GIS in Brownfield Redevelopment in Innovations in GIS 8: Spatial Information and the Environment, Halls, P. (Ed.), Taylor and Francis, London. pp. 241–258, 2001

[8] C. Atturo, C. Cianfrone, V. Ferrara, L. Fiumi, G. Fontinovo & C. M. Ottavi, Remote sensing detection techniques for brownfield identification and monitoring by GIS tools, Brownfield Sites III, WIT Press, pp. 241–250, 2006

Japanese knotweed: impact on brownfield development and discussion on newly implemented innovative solutions

P. Mantzou
Wardell-Armstrong LLP, Consulting Engineers, Cardiff, Wales, UK

Abstract

Japanese knotweed (*Polygonum cuspidatum*) has become an important environmental issue prior to the development of a brownfield site. An invasive plant, it has the ability to spread once fragments are dispersed by natural means and human activity affecting the ecosystem and animal habitat as well as proposed costs and time-scales of any future development. Knotweed is a particular problem in the British Isles, having been introduced as a non-native species from Asia and is likely to spread further throughout Europe and beyond due to its nature of adjusting to different soil types and climates. The legal and financial implications in the UK are explored, as well as roles and responsibilities arising from knotweed presence. The methodologies used once knotweed has been identified are discussed and the liaison with relevant British government authorities and agencies clarified; efforts for the secure and applicable management of the knotweed are also discussed. The liabilities to the landowner or developer for treatment, including the role of environmental consultants to identify the best options for designing and managing the impact, are examined. The British experiences can be presented to a wider audience who may be encountering similar problems with site development. Current strategies used for the treatment of Japanese knotweed and their efficacies are highlighted and a phased, step-by-step approach in managing and treating the impact prior to the redevelopment of a site, is proposed. New innovations utilising geosynthetic technologies for more rapid, amicable redevelopment of Japanese knotweed affected sites, with less disruption and at lower costs, are described.

Keywords: knotweed, development issues, liabilities, treatment methods, eradication, phased approach, geosynthetics, SuDS.

www.witpress.com, ISSN 1743-3541 (on-line)
doi:10.2495/BF080071

1 Introduction

Demand for housing, infrastructure and employment-providing land has meant an increasing reliance on brownfield sites and marginal land in Britain and elsewhere. Indeed, government regulations and laws prevent such development on 'greenfield' sites increasing demand and the need for solutions. Brownfield site development is an important aspect to regeneration of land and nature conservation. Numerous sites in the United Kingdom have been affected by the invasion of Japanese knotweed, causing many concerns to future developers and landowners as it may have a potential impact on the time-scale and cost of the proposed development.

A comprehensive and effective approach to control and eradicate this non-native species should be carried out and a well developed management operation that would be compliant with the relevant legislations that exist, thus minimising the size of impact, its disturbance and potential spread. The methodologies used should be efficient and environmentally friendly as well as cost-effective for the benefit of the developer/landowner and the environment at large.

2 Background

Japanese knotweed was introduced into the UK from Japan in 1825 as an ornamental garden plant and was broadly used for the stabilization of river banks (Bond & Turner [1]). In the early 20th Century, it had spread throughout south Wales where it became prevalent and subsequently escaped to become established in England (ibid). It is estimated to be present in 60% of UK development sites (Clyde & Co [2]). It is located along rivers, railways, highways and waste tips where it has been negligently deposited, often illegally.

2.1 Main characteristics

Japanese knotweed, also known by the scientific name in current use *Fallopia japonica* belongs to the plant family Polygonaceae (the knotweeds), which derives from the Greek 'poly' meaning many and 'gony' meaning jointed (Japanese Knotweed Alliance [3]). This plant has large oval green leaves and a hollow stem, similar to bamboo. In springtime it produces red coloured shoots that can reach a height of 3m by June. It grows rapidly – 20mm per day in any type of soil, fertile or poor and its dense leaves create a large shed above other native species. In August, the plant flourishes and produces sterilised seeds whereas during the autumn and winter period the plant dies back leaving a dry deep brown stem (EA [4]). The knotweed has an intricate root (rhizome) network underground and depending on the ground conditions, it can extend 7m around and 2–3m beneath it. The spread of the plant is vegetative as it can be created and grow from its own pieces once transported by humans or watercourses (ibid). Due to the reason that it does not compete fairly with the country's native species, it has the ability to spread uncontrolled (Complete Weed Control [5]). Japanese knotweed is not considered to cause harm to human health given that it is not toxic but could have an effect on the ecosystem creating a poor habitat for animals by preventing the re-production of adjacent plants. Moreover, this invasive plant can cause extensive structural damage to buildings and infrastructure by emerging through bitumen and concrete, which also results in the destruction of important archaeological sites and flood defence structures. Erosion prevention and control along water courses are effectively reduced whilst the knotweed dies-back in winter; knotweed having effectively suffocated other established vegetation that would have provided root and soil-binding protection in the winter months. It has been estimated that 14,000kg/ha dry weight rhizome can be present at the upper 250mm of topsoil on a site (Brock & Wade [6]). It is worth noting that knotweed can be tolerant of highly acidic soil, topsoil contaminated with heavy metals and air pollution (Bond & Turner [1]). The uncontrolled rapid spread of this invasive species has been affecting different countries worldwide causing implications on future developments, as in the UK. It has been found widespread across Europe from southern France/northern Italy to Norway and from California to Washington in the USA, Canada, New Zealand and Australia (Devon County Council [7]).

2.2 Legal and financial implications

The existence of government legislation for knotweed demonstrates the significance of this UK invasion and worldwide as it can cause delays in construction, create criminal and civil liabilities and can be costly to eradicate.

Regulations and legislation that cover the management and disposal of knotweed (two of which are generally enforced) are:

- *Wildlife and Countryside Act 1981 (s.14)* which creates an offence to spread knotweed and consequently causing it to grow in the wild and applies a heavy fine and imprisonment (EA [4]);
- *Environment Protection Act (EPA 1990) Section 54* which states that Japanese knotweed contaminated material is likely to be classified as 'controlled waste' and its safe disposal should therefore be ensured by waste producers at a licensed landfill site according to the *Environmental Protection (Duty of Care) Regulations 1991* without posing a risk to human health and the environment at large (Waste Management Licensing Regulations 1994 [4]). Failure to comply with the above provisions will be considered as an offence (ibid);
- *Hazardous Waste Regulations 2005 (HWR 2005)* which contain legal provisions regarding the handling and movement of hazardous waste, and Japanese knotweed material treated with certain herbicides can be classified as hazardous waste (ibid);
- *The Control of Pesticides Regulations 1986,* which create a liability for users who handle pesticides for the eradication of knotweed to protect human health and the environment in which they are applied to (ibid).

There can be cases of private or public nuisance from an inadvertent spread of the knotweed to neighbouring sites therefore affecting the landowner or the public in situations where there is evidence that the accused person may have 'foreseen' the spread (Clyde & Co [2]). The presence of Japanese knotweed on a development site can add 10% to the total budget for its complete removal and legal disposal (Van Driesche *et al* [8]). Therefore, developers are advised to obtain legal guarantees that confirm the absence of the knotweed when purchasing a site otherwise depending on how profitable the development is likely to be they could either negotiate a reduction on the original price of the land or come to an agreement with the vendor to carry out a removal operation of the knotweed at his own cost prior to selling the property (EA [4]). A good example of the implications knotweed can cause to the time-scale and cost of a future development are the predominantly brownfield sites in east London hosting the 2012 Olympic Games. The presence of knotweed found spread across the sites has raised the budget to £70m (approx. €100m or $140m) for its eradication and currently remains the most important issue (Booth [9]).

2.3 Roles and responsibilities

There is no single organisation with responsibility for the control of invasive species in the UK, including Japanese knotweed. The responsibility for its control rests with the landowner or tenant of the land. The EA may carry out eradication surveys on land that it owns or flood defence structures that it maintains and being responsible for regulating waste, it can enforce prosecution if the law is not complied with (EA [4]). Treatment options will need to take account of controlled waters present on site and liaison with the EA should be undertaken as the use of an approved herbicide, in or near water, as well as burning of the plant requires their prior written approval. There is no legislation that requires the notification of relevant British Government authorities at the sighting of knotweed on a site, such as DEFRA (Department for Environment Food and Rural Affairs) and local authorities. Although, according to the Town and Country Planning Act (1990) s215 local authorities are empowered to require landowners to remediate land that has been infested by knotweed or undertake a remedial strategy themselves and recover the costs from the landowner by means of affecting the amenity of neighbouring and public areas (County Council of The City and Council of Cardiff [10]). In order to increase public awareness and to encourage the public to take actions to prevent the spread of knotweed there are documents and publications released by the EA and Local Authorities as well as financial support to public and private owners by County Councils. Government funding is also available to local authorities but only for areas of high priority. Also, the Welsh Assembly Government provides funds for biological research purposes in order to create a more sustainable and more effective treatment method.

These actions have increased the knowledge and responsiveness of land owners, tenants, developers, local authorities and consultants (ibid).

2.4 Liaison and methodology used for managing Japanese knotweed on sites

In order to ascertain that land to be given for future development is unaffected by the knotweed infestation or, if found to be infested by it to prevent its spread, a series of actions should be taken prior to the commencement of any works.

Table 1: Actions and responsibilities prior to site redevelopment.

Actions:	Responsibility:
Undertake a full site survey to locate and record all areas of Japanese knotweed	Ecology Surveyor in liaison with environmental consultant and developer
Seek advice once knotweed found on site	Developer
Develop a treatment management plan which involves consultation and discussions with relevant government authorities and the EA	Environmental Consultant
Determine timescale, cost and most appropriate methodology for removal	Environmental Consultant in liaison with developer
Implement eradication programme	Qualified knotweed specialist contracted and supervised by Environmental Consultant

Developers are advised to investigate the site for potential knotweed infestation at an early stage prior to its development in order to avoid excessive costs and potential prosecution. In the presence of watercourses within or adjacent to the site, the EA should be notified in order to gain their approval for the application of pesticides in or near water. Consultation should also be made, where appropriate, with adjacent landowners. The local authority will require a management plan to be implemented in order to grant planning permission. This will involve a survey by an ecology surveyor to be carried out to establish the presence/extent of infestation and most importantly, identify its potential source (Devon County Council [7]). The surveyor will identify the knotweed stands and the rate of spread including a record of other vegetation that is present on site that may be affected by its presence. The results are afterwards presented in the form of a report with photographic material and plans that show the extent. A Risk Assessment is then undertaken by the environmental consultant, based on the survey results along with a remediation strategy that presents the most suitable eradication options taking into account the time-scale of the proposed development and the immediate costs for dealing with the problem. Many sites are open to the public and therefore can be subject to material being imported, which may be contaminated. In this case, it is unlikely to identify the potential source. Most importantly, during the site inspection the presence of stands adjoining the site must also be noted in order to avoid any legal implications with neighbouring landowners. After identifying the best remedial options, a qualified contractor is appointed by the consultant in order to clear the site from the stands and secure its complete eradication. This work is managed efficiently and cost effectively under direct supervision, which ensures that regulations and site safety rules are being followed. The works and treatment should be monitored throughout the year and on-going survey work should be carried out at intervals to establish the success of the treatment or report any failure.

2.5 Japanese knotweed management plan – role of consultants

Treatment methods for the remediation of a knotweed infested site are provided by the environmental consultant to the developer in the form of a management plan that takes into consideration the findings from the ecological survey initially carried out on site. The selection of the most appropriate eradication solutions should balance the time-scale available and cost, and take into account the effectiveness and the surrounding environment where applied. The main aim of the management plan is to ensure that the development remains compliant with the relevant legislation for Japanese knotweed and is intended for use as guidance during the planning and operational phases of the works in order to prevent an accidental spread. The management plan is mainly developed in response to, and in accordance with "The Knotweed Code of Practice: Managing Japanese knotweed on Development Sites" (KCoP) published by the EA in 2006 [4]. The KCoP provides comprehensive guidance on techniques for managing risk on sites infested with knotweed and also provides details of control strategies and eradication methods. Once the appropriate agreed remediation method is selected, a suitably qualified operator of Japanese knotweed treatment is appointed by the environmental consultant to carry out the appropriate works.

2.6 Eradication solutions, costs and effectiveness

Early identification on a site can prove beneficial as it allows the developer to assess the main options available for management and disposal in terms of cost and time. The main treatment methods used for the complete eradication of knotweed, taking into consideration the available time and money, are as follows.

2.6.1 Herbicide application treatment

Used *in situ* and is the most cost-effective method. It enables the containment of an infestation without the possibility of it being spread to other areas. It can be effective although it does not completely destroy the infestation immediately. Herbicide application should be carried out when the plant is in its growing season (July to September) with the most important application in September as the maximum uptake of the chemical is achieved. However, it requires a minimum of nine spraying visits over three growing seasons in order to prove successful. It may not be considered as a suitable solution for big development sites where time can be more important than cost, nonetheless the plant should still be treated once with an appropriate herbicide if found in a flourishing state prior to other methods being used (EA [4]).

The approximate cost may vary from £3–£8 per m^2 (approx. €4–€11 or \$6–\$16/m^2) in the UK. The EA's CoP states that there are a number of herbicides available for knotweed treatment, with Glyphosate and 2, 4-D Amine being the most suitable for preventing contamination to a watercourse, see Table 2 (ibid).

Table 2: Approved herbicides for use in the control of Japanese knotweed.

Herbicide	Affects grasses?	EA approved for use in or near water?	Persistent?
Glyphosate	Yes	Yes	No
2,4-D Amine	No	Yes	Up to 1 month
Triclopyr	No	No	Up to 6 weeks
Imazapic	Yes	No	Yes
Picloram	No	No	Up to 2 years

2.6.2 Excavation and spreading on site

This method can be used only if an *in situ* treatment is not considered feasible and needs to be carried out in combination with spraying as it effectively reduces the time for chemical control. In order to avoid contamination of the soil, a non-persistent chemical such as Glyphosate ("Roundup Pro-Biactive"), which will not cause damage to neighbouring plants, should be applied. The excavation is to be carried out during winter when the plant dies back and at a depth of 3m with a perimeter of 7–10m from the margins of the stand within the site boundaries in order secure the complete removal of the infectious parts, i.e. rhizomes. The soil is sieved and placed on an uncontaminated part of the site that is to remain undisturbed for three growing seasons with continuous monitoring. The typical cost for this method of treatment would be £15–£20/m^3 and depends on the suitability of the site to hold and maintain a clear area for the treatment to take place.

2.6.3 Excavation and removal from site

After the infested material is removed from site through excavation, it is then transferred and disposed of at a suitably licensed landfill site and treated as *controlled waste* while being subject to various legal controls. This method of treatment can cost £150–£350/m^3. These costs include the transportation, tipping fees, tax, as well as backfilling, which may be imported from other sites or balanced from operations with clean soil.

2.6.4 Excavation and burial on site

This method follows the same methodology for excavation as in previous methods mentioned and would ideally be followed by an initial spraying operation to avoid a further distribution of the rhizome network once it has been disturbed. This would also assist in reducing the time period required for chemical control allowing the development of the site to take place at a short period of time. The excavation will be inspected for the presence of rhizome material through a watching-brief by a person competent in the identification of rhizome material. The excavation of the infested material is then placed in a suitable burial area on site, to a minimum depth of 5m. Once the material has been placed it is then covered by a high density polyethylene (HDPE) and/or suitable geotextile, prior to infilling. Due to the contaminated material being present on site a validation report may be required by the EA and the National House Builders Council (NHBC) to verify the location of the burial area and assess if any subsequent development is likely to be affected by it. The approximate cost for this method of eradication would be £30–£40/m^3. Careful design would mean sites could be developed quickly, often immediately, economically, with no delays.

2.6.5 Other treatment methods

Grazing, pulling and cutting of the knotweed stems are further options although they cannot provide complete eradication without the application of an appropriate herbicide. Another option is excavation, then very costly controlled incineration of the infested material, allowing almost immediate development.

2.7 Innovative solutions – geosynthetics/SuDS

Synthetic permeable geotextile materials act as environmental barriers to prevent lateral and vertical soil penetration by knotweed rootlets and their subsequent gradual spread (Haghi [11]). Currently in the UK, geosynthetics have been widely considered where there is a requirement for an immediate remediation solution, while the competitive nature of the market calls for research trials to be carried out to increase their performance in terms of cost and sustainability (Resource & Environmental Consultants Ltd [12]). Applications in the UK at present involve the use of advanced geotextile systems. These systems have been successfully applied to meet the requirements of the developer, by providing complete and safe eradication of the problem as well as huge savings in time and cost. More innovative geotextile design is currently underway as result of the rapidly increasing distribution of geosynthetic companies, which put in time and effort to eliminate any constraints faced during installation. There are two main types of geosynthetics for managing Japanese knotweed currently in the UK market depending on the type of application they are to be used for: permeable geotextiles, which allow filtration (i.e. *RootX*) and extremely low permeable geomembranes, which avert fine material (i.e. mud) from entering (i.e. *DW300/700*) (Haghi [11]). These allow the excavated infested material to be encapsulated within a designed trench. *RootX* is a physical and phytotoxic barrier that prevents water logging, due to its permeable nature, as well as soil instability, due to its ability to provide support to the soil thus avoiding erosion and the creation of soil flip planes. It may also be developed over and laid within landscaping and car park areas to prevent intrusion of knotweed rhizomes (REC Ltd [12]). In addition this root barrier also performs high resistivity to puncturing from sharp materials present in the ground. RootX consists of a copper foil sheet interbedded between a woven and nonwoven geotextile bonded together by needle punching allowing air/water ingress so as to allow surface water infiltration and prevent the build up of high water pressure below. The copper foil releases an inert chemical trace, which controls the penetration of rhizomes through the fabric while its low concentration, below relevant guidelines, does not cause a potential risk of contamination to humans and the environment (ibid). *DW300* is a root barrier that is used to 'wrap' the infested material in the form of envelopes or packages of geotextile creating a containment zone and is mainly used in open-space areas. This polyethylene membrane is of highly low permeability and is joined with double-sided adhesive tape or welded *in situ*. *DW700* is a low density polyethylene (LDPE) membrane, which can allow the fabrication of large pieces joined with double-sided adhesive tape while minimising site joining (ibid). *Tuffline* is a woven geosynthetic that is coated both sides with an impermeable LDPE coating and is suitable as a contemporary containment of infested material. Other geosynthetics include *Lotrak* (woven fabric), *Typar* (nonwoven fabric) and *Terram* (nonwoven fabric), which are applied on contaminated sites as they only work in unison with chemicals and therefore act as a storage medium and therefore cannot be considered as root 'barriers' (Rilem [13]).

New geotextile systems are in development that would be even more effective, increasing the fabric's ability to withstand puncture and widening the rolls, for example, and incorporating features that make the system cheaper.

Sustainable urban drainage systems ("SuDS") are 'the way forward' for sustainable control of surface water run-off in urban environments. They allow surface water to be managed under natural processes while providing temporary rain storage during heavy storm events thus preventing the occurrence of flooding events and subsequent pollution (Wright & Alkhaddar [14]). Prior to the installation of SuDS on a developing site infested by knotweed, consideration should be taken with regards to potential penetration and following damage of services from the spread of rhizomes, which tend to grow around them. Once knotweed has entered these sustainable drainage systems, it could affect the ability of water to drain away by causing overflowing conditions and the eventual spread of the knotweed roots to adjoined sites and remote areas through transportation by controlled waters with inevitable consequences. For that reason, the use of geotextiles for the encapsulation and protection of SuDS is also considered necessary prior to the placement of any infested material within the pit (Water-Lines Solutions Ltd [15]).

The main advantage, notwithstanding, of utilising SuDS on the redevelopment of brownfield sites affected by knotweed is that the systems themselves require careful design for their location and effectiveness followed by excavation and engineered backfill. Hence, during the design stages, locations for knotweed burial sites can be allowed for; during the SuDS construction, burial sites can be incorporated, reducing costs and timings. The same allowance can be made in areas that require landscaping and for noise bunds, aesthetic barriers, etc., which can all serve as knotweed burial sites once encapsulated in geotextile systems.

2.8 Methodology and geotextile application

Prior to the commencement of any excavation works carried out for the removal of knotweed infested material on site, the following considerations should be taken, in an engineered phased approach:

- Identification of most suitable location for the placement of infested material. This area should be 7–10m away from any knotweed patches/stands. This 'distance' should be regularly checked with knotweed regulations and guidelines as it is likely to change;
- Selection of the most appropriate geotextile layer according to the site conditions (i.e. after checking the contaminative status of the site);
- Calculation of the total volume of soil to be excavated and re-used, if suitable for infilling;
- Clarification of drainage service locations prior to geotextile placement.

It is necessary for the excavation to be carried out during the winter period in order for the treatment to prove successful, as knotweed remains dormant. The on-site burial would ideally follow an initial spraying operation before and after the placement of the infested material to provide an additional control measure beneath the barrier system. The following methodology should be followed during on-site burial operations, again following a phased approach:

- Inspection of excavated material to identify the total depth of rhizome spread;
- Supervision of careful knotweed transfer (ideally on geotextiles which can be re-used for the containment of knotweed material in the burial pit);
- Excavation of a trench at a minimum depth of 5m along with a watching brief to inspect for the presence of rhizomes and, if drainage services are placed, the bottom of the trench is lined with a root barrier and sealed with joining tape (geomembrane) prior to the drainage installation to prevent puncturing as well as the blocking the open pores of the SuDS layer from fine sediments;
- Placement of an appropriate geotextile layer and insertion of the infested material, which is encapsulated within the designed trench. Checks carried out that the geotextile is installed correctly;
- On-going monitoring and surveys to be conducted to identify any potential re-growth that will need to be treated ("watching-brief");
- Design of systems should carefully assess the volume of rhizomes and soil that require treatment and the required burial pit dimensions to accommodate, allowing for bulking factors and compaction;
- Locations for knotweed burial can be around the periphery of sites or neighbouring sites, in landscape areas, under bunds/embankments (e.g. noise/aesthetic structures) and in open-spaces.

If the presence of knotweed on a large site delays the sale of land, or affects ownership, a compromise could be reached where the owner keeps possession of a smaller area of open-space/landscaping in which burial has been engineered, carrying out a watching-brief for a set number of months until the presence and/or spread of knotweed can be deemed to have stopped. The small parcel of land can then be handed to the purchaser. This may, therefore, allow redevelopment of large areas of land without delays.

3 Conclusions

Heading towards a sustainable future, the demand for redevelopment of brownfield sites is rapidly increasing whilst one preserves natural landscaped areas and improves the quality of urban areas by restoring lost habitats and reducing potential risks to human health and the surrounding environment. However, important issues that rise prior to the development of brownfield sites such as Japanese knotweed infestation, have created development constraints and financial implications to developers and landowners, who are obliged to comply with regulations enforced by the Government and relevant authorities in order to avoid actions which could result even in prosecution. Delays occur costing time and money.

Japanese knotweed has become a major concern in the British Isles as its uncontrolled spread is causing excessive costs to developers while increasing the timescale for development to take place.

The solution is careful and timely management of this invasive species to help delineate the problem, leading to its complete eradication. A phased approach is encouraged using experienced geo-environmental consultants.

Newly developed innovative solutions, such as the design and application of geosynthetics can provide a rapid and cost-effective remediation solution to knotweed infested land and can speed up its redevelopment.

This sustainable and environmentally friendly treatment will also guarantee its complete removal preventing any future damage to structures and foundations, erosion and flooding events.

Placing such 'geosystems' within already designed-in landscaping and SuDS works could prove to be a boon, if engineered and supervised correctly.

References

[1] W. Bond & R. Turner, The biology and non-chemical control of Japanese knotweed (Fallopia japonica (Houtt)), The Organic Organisation, pp. 1-3, 2006

[2] Clyde & Co., international law firm, Managing Japanese Knotweed on development sites, pp. 6-10 Online. www.clydeco.com/knowledge/articles/managining-japanese-knotweed-on-development-sites.html

[3] Japanese Knotweed Alliance. Online. www.cabi-bioscience.org/html/japanese_knotweed_alliance.htm

[4] Environment Agency, Managing Japanese knotweed on development sites-The knotweed code of practice, Environment Agency, pp. 6–19, 2006

[5] Complete Weed Control Ltd, Japanese Knotweed Online. www.completeweedcontrol.co.uk/invasiveweeds/japaneseknotweed.htm

[6] Brock J. and Wade M., Regeneration of Japanese Knotweed (Fallopia Japonica) from rhizome and stems. Observations from greenhouse trials, Proceedings 9th International Symposium on the Biology of Weeds. Dijon, France. p. 85 – 94, 1992

[7] Devon Knotweed Forum, Devon County Council. Online. www.devon.gov.uk/contrast/japanese_knotweed.htm

[8] Van Driesche R, et al., Biological Control of Invasive Plants in the Eastern United States, USDA Forest Service Publication FHTET-2002-04, 413 p.

[9] Robert Booth, Knotweed sets Olympics £70m challenge, Times Online, 2007. Online www.timesonline.co.uk/tol/sport/london_2012/article1563967.ece

[10] Environmental Scrutiny Committee, Short Scrutiny Japanese Knotweed, County Council of the City and County of Cardiff, pp. 7–15, 2006

[11] Dr. A. K. Haghi, Experimental analysis of geotextiles & geofibres composites, WSEAS Press

[12] Resource & Environmental Consultants Ltd, Geotextiles and Geosynthetics Online. www.recltd.co.uk/geotextiles.htm

[13] Rilem, Durability of Geotextiles, Chapman and Hall, pp. 187–205, 1988

[14] Dr. Amanda Wright & Dr. Rafid Alkhaddar, Sustainable Urban Drainage Systems "The Way Forward", School of the Built Environment, pp. 3–9, 2005

[15] Water-Lines Solutions Ltd, Root Barriers Online. www.root-barriers.co.uk/

Section 3
Remediation studies and technologies

Remediation and development of a former landfill and rail yard in Virginia USA

R. P. Huguenard[1], J. M. LaVelle[2] & R. L. Olsen[3]
[1]CDM, Atlanta, Georgia USA
[2]CDM, Tucson, Arizona USA
[3]CDM, Denver, Colorado USA

Abstract

Approaches to the redevelopment of contaminated properties vary depending upon many factors including type/extent of contamination, risk, regulatory authorities, cost, the resources/desires of the owners, and the value and demand for the property. This paper presents a case study of the Carlyle Site, a 75-acre Brownfields site in Alexandria, Virginia that has been transformed from a property formerly occupied by landfills, a scrap yard, a rail yard, and other commercial and industrial operations to a desirable, mixed use commercial/residential/retail district that includes mid-rise office buildings, upscale high-density residential buildings, and retail space. Environmental management planning played a key role in decision making at each step of the redevelopment process for each property, starting with the conceptual planning and purchase and sale negotiations, and proceeding through construction and environmental closure. The integration of proactive and innovative environmental management approaches with development planning and execution was successfully used to control overall environmental costs, maximize property value, and provide the owner with a larger return on his investment.

Examples of the role of environmental management at each step in the redevelopment process include:

- Considering environmental factors during development master planning to minimize overall development cost.
- Considering environmental conditions in sequencing of property marketing and development.
- Managing perceived environmental risk to maximize property value and minimize costs.
- Using effective risk based remediation goal setting.
- Benefits of regulatory Brownfields or Voluntary Remediation Programs.
- Using *in situ* characterization and soil management plans to obtain regulatory acceptance, minimize handling, and reduce costs and cleanup times.

Keywords: contaminated sites, cleanup, remediation, redevelopment.

WIT Transactions on Ecology and the Environment, Vol 107, © 2008 WIT Press
www.witpress.com, ISSN 1743-3541 (on-line)
doi:10.2495/BF080081

1 Introduction

The investigation, remediation, and development of contaminated sites in the USA occurs in many different ways using various approaches depending upon the type/extent of contamination, the environmental and human health risk, the regulatory authorities, the remediation cost, the site owners/developers, and the property value and demand [1–3]. The Carlyle Site is a 75-acre commercial and residential development located in Alexandria, Virginia near the "Old Town" section of the City. The Carlyle Site is an attractive site for development because of its unique proximity to downtown Washington D.C., Ronald Reagan National Airport, major transportation thoroughfares (commuter rail lines and highways), and the amenities available in the City of Alexandria. The site has been divided into 16 parcels for redevelopment (Blocks A to P, see Figure 1). The Carlyle Site was not a single project or redevelopment effort. Instead the site was developed parcel by parcel by different developers. The common link between the parcels was Norfolk Southern Corporation (NSC), which was the property seller and the overall site developer (i.e., responsible for establishing the site development master plan, zoning approvals, installation of roads, installation of infrastructure, etc.). Each property purchase and sale agreement included negotiated language defining the distribution of short-term and long-term environmental liability and responsibility. Remediation on each parcel was completed concurrent with development and involved a coordinated effort between NSC and the parcel developer. The focus of this paper is the development of a 15-acre parcel for the U.S. Patent and Trademark Office (USPTO) campus. The development was performed in parcels J, K, M, N, F (1/2), and G (1/2) (see Figure 1).

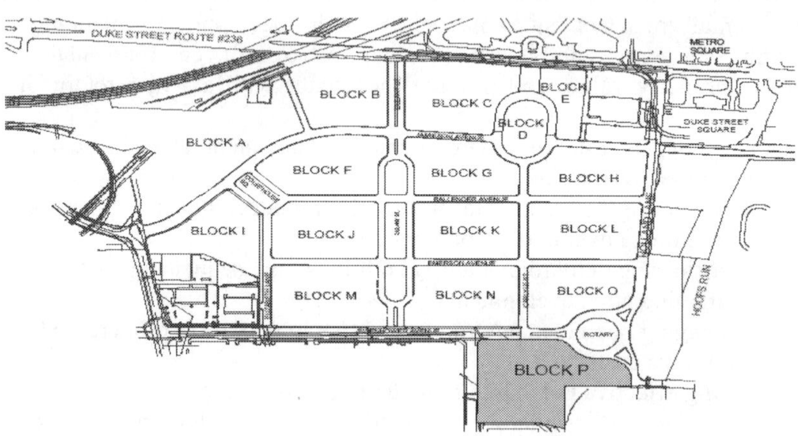

Figure 1: Site location.

The development was made possible through the cooperative efforts primarily of the property owner and project developer (Carlyle Development Corporation, a subsidiary of NSC), the parcel developer (LCOR Alexandria, LLC), the environmental consultant for the land transfer, environmental management planning, and remediation (CDM), the project architect (Skidmore, Owings & Merrill LLP), the general contractor (Turner Construction Company), and the remediation contractor (Weston Solutions Inc.).

For this site, the following items are discussed:

- Site background including types and sources of contamination.
- Remediation approaches.
- Soil Management Planning.
- Conclusions.

2 Carlyle Site description

2.1 Site background

The Carlyle Site is situated in south central Alexandria, Virginia in an area formerly known as West End. Native Americans inhabited the area for thousands of years before the area was explored by Europeans in the early 17th century. Royal grants brought the area into private ownership in 1669, and plantation settlements began in the early 18th century. The eventual intersection of three early colonial roads encouraged trade in the area and the founding of the Village of Cameron, on the site's western edge.

Cameron, later to become known as West End, established itself as a thriving community and expanded to include what is now the new USPTO site. Alexandria annexed the West End in 1915 and the city's growth as a seaport enhanced the importance of the roads that fed the West End. The Orange and Alexandria Railroad established rights-of-way and constructed tracks immediately north of the site in 1851 to provide service to the Potomac River, a couple of miles east of the site. The railroad further stimulated the area's growth.

During the Civil War, it became of strategic value to the Union Army, which constructed a major hospital and the Slough Barracks. Following the war, industrialization came to West End with the establishment of a glass container manufacturing plant, construction of Cameron Yards by Southern Railway, and operation of railroad repair and servicing facilities. The rail yard attracted other industries, and in 1953, landfilling began in the Cameron Run floodplain south of the rail yard (including the southern portion of the USPTO site). Landfilling was terminated in 1978, and the landfill was closed and covered. A scrap yard also was established on a parcel adjacent to the rail yard in mid-1953. The scrap yard consisted of about 10 acres of land that was leased from the railroad from 1954 until the early 1990s.

The railroad yard, which was built after the Civil War, consisted of a switching yard and was expanded in 1901 to include a steam locomotive roundhouse and again in 1944 to include a diesel locomotive repair shop. The roundhouse ceased to be used for railroad purposes in the early 1970s and was leased to a lumber company for warehouse purposes until 1997, when it was demolished as part of the Carlyle infrastructure development on that part of the site. After the merger of Southern Railway and Norfolk and Western in 1982 and subsequent consolidation of certain facilities, the rail yard and diesel shop were abandoned and eventually removed in the early 1990s in connection with the initial Carlyle infrastructure development.

Figure 2 provides an aerial view of the site prior to remediation and development.

Figure 2: Aerial view prior to remediation and development.

2.2 Site environmental setting

The Carlyle Site is relatively flat with elevations ranging between 10 feet to 50 feet above sea level. Elevations are greatest along the northern boundary of the site and gradually slope toward the southwest corner of the site. Regionally, the highest elevation is Shooters Hill, at about 150 feet above mean sea level (msl). The principal surface water bodies in the vicinity of the property are Old Cameron Run (about 500 feet to the south), Hooffs Run (about 200 feet east), Cameron Run (about one-third mile south), and the Potomac River (about two miles East). The elevation of these streams approaches sea level. The original land surface elevation ranged from 22 feet above msl in the north to five feet above msl in the south.

2.3 Site geology

The Carlyle Site is located near the western edge of the Atlantic Coastal Plain physiographic province, which consists of unconsolidated sediments (e.g., clays, silts, sands, and gravels) formed by erosion of the inland mountains. Geologic maps indicate that most of the site is covered with artificial fill underlain by terrace and alluvial deposits and clays, silts, and sands of the Cretaceous Potomac Group [4]. This formation consists of an interbedded series of silt, sand, clay, and gravel. At the fall line, these sediments are very thin, while near the Potomac River, they are up to 600 feet thick.

At the City of Alexandria's southern border with Fairfax County, the lower sands of the Potomac Formation act as a deep aquifer. However, the surficial soils, where the Potomac Formation occurs on the site, are predominantly composed of clays and silts. East of the Potomac sediments lies a loose, heterogeneous material composed of fine grained soil, decomposed rock, and coarse angular rock fragments. At the surface, the fragments have been removed by weathering or erosion. Collectively, these deposits are known as colluvium, and the majority of the site lies over this collection.

Boring logs at the Site indicate that the northern portion of the site is underlain by two to three feet of man-placed fill overlaying clays and silts occasionally interbedded with thin layers of silty or clayey sands. Borings on the southern part of the Site indicate that up to 35 feet of fill soil and landfill material have been placed over natural soils. The natural soils include 5 to 25 feet of a mixture of organic alluvium and Pleistocene terrace deposits underlain by deposits of clays and gravelly, silty, or clayey sands, which are presumed to be deposits of the Potomac Group.

2.4 Groundwater

The geologic materials present at the site are generally low permeability clays and silts with thin lenses of slightly higher permeability material. However, the higher permeability materials do not appear to be consistently continuous across the site. Because of this low permeability base, groundwater movement occurs mostly laterally toward Old Cameron Run and Hooffs Run to the south and the east, respectively. No drinking water wells are known to exist in either the surficial aquifer or the deeper aquifer at the site or downgradient of the site.

While the original groundwater levels and flow directions were ultimately controlled by water levels in Old Cameron Run and Hooffs Run, certain engineered controls on the parcels significantly alter the groundwater regime. For example, the properties in Block O and Block L contain buildings with basements near elevation 0. To protect the buildings, permanent underdrain systems were installed below the bottom slabs. The USPTO Site also includes engineered groundwater controls. Each of the buildings on the USPTO site is equipped with below slab underdrain systems to protect the buildings. In addition, a groundwater barrier (an interlinking system of clay subsurface barriers and synthetic liner barriers) was installed in an east-west direction across the southern part of the USPTO property to minimize the need for groundwater management (pumping and treatment) in association with the buildings located above the former landfill.

3 Carlyle Site remediation

3.1 Contamination

The primary contaminants at the site included lead, arsenic, polychlorinated biphenyls (PCBs), and petroleum hydrocarbons (TPH). Lead, arsenic, PCB, and TPH concentrations in soil ranged from non-detectable to about 24,700 mg/kg, 90 mg/kg, 48 mg/kg, and 20,000 mg/kg, respectively. In addition, about half of the USPTO site had been used previously as a municipal landfill site and was underlain with buried landfill material, incinerator ash, tires, scrap yard remnants, and an occasional drum, tank, and unexploded ordnance. The contaminated soil and landfill material extended over the entire 15-acre site.

3.2 Regulatory history

NSC has a long history of regulatory and community interactions as part of the development plans for the Carlyle Site. In 1989, Norfolk Southern Railway Company began discussions with the Virginia Water Control Board and the Virginia Department of Waste Management (VDMW), both now part of the Virginia Department of Environmental Quality (VDEQ), and the City of Alexandria Health Department on the voluntary cleanup at the Carlyle Site. Subsequently, NSC (through subsidiary corporations) has entered several properties at the Carlyle Site into the voluntary remediation program. Remedial actions and development has been completed and certifications of completion have been obtained on properties entered into the program. Thus, VDEQ and the City have been closely involved in the decision making related to assessment and cleanup activities at the property since 1989. As a result of these interactions, remedial activities have been successfully completed on the majority of the site.

3.3 Cleanup goals

The USPTO property was enrolled in the VDEQ Voluntary Remediation Program (VRP). Site characterization work was performed according to work plans. Based on the characterization, a risk assessment was performed to establish risk-based cleanup goals [5,6]. Results of the *in situ* sampling and coordination with the VDEQ Solid Waste Division resulted in preapproval of soil and waste disposal characteristics and disposal requirements (see Section 4). Additional negotiations resulted in limiting the removal of contaminated soil and buried waste to the depth of the building foundations. In addition, agreements were reached with landfills on special low cost disposal options (e.g., as daily cover) for certain categories of material. Negotiations with the local POTW established temporary industrial discharge permits to allow discharge of partially treated impacted groundwater to the sanitary sewer system. Plans and specifications for the excavation and disposal of soil and waste and the management and treatment of groundwater were prepared concurrent with development.

3.4 Remediation

Remediation alternatives were evaluated based on effectiveness in meeting cleanup goals, implementability, costs, and time to achieve the cleanup goal. In addition, remediation was performed to facilitate phased property development in accordance with economically driven build-out plans and demand for the property.

For the USPTO Site, a site investigation was performed to characterize soil, landfill material, and groundwater. This occurred concurrent with negotiations between the owner, developer, and purchaser. A risk assessment was then performed and risk-based remediation goals were developed, resulting in the necessary removal of soil and landfill material for foundation excavation while leaving other soil and landfill material in place. Residual risks were managed using a combination of deed restrictions and engineering controls. Deed restrictions included prohibitions on potable water well installation and constraints on water use and residential use restrictions. Engineering controls included installation of vapor barriers and subslab gas ventilation systems under each building, and placement of two feet of clean soil over all existing soil that was not covered by pavement or buildings.

To meet schedule constraints, soil and landfill material was characterized for disposal *in situ*, and a soil management plan/excavation design was developed to expedite material removal (see Section 4). Under this approach, the remedial contractor was able to move soil and waste directly from the ground to trucks with a predetermined disposal destination. As a result, as many as 600 tandem truckloads of soil and waste were removed from the site each day, and a total of approximately 450,000 total cubic yards of soil and waste were removed from the site during a six-month period.

The new USPTO development included construction of five mid-rise office buildings (2,400,000 square feet of office space) and two large parking garages. Foundation excavation work progressed from structure to structure, followed immediately by piling installation, foundation forming, and then concrete placement. The integrated planning of the environmental and construction components was robust so that schedules were maintained even with the additional challenges of weather and archaeological investigations.

The remediation and redevelopment process took approximately nine years, starting with the development of a proposal for construction of the USPTO offices at the Carlyle Site in 1996 and culminating with the issuance of a certificate of completion by the VDEQ VRP in 2005. The major milestones in this process were:

- 1988 – Plans to consolidate the USPTO offices were initiated
- 1990 – Zoning approval issued by the city of Alexandria
- 1995 – Congressional approval was granted to lease two-million square feet of office space in Northern Virginia for a period of 20 years

- 1996 – The General Services Administration (GSA) solicitation
- 2000 – The GSA and the USPTO selected the LCOR proposal for development of the new USPTO offices at the Carlyle site
- 2000 – Site environmental investigation and environmental planning were initiated
- 2001 – Construction began
- 2005 – Building construction was completed
- 2005 – A Certificate of Completion was issued by the VDEQ, VRP

Project costs by category are:

Land purchase	$92,000,000
Environmental management planning, permitting, design, and remediation oversight	$2,000,000
Environmental remediation	$24,000,000
USPTO campus design	$31,000,000
Campus construction costs	$518,000,000
Finance	$191,000,000
Reserves	$16,000,000
Miscellaneous	$38,000,000
Total	$912,000,000

Figure 3: Dulany Garden and surrounding USPTO campus.

Innovative thinking and cooperation between the seller (a subsidiary of NSC) and the buyer (LCOR Alexandria, LLC) was the key to arriving at an acceptable agreement for transfer and development of the contaminated property that would become the site of the new USPTO campus. Cost and environmental liability concerns were managed through a combination of a negotiated cost sharing arrangement and a cooperative environmental management approach.

The resulting USPTO project is a model for positive economic development and smart growth. While directly adding 8,000 jobs in the City of Alexandria, its proximity to two metro subway stations, Amtrak, the Virginia Railway Express, and numerous commuter bus lines resulted in manageable impacts to the local traffic.

The USPTO project also included the development of park area. Dulany Gardens, one of the two largest open spaces planned for Carlyle, features two distinct plazas—one with primarily hardscape finishes designed for outdoor seating and dining and the other with extensive lawn, plantings, and a distinctive fountain (Figure 3). The Gardens is designed to terminate at the monumental atrium of the Madison Building.

4 Soil management planning

4.1 Objectives and scope of the soil management planning

The overall goal of soil management plans was to obtain predevelopment buy-in from the VDEQ on soil and landfill material management and disposal to allow remediation to occur concurrent with development while minimizing potential delays for environmental decisions [7]. The soil management plans were not a regulatory requirement, but were a cooperative approach developed by CDM and the VDEQ to solve problems each party faced. Potential large delays would be encountered if disposal decisions and approvals were made with each batch of material removed from the site and the VDEQ faced management of a tremendous number of special waste approval requests. The following specific objectives were accomplished by soil and waste management plans:

- Present analytical data and field observations.
- Horizontally and vertically delineate soils and waste with regards to handling and disposal requirements.
- Delineate the approximate vertical extent of the landfill when present.
- Develop contingency plans to identify and address potential problems that may be encountered during development excavation.

4.2 Potential environment issues

The following environmental issues were typically encountered during development:

- Landfilled Material – Landfilled material was encountered during excavation on the southern portions portion of the site and required proper handling and disposal.
- Landfill Gases – Landfill gases were a common problem that had to be addressed.
- Groundwater – Much of the excavation required digging into the groundwater table. Some groundwater required treatment and special disposal, while other required only standard silt/sediment control.

- Resource Conservation and Recovery Act (RCRA) Hazardous Waste – A small portion of the waste was hazardous due to lead concentrations.
- Soils Impacted by Metals – Lead and arsenic were common contaminants across the site and required special handling and/or disposal if they were removed from the site or reused onsite.
- Soils Impacted by TPH and/or PCBs – Some soils removed from the site or reused onsite also required special handling and/or disposal due to slightly elevated levels of TPH and/or PCBs. A small amount of the waste had PCBs over 50 mg/kg and required disposal to TSCA waste facilities.

4.3 Soil and landfill material characterization

The purpose of the site investigation was to characterize soils and landfill material that will be excavated during development for disposal or reuse [5]. The resulting soil and landfill material chemical and physical characterization results allowed predevelopment planning of environmental management during construction and ultimately minimized delays in development due to environmental issues. The sample frequency established for the site investigation provided sufficient data to satisfy the soil and waste characterization requirements of the landfills that will receive the soil and waste. Specific objectives of the site investigations included:

- *In situ* characterization of the soil and landfill material that will be excavated for development. Characterization was sufficient to 1) allow horizontal and vertical delineation of soils and waste with regards to disposal requirements, and 2) allow pre excavation acceptance of the soils and waste by the selected landfills.
- Examine soil and landfill materials in soil boring cores to visually characterize the landfill contents by horizon.

The soils and landfill material were characterized both visually through boring logs and chemically through laboratory analysis. In known landfill areas, borings were performed on a 50-ft grid spacing. On nonlandfill areas, the grid spacing was 100 ft. The boring depths were selected to coincide with the proposed excavation depths. Cores from soil borings were visually characterized and then sampled at three-foot intervals and sent to laboratories for analysis. The specific chemical analyses performed from borings in landfill areas are described below in Table 1.

In nonlandfill areas, samples were analyzed for total arsenic, total lead, TPH gasoline range organics, and TPH diesel range organics. If TPH was detected, the samples were also analyzed for BTEX, TOX and PCBs. If total metals exceeded twenty times the TCLP limits, the samples were analyzed for TCLP metals (only the specific metals). Visual observations of the physical characteristics of the soils and landfill materials were made and recorded during boring installation. Each sample was classified according to geologic characteristics, color, texture, and landfill waste content. Soil and landfill material chemical characteristics were obtained through testing at an analytical laboratory. The chemical and physical data for each boring location and depth were then evaluated to characterize the materials in terms of reuse or disposal criteria. Cross-sections presenting the chemical data and the disposal characterization were constructed. A cross-section was presented for each of the analytical parameters that had an impact on determining the disposal criteria (TPH, Arsenic, Lead, BTEX, PCBs, and TOX).

Table 1: Analysis of material samples.

Parameter	Frequency
Total petroleum hydrocarbons (TPH) gasoline range organics	All samples
Total petroleum hydrocarbons (TPH) diesel range organics	
TCLP arsenic and lead (for classification as hazardous waste)	
Full TCLP (i.e., metals, volatiles, semivolatiles, pesticides, herbicides) (for classification as hazardous waste)	Every eighth sample
PCBs in solids	Samples in which TPH is detected
Benzene, toluene, ethylbenzene, xylenes (BTEX)	
Total organic halides (TOX)	

The reuse and disposal criteria identified in the cross-sections were also presented in plan view by horizon to better facilitate excavation planning. The plan views were presented in horizons of at least two feet starting at the land surface and ending at the deepest excavation depth. Typical disposal and reuse categories used for classification of the samples are presented and explained in Table 2.

Some soils (see Table 2) were reused onsite. However, reuse of soils was only allowed in locations that were covered by buildings or two feet of clean fill as part of the site development. In addition, reuse of soils was not allowed in utility corridors.

Temporary stockpiling or staging of soils to be reused onsite was necessary. Where creation of soil stockpiles was necessary, the stockpiles were plastic lined and had surface water run on and run off controls and sedimentation controls. The stockpiles were covered with plastic at the end of each day.

Materials coded as RCRA hazardous waste or PCB wastes were either directly loaded into trucks for hauling to an appropriate disposal site or loaded into covered hazardous waste roll-off containers for staging onsite. All other excavated soils or materials were directly loaded into trucks for offsite disposal.

One of the primary goals of soil and landfill material management plans was to maximize the efficiency of the development excavation process by minimizing delays required for management of environmental issues. Contingency plans were a critical tool for meeting this goal. The plans were developed to establish general protocols and procedures for dealing with issues and problems that were not necessarily identified by the site investigation, but have a reasonable potential for occurring. Contingency plans were included to establish general protocol and procedures to use when the following issues and problems were encountered.

Table 2: Material classification.

Material Description	Disposal/Reuse Requirement
Soil with TPH <500 mg/kg and remaining constituent concentrations at or below prevailing site concentrations	Restricted onsite reuse or disposal at an appropriate, permitted lined landfill
Soil with TPH between 500 mg/kg and below 3,000 mg/kg	Disposal at an appropriate, permitted lined landfill
Soil with TPH above 3,000 mg/kg	Treatment and disposal at an appropriate, permitted TPH incineration facility or other appropriate offsite treatment and disposal facility
Landfill material with TPH below 500 mg/kg	Disposal at an appropriate, permitted lined landfill
Landfill material with TPH between 500 mg/kg and 3,000 mg/kg	Disposal at an appropriate, permitted lined landfill
Landfill material with TPH greater than 3,000 mg/kg	Treatment and disposal at an appropriate, permitted TPH incineration facility or other appropriate offsite treatment and disposal facility
RCRA hazardous waste, soil, or landfill material	Treatment and disposal at an appropriate, permitted RCRA hazardous waste facility
TSCA PCB contaminated soil or landfill material (PCB above 50 mg/kg)	Treatment and disposal at an appropriate, permitted TSCA PCB waste facility

- Buried Ordnance or Other Unidentified Objects – A limited amount of unexploded ordnance (unarmed) and other unidentified objects were encountered during remediation efforts in the landfilled areas.
- Compressed Gas Cylinders – A limited number of compressed gas cylinders were encountered during remediation efforts in the landfilled areas.
- Underground Piping and Other Utility Lines – Due to the long history of the Carlyle Site, previously unidentified piping and utilities were sometimes encountered during excavation.
- Tanks – In view of the historic use of the property, it was considered prudent to establish a contingency plan for this issue.
- Drums – Some drums were encountered during remediation efforts in the landfilled areas.
- Material Varying from Assigned Classification – Soil or landfill material that was inconsistent with the assigned disposal classification was occasionally encountered.
- Buried Structures – This contingency plan outlines procedures and protocols that should be followed in the event that additional structures were encountered.

- Rejection of Waste by the Landfill – Because of the extensive waste characterization activities that have been performed prior to waste disposal, no waste from the Carlyle Site should be rejected by a receiving landfill. However, it was considered prudent to establish a plan that addressed this potential issue.

5 Conclusions

Approaches to redevelopment of contaminated properties vary depending upon many factors including type/extent of contamination, environmental/human health risk, regulatory authorities, costs, the resources/ desires of the owners/developers, and the value and demand for the property. Overall, the remediation and development on the Carlyle Site demonstrated the importance of integrating environmental management with development planning and execution. Specific examples of this integration and lessons learned include:

- Risk based exposure pathways can be minimized through use of institutional controls (e.g., deed restrictions) and development features (e.g., barriers such as subslab ventilation, clean soil cover and pavement; placement of buildings to avoid groundwater contamination; placement of recreational areas on less contaminated property).
- Up front land use planning should include environmental implications. The development configurations should be flexible if risk assessment provides acceptable solutions. If feasible, acceptable residual risk should be the goal versus fixed remediation goals.
- Property sale prices are influenced more by perceived environmental risk than by actual risk. The perceived risk should be managed by securing regulatory support and up front concurrence on management approaches. The regulators should be continually involved and informed.

References

[1] Olsen, R.L., Woods, A.B. & Edgar, M.H., *Remediation and Development of a Former Military Manufacturing and Test Site in Florida USA,* Third International Conference on Prevention, Assessment, Rehabilitation and Development of Brownfield Sites, WIT Transactions on Ecology and the Environment, Vol. 94, WIT Press, Southampton and Boston, pp 121 -130, 2006.

[2] Olsen, R.L. & Burgess, M.A., *Case Histories and Comparison of Two "Brownfields" Sites in Kansas and Indiana USA*, Second International Conference on Brownfield Sites: Assessment, Rehabilitation and Development, WIT Press, Southampton and Boston, pp 191-200, 2004.

[3] Whitman, I.L., *Brownfield Redevelopment by the Private Sector: Market Driven Decision-making*, Third International Conference on Prevention, Assessment, Rehabilitation and Development of Brownfield Sites, WIT Transactions on Ecology and the Environment, Vol. 94, WIT Press, Southampton and Boston, pp 21 - 27, 2006.

[4] U.S. Geological Survey (USGS), *Geology and Groundwater Resources of Washington, DC, and Vicinity*, USGS Water-Supply Paper #1776. U.S. Government Printing Office, Washington, DC, 97 pp, 1983.
[5] CDM, *Site Characterization and Remedial Action Planning Report*, Block P, Carlyle Site, Alexandria, Virginia, Sept. 2006, submitted to VDEQ on behalf of Carlyle Development Corporation, 2006.
[6] Virginia Department of Environmental Quality (VDEQ), *Voluntary Remediation Program Draft Risk Assessment Guidance,* Richmond, VA, 1999.
[7] CDM, *Soil and Landfill Material Management for the Development of Block P, Carlyle Site, Alexandria, VA*, submitted to VDEQ on behalf of Carlyle Development Corporation, 2007.

Bridging mining theory with soil remediation

T. Karachaliou & D. Kaliampakos
Laboratory of Mining and Environmental Technology,
School of Mining Engineering and Metallurgy,
National Technical University of Greece, Greece

Abstract

Soil contamination has been a major problem all over the world posing great risks to human health and the environment. Currently there are many remedial alternatives that can be applied, yet the available funds are not enough to entirely face the problem. The optimal use of the available resources by maximising their environmental benefits is of great interest. With this aim in mind, a method based on mining theory is proposed in this paper. The core idea is contamination to be treated as a "negative" ore. The meaning of "negative" is attributed to the fact that contamination, contrary to the ore, is an unwanted asset. In this case, what is actually waste is considered valuable. However, the rationale is the same since in both cases the profit is proportional to the grade of the extracted ore or the concentration of the removed contaminant. This approach enables the use of pit optimisation tools such as the Floating Cone method suitably developed to be implemented in soil remediation. The main problem to overcome seems to be the absence of an economic value attributed to the removal of contamination. The paper also introduces a method to define a shadow price in order to compare the profit of contaminated soil removal to the corresponding total cost of this action. As a case study, the method is applied in a contaminated site in Lavrion, Greece.

Keywords: soil remediation, environmental risk, block modelling, pit optimisation.

1 Introduction

During recent decades the modern world has been increasingly concerned about contaminated land. The problem of soil contamination seems to be expanding since new brownfield sites are discovered at every turn, whereas the available funds remain inadequate to rehabilitate them all. According to some estimates,

WIT Transactions on Ecology and the Environment, Vol 107, © 2008 WIT Press
www.witpress.com, ISSN 1743-3541 (on-line)
doi:10.2495/BF080091

there are about 1,500,000 possibly contaminated sites in the European Union and their remediation cost may exceed 100 billion euro [1]. The need for methodologies aiming at the optimisation of the available funds is strongly emerging.

The methodology described in this paper is based on techniques of the mine design theory, and the pit optimisation in specific, and is suitably developed so as to be used in the remediation planning. The concept is to treat contamination as a "negative" ore and evaluate alternative remediation schemes on a cost-benefit basis. The soil remediation project that was undertaken at a former metallurgical site in Lavrion, Athens is used to demonstrate the applicability and utility of the methodology.

2 Pit optimisation theory

The purpose of any pit optimisation methodology is to estimate the actual ore reserves (tonnage and grade) by combining economics, geometries and ore distribution. The process involves the superposition of a geometric surface called a pit onto the mineral inventory. The size and shape of the pit depends upon economic factors and design/production constraints. With an increase in price the pit would expand in size assuming all other factors remained constant. Within the pit are found materials of differing value. Economic criteria are applied to assign destinations for the materials based on their value (i.e. mill, waste dump, etc.), see fig.1.

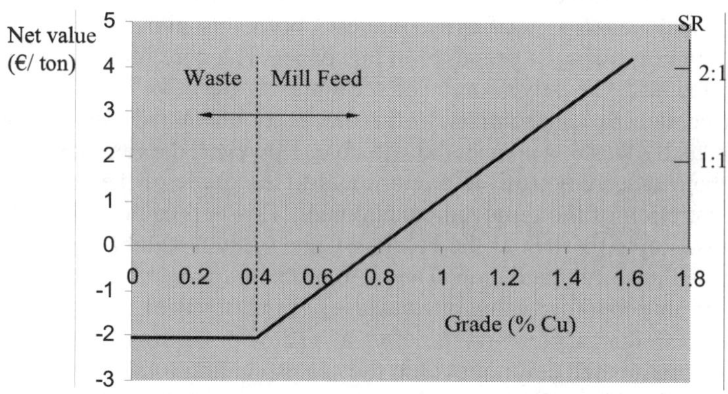

Figure 1: Net value-grade curve showing the waste/mill split.

In order to uncover the ore, waste has to be removed. Ore is distinguished operationally from waste by the cut off grade. The cut off grade is the grade at which the mineral resource can no longer be processed at a profit [2]. Ore above cut off can be treated and sold at a price equal to or above 'break even'. Material below this cut off is waste [3]. The choice of the cut off grade in mining influences the profitability and life of individual mines and thereby the quantity of a resource that is available to society. The optimal cut off grade depends on all the salient technological features of mining, such as the capacity of extraction and of milling, the geometry and geology of the orebody, and the optimal grade of concentrate to send to the smelter [4].

The amount of waste that must be removed to release a given ore quantity is described by the "stripping ratio". The ratio is most commonly expressed as in eqn (1).

$$SR = Waste\ (volume) / Ore\ (volume) \tag{1}$$

The break even stripping ratio describes the situation when the costs involved in mining the strip just equal the revenues. The break even cut off grade is defined as that grade for which the net value (gross value minus total cost) is zero [2].

An important input into the economic viability of a mine is the determination of the ultimate pit limit of the ore body. That is, that contour which is the result of extracting the volume of material that provides the total maximum profit whilst satisfying the operational requirements of safe wall slopes. The ultimate pit limit gives the shape of the mine at the end of its life [5]. The standard procedure of pit optimisation is as follows.

An important task in mine management is the establishment of an accurate model for the deposit. The block model is extensively used in optimisation. The regular 3D fixed-block model is the most commonly used and is best suited to the application of computerised optimisation techniques. This model is based on the ore body being divided into fixed-size blocks. The block dimensions are dependent on the physical characteristics of the mine, such as pit slopes, the dip of the deposit and grade variability as well as the equipment used. The centre of each block is assigned, based on drill hole data and a numerical technique (such as inverse distance weighting or krigging), a grade representation of the whole block. Using the financial and metallurgical data the net profit of each block is determined. To satisfy the mine site safety and stability requirements, wall slope restrictions are imposed on each block. From these we can identify for each block x the set S_X of blocks that must be removed before block x can be mined. This collection of blocks is usually referred to as "cone".

The ultimate open pit limit problem is that of determining the contour that satisfies the safe wall slope and which yields the maximum profit. Mathematically, this problem can be formulated as follows. Consider an ore body with N blocks. Let p_i be the net value (profit) of block I and S_i the set of overlying blocks associated with block I [6]. The ultimate pit problem can be written as in equation 2.

$$\text{Maximise} \quad \sum_{i=1}^{N} p_i \times x_i \tag{2}$$

subject to

$$x_i - x_j \leq 0 \text{ for all i and j and } j \in S_i$$
$$\text{and } x_i = 0, 1 \text{ for all i}$$

The limits define the amount of ore minable, the metal content, and the associated amount of waste to be moved during the life of the operation. The material contained in the pit will meet two objectives. A block will not be mined unless it can pay all costs for its mining, processing, and marketing and for stripping the waste above the block. For conservation of resources, any block meeting the first objective will be included in the pit. The result of these objectives is the design that will maximize the total profit of the pit based on the physical and economic parameters used.

The stripping ratio is used to set the pit limits on each section. The pit limits are placed on each section independently using the proper pit slope angle. The pit limits are placed on the section at a point where the grade of ore can pay for mining the waste above it. When a line for the pit limit has been drawn on the section, the grade of the ore along the line is calculated and the lengths of the ore and waste are measured. The ratio of the waste and ore is calculated and compared to the breakeven stripping ratio for the grade of ore along the pit limit. If the calculated stripping ratio is less than the allowable stripping ratio, the pit limit is expanded. If the calculated stripping ratio is greater, the pit limit is contracted. This process continues on the section until the pit limit is set at a point where the calculated and breakeven stripping ratios are equal [7].

The ultimate pit limit problem is easy to formulate mathematically, but not so easy to solve because of its size. One of the methods that are widely applied in pit optimization is the “floating cone”. It works by searching through the block model for ore blocks and then assessing the value of the inverted cones that have to be mined to expose them. If the value of a cone is positive, it is mined out and all the blocks it includes are changed to air blocks. The search then continues. The process is repeated for each ore block in a deposit, considering cone overlaps. The term "floating" is derived from the "movement" of the cone throughout the model. The optimal pit could be defined as the one yielding maximum profit, maximum net present value or maximum extraction.

3 Contamination as a “negative” ore: the basic concept

Pit optimisation techniques can be adjusted to optimise the allocation of the funds in soil remediation. In this case, what is actually waste (contaminated soil) is considered as the valuable ore, and the profit of extraction derives from the elimination of environmental risk. The process is quite similar. Contamination is first of all explored by drilling probe holes in the area of interest. The contaminated area is then divided into blocks. Each block is assigned a contamination value (such as contaminants’ concentration) using interpolation methods. The economic value of each block is then calculated. The extraction of a contaminated block is obviously profitable, in terms of human health and environmental protection. However there is no actual “price” (e.g. euro per ton of removed contaminated soil) that can be used to estimate the economic value of each contaminated block. In order to determine a shadow price a basic assumption is made that the profit of excavating a block is zero when the contamination value is equal to the applied standard. The net value of the removal of contaminated soil above the applied thresholds is considered positive. The net value of the removal of soil below the applied thresholds is considered negative. This limit is corresponding to the break even cut off grade, the contamination level for which the net value (gross value minus total cost) is zero.

4 Application in Lavrion

The site under consideration is located in Lavrion, Athens, within an area of 24.5 hectares. It has a long industrial past, which resulted in a severe environmental problem [8, 9]. Contamination was detected through out the site, to an average depth of 5 meters. Given the high volumes of contaminated soil and the limited budget that was available, a special application of the "dry tomb" technique was implemented ex situ but on site [10]. Contaminated soil was excavated, transferred and disposed off in a secure, water-tight construction within the boundaries of the site. In total 113.000 m^3 of contaminated soil were excavated and transferred in the repository. The total cost of the project was approximately 3.5 million euro corresponding to about 31 euro per ton or 16 euro per m^3 of contaminated soil. With regard to these economic data, the optimal excavation limits and depths will be defined.

The contamination value that needs to be investigated is the leaching of arsenic. The described technique is applied in a subarea of the site to define the optimal excavation contour that maximises the environmental risk reduction given the available budget. Eighty samples through sixteen drill holes to a final depth of five meters were used for the analysis. Table 1 lists the arsenic leaching values based on the procedures described in 2003/33/EC Council Decision [11]. The area was divided into blocks 25m long x 25m wide x 1m high. Figure 2 shows a plan and a section view of the block grid and the location of the drill holes.

Each block is assigned a leaching value using the inverse distance weighing method. The shadow price is then calculated based on the rationale described

Table 1: Arsenic leaching values (mg/kg dry substance).

Drill hole	Depth				
	0 m	1 m	2 m	3 m	5m
Dh5	0.05	0.20	0.07	0.13	0.42
Dh6	0.07	0.10	0.06	0.08	0.13
Dh7	0.54	0.22	0.24	0.6	0.05
Dh8	0.1	0.11	0.05	0.05	0.05
Dh9	0.16	0.06	0.05	0.05	0.05
Dh10	0.05	0.09	0.05	0.17	0.05
Dh11	0.13	0.58	0.13	7.3	252
Dh12	0.39	0.07	0.05	0.05	0.05
Dh13	0.05	0.05	0.05	0.11	0.36
Dh14	0.13	0.07	0.07	0.1	0.05
Dh15	0.41	0.05	0.05	0.05	0.05
Dh16	0.11	18.50	0.05	0.66	0.05
Dh17	0.05	0.09	0.38	1.21	0.08
Dh18	223.8	46.40	56.3	0.28	0.05
Dh19	0.18	0.28	0.08	0.07	0.05
Dh20	0.05	0.05	0.07	0.05	0.05

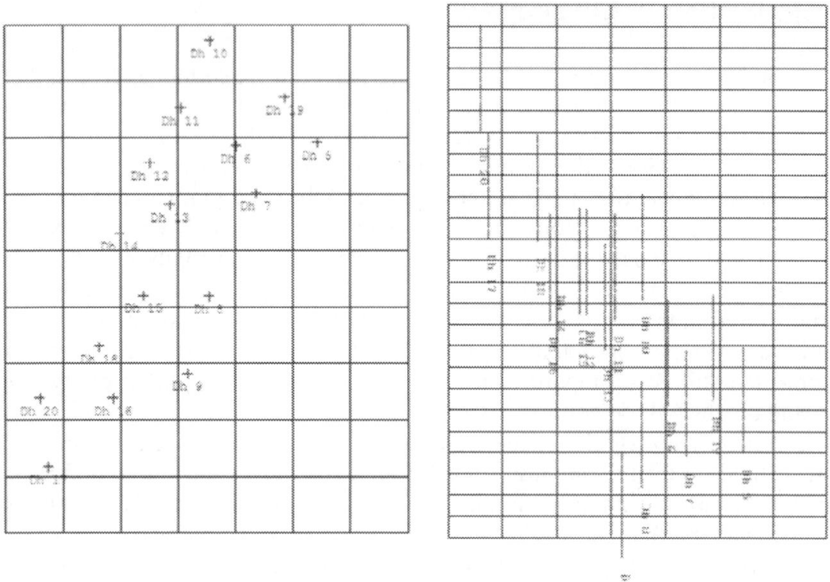

Figure 2: Plan and section view of the block grid and the drill holes.

above. The leaching limit value for non hazardous waste is 2 mg/kg dry substance, $2*10^{-3}$mg/ton. The net value (gross value-cost) of excavated blocks with this value is zero (eqn.(3)). This is expressed as follows:

$$V - C = O \tag{3}$$

$$L \times SP = C$$

$$SP = \frac{C}{L}$$

$$SP = \frac{16 euro / ton_{soil}}{2mg_{As} / 10^3 ton_{soil}}$$

$$SP = 8 \times 10^{-3} euro / mg_{As}$$

where V denotes the gross value (euro/ ton_{soil}), L the leaching limit value ($mg_{substance}$/ ton_{soil}), C the cost (euro/ ton_{soil}) and SP the shadow price (euro/ ton_{soil})

The shadow price per ton of the contaminated soil is estimated to be $8*10^{-3}$euro/ mg_{As}. Thus the net economic value P (euro/ton) is calculated from the leaching value, l (mg_{As}/ ton_{soil}= 10^3 mg_{As}/ kg_{soil}) as in eqn (4).

$$P = l \times SP - C \tag{4}$$

$$P(euro / ton_{soil}) = l(mg_{As} / ton_{soil}) \times 8 \times 10^{-3} euro / mg_{As} - 16 euro / ton_{soil}$$

Therefore blocks that have a leaching value less than 2 are assigned a negative economic value, whereas blocks that have a leaching value more than 2 are assigned a positive economic value.

A computerised floating cone method, by means of CSMINE software, is implemented. CSMINE is a mine planning and design software accompanying the book by Hustrulid and Kuchta [2]. The purpose is to define the optimal excavation contour, in other words the blocks that need to be excavated in order to optimise the use of the available funds and maximise the environmental profit. The maximum depth of excavation is quite low (5 meters), so it was decided to consider the sides almost vertical. A slope angle of approximately 75° was selected that is proved not to cause any stability problems. Table 2 provides information on all the blocks that shape the optimal excavation outline.

Table 2: Leaching value and net profit of the blocks that should be excavated.

Block number	Leaching value (mg/kg)	Net profit (€)	Block number	Leaching value (mg/kg)	Net profit (€)
1	0.05	-4,875	17	0.12	-4,688
2	0.05	-4,875	18	0.22	-4,440
3	144.64	356,603	19	0.17	-4,567
4	129.75	319,373	20	3.85	4,615
5	101.75	249,366	21	2.41	1,033
6	48.97	117,430	22	3.6	3,988
7	18.55	41,376	23	6.32	10,791
8	6.83	12,082	24	23.42	53,540
9	10.31	20,769	25	104.7	256,760
10	25.12	57,806	26	3.19	2,965
11	33.51	78,786	27	5.06	7,649
12	12.45	26,119	28	9.08	17,703
13	4.11	5,285	29	15.71	34,280
14	4.42	6,038	30	34.17	80,432
15	4.24	5,606	31	159.74	394,355
16	0.31	-4,213	32	15	32,498
			33	14.21	30,532

Figures 3 and 4 show two sections (East-West and North-South) of the final pit limit. The discontinuous line shows the surface elevation and the thick line marks the ultimate pit outline. The economic net value of each block is also shown. The blocks that need to be removed are shown in grey.

The figures show that not all positive valued blocks can be excavated. For instance, block (504050, 4175035, 20) in Figure 4 valued at +2.709 shouldn't be removed because the cost to excavate the overlying blocks is more than the net profit from that action. Figure 5 shows in plan view the number of blocks that should be removed in the downward direction. The discontinuous lines indicate the orientation and location of the mentioned sections.

According to the floating cone technique 33 blocks (10,313 tons) should be removed, 27 of them have positive economic value (leaching value more than 2)

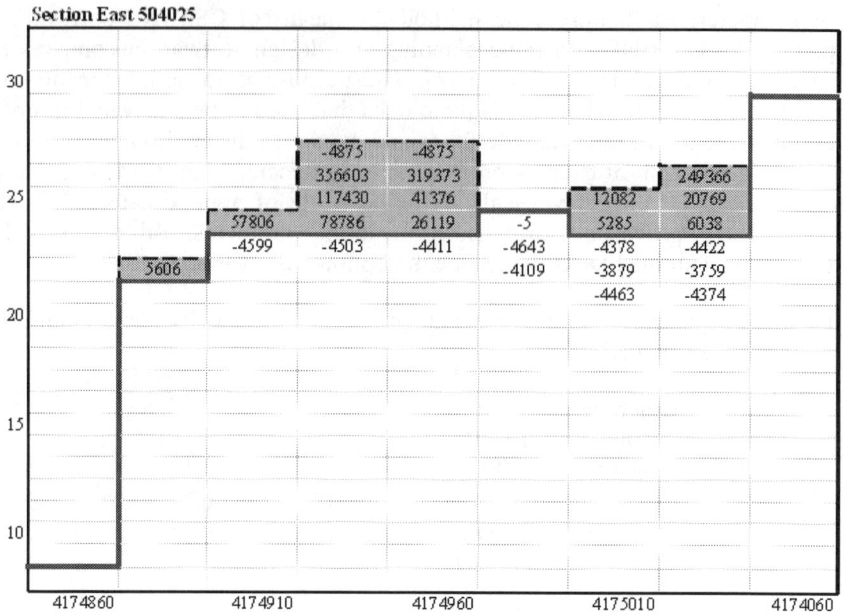

Figure 3: Section North-South at Easting 504025.

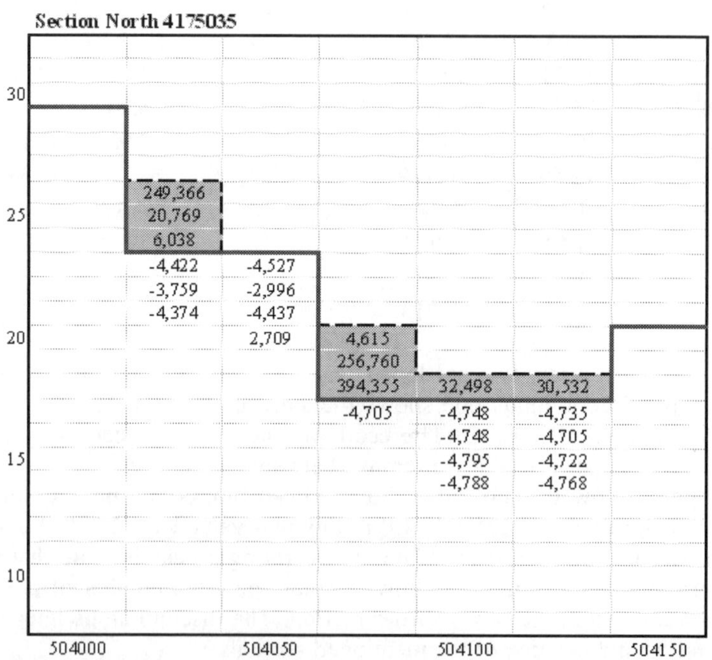

Figure 4: Section East-West at Northing 4175035.

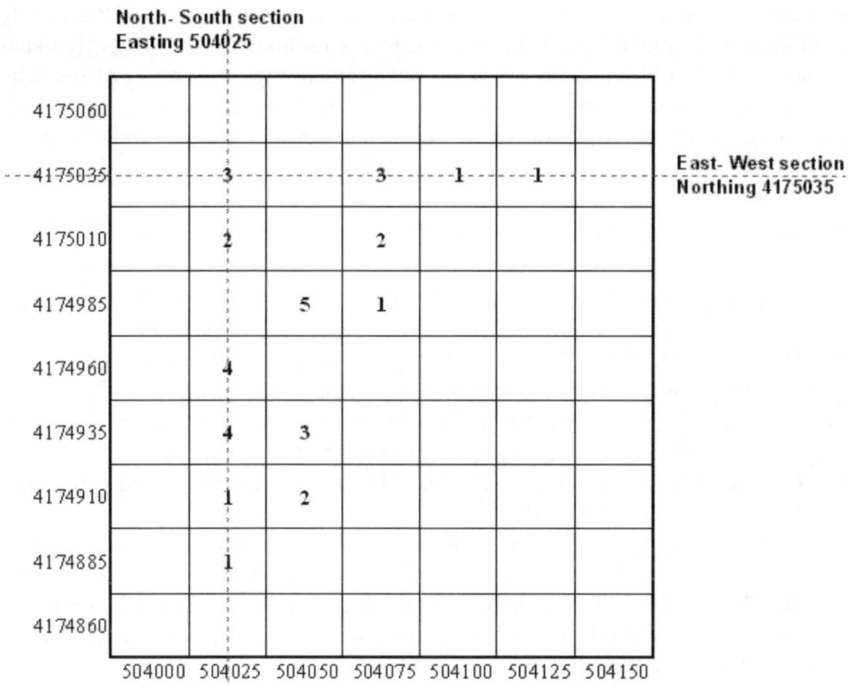

Figure 5: Plan view showing the number of blocks that should be removed in a downward direction.

and 6 have negative value. The average leaching value of these blocks is 28.7 mg/kg dry substance. The net profit of this pit is estimated to be 2,169,588 euro. This number, obviously, doesn't have an absolute meaning. It depends on the basic assumptions that were made.

5 Conclusions

By transferring mining theory into soil remediation, an approach aiming at the optimisation of the available remediation funds is developed and presented in the paper. Contamination is treated as a negative ore. Although it has a negative meaning, the removal of contaminated soil, as with ore extraction, has a positive value. It is considered profitable, in terms of environmental protection. In fact the environmental benefit is proportional to the level of the contamination (e.g. the concentration of the contaminants).

Corresponding to the pit optimisation theory, the Floating Cone method can be used to determine the optimal excavation outline. The absence of an economic value attributable to contaminated soil is overcome by a basic assumption. The contaminants' concentration limit value is the break even limit at which the net profit is considered zero. This way, a shadow price is produced to be assigned to contaminated soil and the net profit of the excavated soil can be estimated. The methodology can be of great value especially in cases where the available budget is not enough to clean up all the volume of contaminated soil, which is usually the case. The results most probably do not indicate the excavation of the whole range of contaminated soil. The optimal excavation contour, the exact location and depth, is identified in order to guide the optimal use of the remediation funds.

References

[1] European Environment Agency, Environment in the European Union at the turn of the century. Soil degradation, Ch. 3.6, (1999), pp. 192.

[2] Hustrulid, W. & Kuchta, M., Open pit mine planning and design. Volume 1-Fundamentals, Balkema Publishers, Brookfield.

[3] Lane, K. F., The economic definition of ore cut-off grades in theory and practice, Mining Journal Books Ltd, London, 1988, 149pp

[4] Cairns, R.D. & Shinkuma, T., The choice of the cutoff grade in mining, Resources Policy 29 (2003) 75–81

[5] Caccetta, L., Application of optimisation techniques in open pit mining

[6] Caccetta, L.& Kelsey, P.J., Models for Mine Site Rehabilitation, Proc. MODSIM 2001 International Congress on Modelling and Simulation

[7] Laurich, R., Planning and Design of Surface Mines, Society for Mining, Metallurgy, and Exploration, Inc. (SME).

[8] Karachaliou, T. & Kaliampakos, D., Redeveloping derelict urban space, the case study of Lavrio, Greece. CABERNET 2005 – The International Conference on Managing Urban Land, Belfast, Northern Ireland, UK, 2005.

[9] Karachaliou, T., Damigos, D., & Kaliampakos, D., Risk assessment in heavily contaminated lands. CEST 2007 – 10th International Conference on Environmental Science and Technology, September 5th–7th, 2007, Greece.

[10] Kaliampakos, D., Damigos, D. & Karachaliou, T., Using the "dry tomb" technique in the remediation of heavily contaminated land, (SWEMP 2007), December 11–13, 2007, Bangkok.

[11] 2003/33/EC: Council Decision of 19 December 2002 establishing criteria and procedures for the acceptance of waste at landfills pursuant to Article 16 of and Annex II to Directive 1999/31/EC.

Simplified volume estimation techniques for contaminated land remediation: a UK example

N. Cropp[1,2], E. Hellawell[1] & R. Woods[1]
[1]*Faculty for Engineering and Physical Sciences, University of Surrey, UK*
[2]*Tony Gee and Partners, UK*

Abstract

The need for contaminated land assessment is increasing in the UK as Brownfield sites are being targeted for development. For sites that are deemed to be contaminated, the practical application of a remediation strategy often leads to approximations of volumes of material to be treated. The extent of contamination on the site is assessed based on a limited number of data points within a defined area. At each data point the level of contamination is known for a given sample depth. In the UK a risk based approach is used to determine whether the soil is 'contaminated' and in need of treatment. In a commercial context, time and cost pressures lead to simplifications of the volume estimation process. These simplifications must strike a balance between the environmental risk from underestimates of the contaminated volume and the cost of wasted resources associated with overestimates. This paper presents a comparison between three practical estimation techniques used to assess the volume of 'contaminated' soil on a development site, formerly a gas works. The methods used are; areas of influence, proportional method and interpolation using Kriging. All techniques were found to have a useful application although the limitations of each must be recognised. There is inevitable uncertainty associated with the simplification of any practical situation. In comparing these methods the main uncertainties are identified and management approaches discussed.
Keywords: volume estimation, contaminated soil.

1 Introduction

In the UK the previously developed land (PDL), also referred to as Brownfield land, is being targeted for development. The government have set a target of

WIT Transactions on Ecology and the Environment, Vol 107,
www.witpress.com, ISSN 1743-3541 (on-line)
doi:10.2495/BF080101

60% of all new housing to be located on Brownfield land [1]. Some of this land has been subject to polluting industrial land uses in the past leading to contamination of the soil. A key information source for assessing contaminated land is site investigation (SI) data, whereby contamination levels are identified at discrete locations through sampling and testing procedures [2,3]. This leads to a series of data points where the level of contamination is known and can be used to determine a representative concentration of contamination across the whole site. In the UK a risk based approach is used to determine whether the level of contamination is acceptable with regard to the risk to human health and the wider environment [4,5]. Should the concentration of contamination on site be found to pose an unacceptable level of risk the site is considered to be "contaminated land", as defined by the regulations [4], and will require some form of remediation.

In the past the most cost effective option for dealing with contaminated material was 'dig and dump' [6]. There are a number of draw backs to this approach including the fact that the problem is simply being relocated and also the availability of landfill is not infinite [7]. The limited availability of landfill has been magnified by legislative changes; most prominently the ban on co-disposal of waste [8]. The subsequent rise in the cost of disposal is leading to an increase in the market for, previously more expensive, process based remediation techniques [9]. The overall increasing cost associated with developing contaminated land drives a need for better delineation of the areas that actually require excavation for treatment or disposal.

The nature of estimation means that there is inevitably some level of uncertainty involved in the assessment process. In the case of contaminated land this is predominately related to the limited amount of information available for the assessment compared with the complexity of the spatial distributions of contamination across the site [10,11]. Part of the solution to improving the estimate of soil volumes is to improve the quality and amount of data available. Several studies into optimised site investigation techniques have been carried out (*e.g.* Demougeot-Renadrd and De Fouquet [12]). However, in a commercial context inevitable cost and time pressures limit the resources available for complex site assessments and collection of additional data.

The aim of this paper is to assess three volume estimation techniques that can be applied to contaminated land where data is limited. The methods used are: areas of influence, proportional method and interpolation using Kriging. Each has been applied to a former gas works case study using different aspects of the data obtained through the SI. The methods have been assessed for their ease of use and appropriateness for the specific site used in the case study.

2 Experimental materials and methods

The volume estimation methods used are:

1. Area of influence: This method is based on the assumption that each data point is representative of the area surrounding it. This method does not consider any spatial relationships between adjacent data points.

2. Proportional method: Descriptive data from borehole logs is combined with test results to calculate the proportion of each stratum that is likely to be contaminated.
3. Kriging: This method uses the Kriging interpolation method to create contour plots of the contamination distribution across the site. The method is based on an assumed spatial relationship between data points.

Each of the above methods has been applied to a case study, the expected volume of contaminated material calculated and compared.

2.1 Volume estimation method 1: area of influence

This method is based on the assumption that SI data from a specific sampling location can be considered representative of the ground conditions surrounding it. The method uses the spatial distribution of sample points to describe the contamination conditions of site as a whole. The contamination test data for each stratum is used to classify each point as contaminated or not. The method comprises the following steps (Figure 1a to d):

1. Sample points for a given stratum are plotted across the site using a computer aided design package such as AutoCAD [13] (Figure 1a)
2. The data points are connected to their nearest neighbours to produce a series of non-overlapping triangles across the site, similar to the triangular irregular network (TIN) (Figure 1b). To represent ease of application under time pressure the points have been connected by eye only.

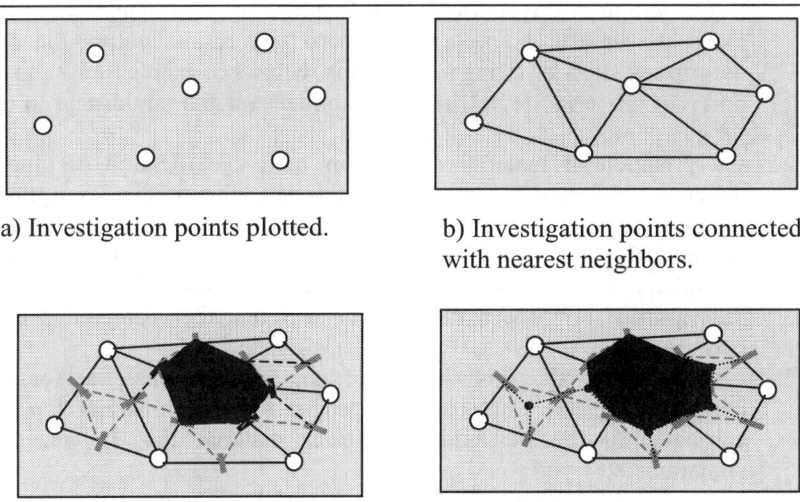

a) Investigation points plotted.

b) Investigation points connected with nearest neighbors.

c) Bisect lines between investigation points.

d) Area of influence extended to centroid of remaining areas.

Figure 1: The area of influence method.

3. The mid point of each of these connecting lines is joined to form a polygon around the sample point, creating an area of influence. (Figure 1c)
4. At this point the areas of influence of the sample points do not cover the entire site; the parts of that site that fall between the assigned areas of influence are allocated using the centroid as the intersection point. (Figure 1d)
5. Areas for the outermost data points are extended to the boundary for the site
6. The volume to be treated is calculated multiplying each area by its respective thickness of contaminated material. These volumes are then summed.

2.2 Volume estimation method 2: proportional method

This method is useful for gaining a general overview of the volume of contaminated soil on a site. The proportion of each stratum that is contaminated is estimated based on descriptive borehole logs and contamination test data. The proportion of a stratum that is classed as contaminated is then applied to the total volume of that stratum to calculate a volume of material requiring treatment. The process has the following stages:

1. Collation of borehole data and classification of material as contaminated based on test results. Figure 2 shows an example log with two test points A and B within Material 1. It is assumed that a test result within a given described material is representative of that material. In the example shown two test results within the same description show differing results (A is within acceptable limits and B is not). In this case the test result is applied a depth equidistant to each sample point.
2. Interpretation of material descriptions and classification of untested material. In Figure 2, Material 2 is untested. Should the description of the material be sufficiently similar to Material 1 above that the material can be considered to be the same, the test result of sample B would be considered to be representative of Material 2 also. However, if the descriptions show the material to be different then Material 2 is not classified.
3. Calculation of the total length of contaminated material for each material type, the total recorded length for each material type and subsequently the percentage of each material that is considered contaminated.
    a. All logs that record a given material are summed to give a total recorded length for that material ($\sum L_M$)
    b. The total contaminated length for that material would be calculated for tested data ($\sum L_{TEST}$) and interpreted data ($\sum L_{INTERP}$).
    c. From this, the percent contaminated for a given material can be calculated ($Contam_M$) as shown in Equation (1) below;

$$Contam_M = 100 \times \frac{\sum L_{TEST} + \sum L_{INTERP}}{\sum L_M} \tag{1}$$

4. Apply the percent contaminated for each material type to the total site volume for that material type to calculate volume of contaminated material.

The total material volume is calculated from a three dimensional ground model. This was done by plotting the material thickness recorded at each location and then interpolating, using Kriging, to establish the volume of each material across the whole site. The programme Surfer v8.0 was used as described in Section 2.3 below. The process can be repeated to calculate an uncontaminated volume and an unclassified volume of material for each stratum as required.

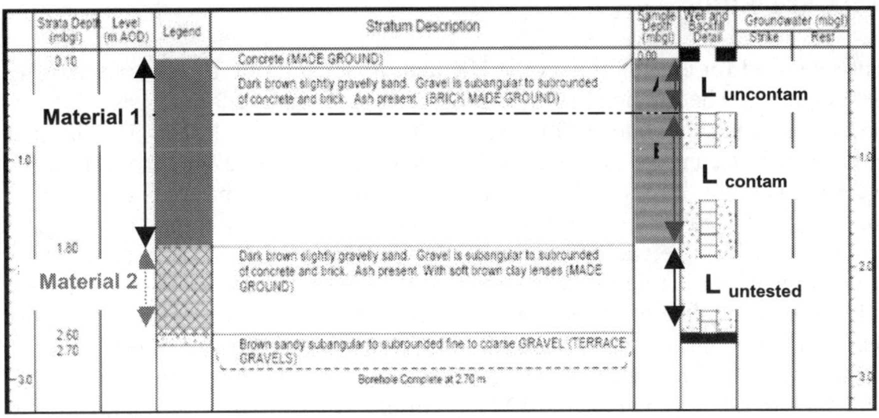

Figure 2: Example borehole log used in the proportional method.

2.3 Volume estimation method 3: Kriging

Surfer v8 [14] was used to carry out this method. Surfer allows data to be plotted and displayed in a number of ways including; data points, contour plots and 3-dimentional surfaces. Multiple maps can be overlain to present different data sets on a single plot. Areas within a surface and volumes between surfaces can be calculated, making the programme ideal for this study. To create a map data points are interpolated to produce regular grid across the area of interest. Ordinary Kriging was selected as the interpolation method for this stud; the default method for the programme. Considered to be the most appropriate as the study is aimed at reproducing simple methods that are likely to be used under time pressures. The Kriging interpolation method is based on the assumption that there is an underlying spatial relationship between data points; i.e. the concentration of contamination varies as a function of the distance between data points. For a full explanation of Kriging refer to Matheron [15] and Matheron and Kleingeld [16].

The process for this method is as follows (repeated each stratum separately):

1. The concentration ratio data is interpolated using Kriging to produce a regular grid of contamination concentrations across the site. This data was then used to produce a contour plot for each contaminant
2. Contour plots for each of the assessed contaminants are overlain to produce a single combined plot indicating areas of contaminated material where concentrations exceed acceptable limits.
3. To assess the depth of affected material Surfer v8 can then be used to plot the total strata thickness and calculate the total site wide volume of each material type.
4. The total areas of contamination exceeding the allowable concentration values are then overlain onto a plot of the thickness of the assessed stratum and the volume of material within these areas calculated.

3 Case study

The site used for the study is in the UK and the location for a proposed housing development. The previous land uses on the site include a former gas works in operation from the late 1800's to 1970 when it was closed. The limited environmental controls in place in the UK during the time that the gas works were in operation lead to polluting operations on the site. Since this time part of the site has remained unoccupied and part has been used as offices and warehouses. It is the vacant portion of the site that is of immediate concern for development and is referred to as Phase 1. The area of the site is approximately 1.1 hectares. SI data has been collected from a series of investigations; the most recent (59 points within Phase 1) has been used for the assessment of contamination with historical information used only for assessing stratigraphy. The site stratigraphy is generally Made Ground (of various types) underlain by alluvial deposits (sandy clay/silt across part of site) and flood plain gravels and sands.

3.1 Contaminants of concern

Based on the results of the initial risk assessment of the site the following contaminants have been identified as posing significant risk to human health, the wider environment or structures on the site. Excavation and remediation or disposal off site is applied to material "contaminated" with respect to the agree remediation targets listed in Table 1 below.

Table 1: Acceptable limits for key contaminants.

Contaminant of concern	Remediation Target (mg/kg)
Ammonium	100
Benzene	8
Naphthalene	23
Bezo(a)pyrene	55

4 Results

For each method described above the volume of material classed as contaminated was calculated for the Made Ground and Alluvial clay layers as the strata of concern for excavation. Table 2 below summarises these results.

Table 2: Calculated volumes.

		Volume of Contaminated Soil		
		Kriging (m^3)	Area of Influence (m^3)	Proportional method (m^3)
Made Ground	*Total Volume*	*14,400*	*11,850*	*14,400*
	Contaminated Volume	5,370	2,585	3,744 (26%)
Alluvium	*Total Volume*	*3,650*	*2,635*	*3,650*
	Contaminated Volume	2,050	880	1,278 (35%)
Total Contaminated Volume		7,420	3,465	5,020

5 Discussion

The application of each method is discussed below followed by a general discussion of common issues.

5.1 Area of influence

The application of the area of influence method is very easy and requires little specialist judgement in its application. The methodology described permits the user to complete a volume calculation based on visual data and can be carried out with the use of readily available software. The method could be improved by more accurately identifying the nearest neighbours when triangulating the data, however this would require another level of sophistication in the software used.

The method may be best used to highlight where more information is required as it incorporates a simple visual plot. If there is a particularly large area of influence attributed to a borehole, it may suggest the need for further investigation. The areas calculated can be compared with the expected hot spot size to indicate whether the SI distribution has been sufficient to find them [17].

The main limitation of the method is that it excludes any spatial relationships between data points. It is also sensitive to data gaps, and uneven sampling distributions across the site. In this case the method consistently predicted the lowest volumes for remediation indicating the SI may be insufficient.

5.2 Proportional method

The application of this method requires much more expert judgement than either of the others. In reading the SI logs the assessor must understand the descriptions and be able to filter the key features that can be used to group materials of a similar nature. For contamination assessment a key challenge is in describing Made Ground and identifying its origin, and associated contamination. The problem is the inherent variability of Made Ground; at the case site seven different types were identified based on contamination test data, material descriptions and colour. Historical maps can be used determine the timing of the placement of the material with respect to site activities, aiding in the classification. As it is impossible to test the whole stratum, the descriptions and history of the material become more important as an indication as to the likelihood of contamination.

The main disadvantage of this method is that it does not identify where the contamination is located, just approximately how much to expect. As such it is really only useful for early design stages and best used in conjunction with some form of plot of test locations.

5.3 Kriging

This method assumes a spatial relationship where one may not always exist, for example ashy patches were found on the case study site, which are isolated hotspots of contamination. Without modification of the Kriging process itself contamination hotspots can become smeared across the site, increasing the affected area. In general this smearing of information may be useful for an overall view of the contamination level of the site; however the delineation of contaminated areas may not represent the variability of the material. In applying contaminated areas to the total thickness of the stratum the method does not consider variation of contamination levels with depth within the stratum. This contributes to overestimated volumes as shown in the case site. This could be improved with more detailed assessment of the thickness of the affected stratum in the calculated volume. On the whole the method is more rigorous as the interpretation process uses all of the available data to predict the location of contamination. The process is most useful for mobile contaminants where there is more of a spatial relationship between data points.

5.4 General discussion

There are a number of general practical issues that need to be considered. For example if a contaminated stratum is overlain by clean stratum the clean stratum may also need to be excavated to assess the contaminated material beneath. In addition the practical issue of 'over dig' has not been included. During excavation works on site the difficulties of excavating to the exact base of a strata is accounted for by allowing an additional depth of excavation.

A disadvantage of Kriging and the area of influence methods is that the irregular contaminated areas identified are unlikely to offer a practical remediation plan for the site. In the case of the percent contaminated it is not possible to identify the areas of the site that require remediation at all. All of the methods require care when extrapolating data to the site boundaries. The amount of data available often diminishes at the boundaries and data outside of the boundary is rarely available. The development of these calculations to form a remediation plan would need to allow for these limitations.

With all of these methods there is a need to have a good understanding of the conceptual model for the site, what the nature of the contamination is, where it has come from and the behaviour of the particular contaminants in the ground. With this understanding it is easier to apply an appropriate volume estimation method and subsequently design a practical remediation plan.

6 Conclusions

The methods presented can help to give structure to the volume estimation process. The most appropriate method will depend on the contaminant of concern and its physical and chemical behaviour in the ground. Accepting that, in a commercial context, time and cost pressures mean that problems are simplified by necessity; the issue becomes how to best deal with the associated uncertainty. With all of the methods there is a need to apply an understanding of the chemical behaviour of the contamination, and a practical approach to developing a remediation strategy to be implemented on site.

Acknowledgements

The authors wish to thank Enviros Consulting Ltd, Tamdown Regeneration Ltd and Explore Living Plc for the supply of data used in the case study and EPSRC for support of the Engineering Doctorate Programme at University of Surrey of which this project is part.

References

[1] Office of the Deputy Prime Minister (ODM), Annual Report 2003 (Cm 5906), 2003.
[2] British Standards Institute (BSI), BS5930: 1999 Code of practice for site investigations, BSI: London, ISBN 0 580 33059 1, 1999.
[3] BSI, BS 10175:2001 Code of Practice for the Identification of Potentially Contaminated Land and its Investigation, BSI: London, ISBN 0 580 33090 7, 2001.
[4] ODPM, Environmental Protection Act (Part IIA), HMSO: England, 2000.
[5] Department for Environment, Food and Rural Affairs (Defra), CLR 11: Model Procedures for the Management of Land ODPM: England, 2004.
[6] Rivett, MO, Petts, J, Butler, B and Martin, I, Remediation of contaminated land and groundwater: experience in England and Wales, Journal of Environmental Management, 65 (2002), pp 251–268, 2002.

[7] Wood AA, Contaminated land – an engineers view point. Polluted and Marginal Land 1994, Proceedings of the 3rd International Conference: Re-use of contaminated land and landfills, 1994.
[8] ODPM, Environmental Protection Act England and Wales: The Landfill (England and Wales) (Amendment) Regulations 2004, HMSO: England, 2004.
[9] Market & Business Development Ltd., UK Contaminated Land Treatment Market Development Report 2006, Market & Business Development Ltd: England, 2006.
[10] Demougeot-Renard H, de Fouquet C and Renard P, Heavy Metals in the Environment: Forecasting the Number of Soil Samples Required to Reduce Remediation Cost Uncertainty, Journal of Environmental Quality, 33 (2004), American Society of Agronomy: USA, pp 1694–1702, 2004.
[11] Ramsey, MH and Argyraki A, Estimation of measurement uncertainty from field sampling: the implications for the classification of contaminated land, The Science of the Total Environment, 198 (1997), Elsevier, pp 243–257, 1997.
[12] Demougeot-Renadrd H and De Fouquet C, Geostatistical approach for assessing soil volumes requiring remediation: validation using lead polluted soils underlying a former smelting works, Environmental Science and Technology, 38 (2004), American Chemical Society: USA, pp. 5120–5126, 2004.
[13] AutoDesk, AutoCAD© 2007.
[14] Golden Software Inc. Surfer® Version 8.
[15] Matheron, G, The theory of regionalized variables and its applications, Paris School of Mines publication, pp. 211, 1971.
[16] Matheron, G and Kleingeld, WJ, The evolution of geostatistics, Proceedings of the 20th APCOM International Symposium, SAIMM: Johannesburg, 1987
[17] Department of the Environment (DoE), Contaminated Land Research Report 4: Sampling Strategies for Contaminated Land, DoE: England, 1994.

Modern environmental technology tests in the Old Gasworks area in Bydgoszcz (project PROMOTE ETV-SGS)

W. Irminski & M. Wroblewska
Polish Geological Institute, Warsaw, Poland

Abstract

PROMOTE is one of the currently running research projects evaluating and implementing ETV (Environmental Technology Verification). It is funded by the European Union in the 7th Framework Program. An ETV certificate guarantees that new equipment or innovative technology corresponds to the producer's description of advantages and simultaneously responds to the environmental requirements of EU experts.

ETV-SGS (Soil-Groundwater Systems) has to answer several logical requirements to be useful and understandable. The general rules of system operation are compliant with the PRINCE2 methodology applied in many countries. This involves laboratory and field test stages. In the PROMOTE project the research site in Poland was chosen for field tests of innovative measurements and monitoring technology. The site was located at the Old Gasworks in Bydgoszcz whose terrain is strongly contaminated. The area is recognized and documented with contamination by organic compounds of ground and groundwater – vestiges of 140 years of gas production from coal – hence became for PROMOTE project purposes and the ETV system an ideal research site. Despite the number of years since the site has been used, tests conducted in cooperation with the Municipality of Bydgoszcz and the land owner i.e. Pomorska Spolka Gazownictwa, confirmed the longevity of pollutants and the high risk assessment for the ground and groundwater environment. The results obtained are all the more credible as the innovative technology tests were verified with classical methods and simultaneous analysis in three different, independent European laboratories in Stuttgart, Barcelona and Warsaw.

Keywords: brownfield, old gasworks, groundwater contamination, Environmental Technology Verification.

WIT Transactions on Ecology and the Environment, Vol 107, © 2008 WIT Press
www.witpress.com, ISSN 1743-3541 (on-line)
doi:10.2495/BF080111

1 Introduction

PROMOTE is one of the currently running EU research projects evaluating and implementing ETV (Environmental Technology Verification) [10] coordinated by DECHEMA e.V. (Germany). ETV systems are already working in the USA [4], Canada [6], Korea and Japan [5]. It is reasonable to take advantage of existing patterns and experiences to implement the system in EU area. An ETV certificate guarantees that new equipment or innovative technology corresponds to the producer's description of advantages and simultaneously responds to the environmental requirements of EU experts. The objectives of PROMOTE are: 1) strengthening the competitiveness of technology developers and the acceptance of European technologies in the field of soil-groundwater remediation and monitoring systems. 2) Faster entrance and full access to innovative technologies in the European market.

ETV-SGS (Soil-Groundwater Systems) has to answer several logical requirements to be useful and understandable – "cost-efficient and fast", "valid", "un-bureaucratic" and "fair and generally comprehensive". The general rules of system operation are compliant with the PRINCE2 methodology that has already been applied in many countries. The ETV system involves laboratory and field test stages.

The PROMOTE field tests of innovative measurements and monitoring technology took place in Poland. The site was located at the Old Gasworks in Bydgoszcz whose terrain is strongly contaminated. The brownfield area had been examined by the PGI Working Group in the frame of INCORE in the 5th FP of the European Union (Irminski and Konieczynska [3]). The area is recognized and documented with contamination by organic compounds of ground and groundwater – vestiges of 140 years of gas production from coal (Hoppe and Perlinska [2]) – hence became for PROMOTE project purposes and the ETV system an ideal research site. Despite the number of years since the site has been used, tests conducted in cooperation with the Municipality of Bydgoszcz and the land owner i.e. Pomorska Spolka Gazownictwa, confirmed the longevity of pollutants and the high risk assessment for the ground and groundwater environment. The results obtained are all the more credible as the innovative technology tests were verified with classical methods and simultaneous analysis in three different, independent European laboratories in Stuttgart, Barcelona and Warsaw.

The city of Bydgoszcz was the first user of the Polish stage of PROMOTE deliverables (the investigation of industrial terrain located in the center of City). However the main goal of the field tests was an evaluation of several tools and technology being a "guinea pig" of the planned European ETV system. Within the project activity there were verified as follows: a photometer LF 300 (made by SLANDI, Poland), a sensometric sond MOX (made by VEGAS, University of Stuttgart, Germany), a minipressure pump (MPP made by IMW - Innovative Messtechnik Weiß, Germany) in combination with a fluorometer (made by VEGAS, Germany), a MPP with double packer, a minipiezometer system CMT pipe (provided by IMW, Germany), and ceramic dosimeters in the form of passive samplers (made by IMW, Germany).

Each of the tools by design will facilitate and festinate field work in environmental protection. In consequence it will be economic with less impact on environment.

This presentation will show the results of field work and comparison to the traditional, classical research methods.

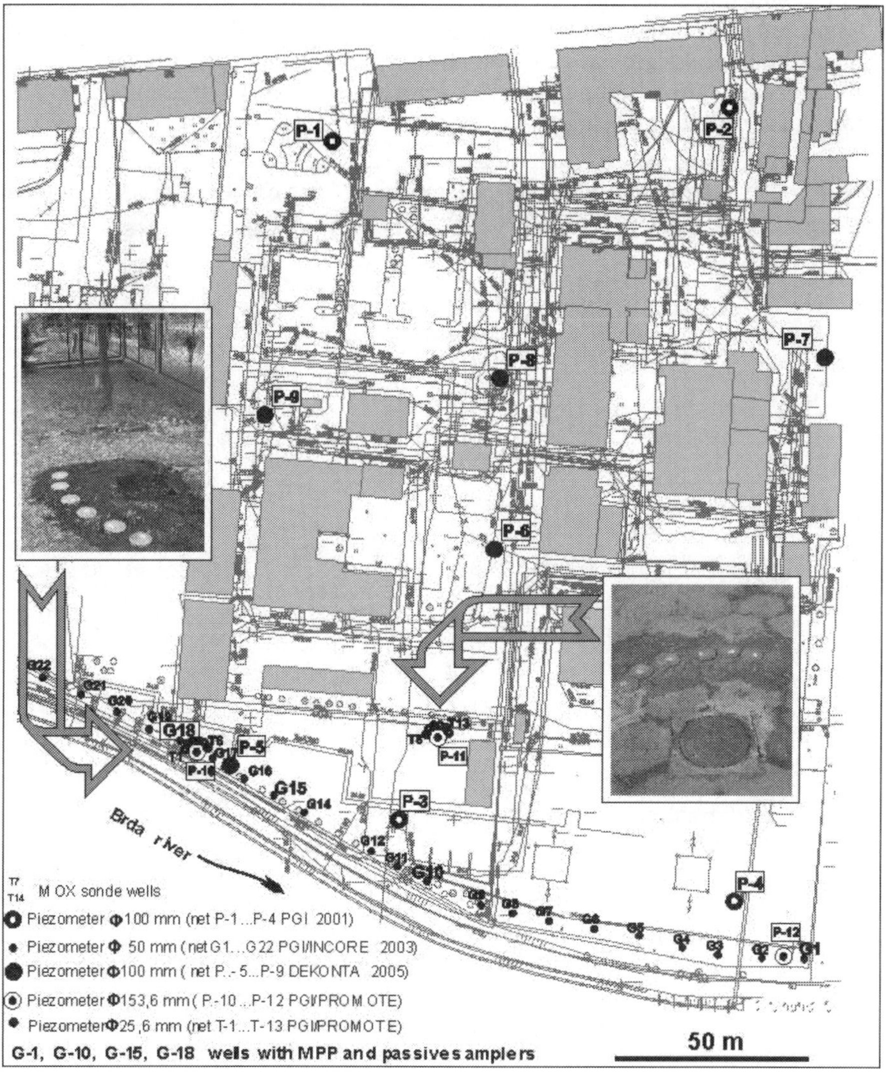

Figure 1: Localization of all investigation boreholes at the Old Gasworks area in Bydgoszcz (Poland).

2 Field ETV tests

For PROMOTE purposes (testing the innovative technologies) existing 2 inch piezometers from the INCORE project and new ones, designed in two additional research reference sites were used. Each of them constitutes a separate system of 1 inch piezometers in the very close neighborhood to some standard 5 inch piezometers which were treated as the comparative well (figure 1).

The holes were drilled in sand and gravel Quaternary deposits, to a depth of 7,5 m. Below this depth there are Tertiary silts and brown coal.

Both reference sites show insignificant differences of the level and type of contamination of the ground and groundwater consequent of location in different pollutant source areas (old pitch pits, underground containers of ammonia water, benzene and naphthalene etc.).

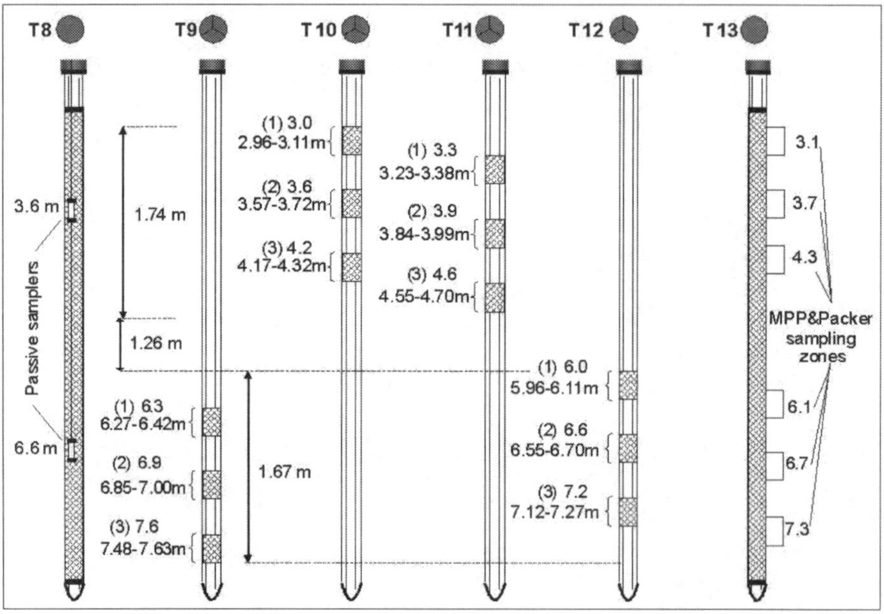

Figure 2: Sampling system of CMT pipe and 1 inch piezometer next to the well P11.

This piezometer system (figure 2) enabled testing of the horizontal diversification, either organic or inorganic contamination, in the water bearing layer. It was attained by providing triple comparative tests in a standard well (5 inch) using a set of MP-1 Grundfoss pumps with a double packer with a test in the CMT piezometer using a manual pump and a last test in the 1 inch hole using a minipressure pump (MPP) in combination with a double packer. Additionally passive samplers were installed in defined depth levels in 5 inch and 1 inch wells.

Similarly, the MPP results were checked with passive samplers in a set of nine pieces in the same four 2 inch holes located at the outflow of contaminated water into the Brda River.

The whole research site was controlled by the electronic measurement of the water table and water-air temperature in holes with the device called a diver. It recorded data every 15 minutes giving almost continuous information about the changes of the conditions at the site.

3 Tested technologies

The minipressure pump (MPP) is particularly useful for precise sampling of groundwater in aspects of volatile compound analysis such as naphthalene and BTEX [7]. The pump driving it is chemically inactive compressed nitrogen. The MPP size is small and its construction simple. It can be installed in small diameter piezometers at the water bearing layer or directly in the ground.

The small size and simplicity of operation give the MPP the greatest advantages. It was applied in two test reference sites at the Brda River in the Bydgoszcz Gasworks.

It is possible to obtain different combinations of several minipressure pumps at the different depth levels of the investigated water bearing horizon. Each pump was sampling water independently thanks to packer installation in the 5 inch hole (figure 4).

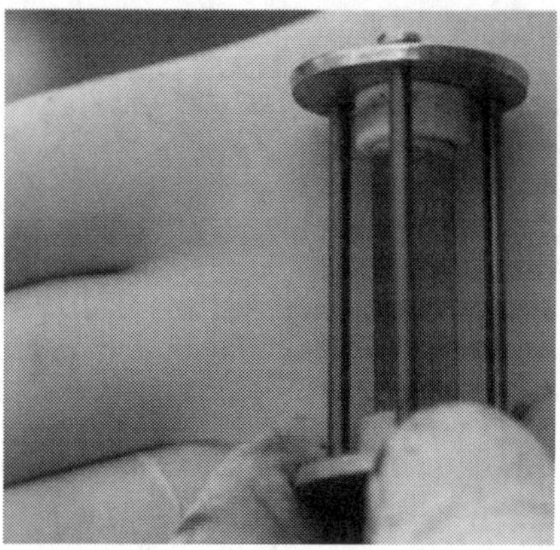

Figure 3: Disassembled sampler contaminated with polycyclic aromatic hydrocarbons. A stainless steel "cage" secures the ceramic tube in the field and during transport to the laboratory.

The photometer LF 300 is the newest product of the SLANDI company, designed for field applications to determine almost 150 substances in water or wastewater [11]. Because of instability of some of the chemical compounds a direct diagnostic at the borehole site is required. This research method doesn't require a high budget and allows for speedy field work. A repeated analysis with the photometer conducted in the mini field laboratory against the chosen chemical compounds was verified by analysis at certified laboratories in Barcelona (CSIC - Consejo Superior de Investigationes Cientificas, Spain) and Warsaw (PGI - Polish Geological Institute). It was possible thanks to the sampling methodology, which took three water samples simultaneously.

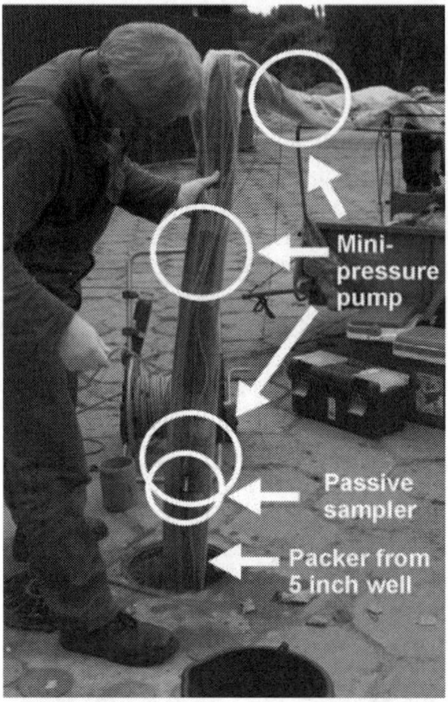

Figure 4: Packer disassembling in classical 5 inch well. A small sampler is seen tested in combination with the minipressure pump MPP (inside the protective cover of the packer).

Minipiezometers CMT are relatively cheap and easy to construct, mount and disassemble [8]. They enable drawing of the water samples from strictly determined depth levels (figure 2). Their disadvantage is the necessity of using the manual pump for a single application. It excluded application of the method for investigation of volatile compounds. The piezometer is a triple channel pipe of 1 inch diameter that can be applied for single tests and monitoring cases. Each channel has a different length to reach a different depth level that enables strict investigation of contamination variation with depth in the water bearing horizon. Drawing of the samples from the CMT triple channel piezometer is conducted with the simplest pump – a pipe with an inertial footvalve.

A special holes configuration was designed for CMT testing in Bydgoszcz. Their mutual localization together with classical 5 inch piezometers allowed evaluation of the advantages and disadvantages of this method of water sampling.

CMT 1 inch piezometers were installed in holes drilled with the method of lost cone.

A Fibre Optic Fluorometer, made by VEGAS, University of Stuttgart, was constructed for detection of dissolved PAHs in groundwater, highly resolved over depth. The MOX – Metal Oxide Sensor System (made by VEGAS) detects chlorinated and non-chlorinated volatile compounds in soil air (Braun and Koschitzky [1]).

All the verified tools within the PROMOTE project were compared with a standard sampling method. There were double packer constructed on the base of the classic water pump MP-1 Grundfoss.

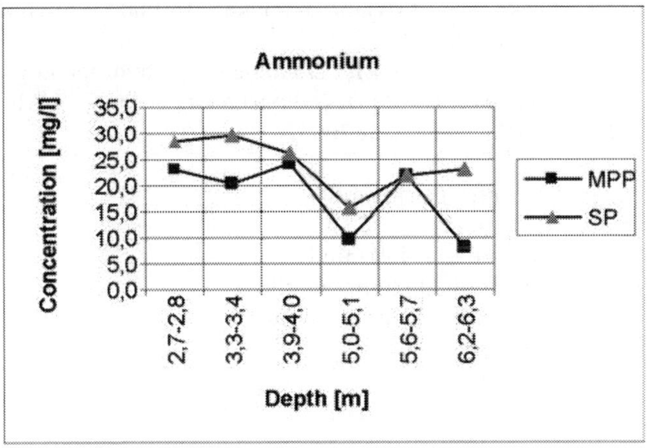

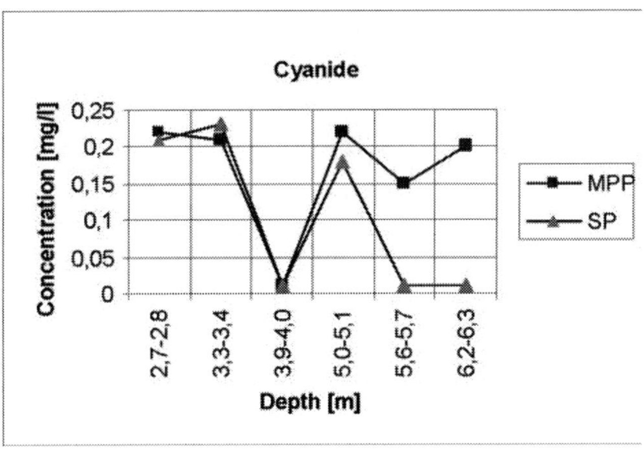

Figure 5: Preliminary comparison of the chemical analysis results of the water samples taken at the same depth level with different equipment (MPP – minipressure pump, SP – standard pump with packer system).

The results of all field test and laboratories analysis are currently being analysed by the international PROMOTE working group [10]. They are expected in April 2008.

Proper test execution verified the important part that can be played by operating the European ETV system in the future.

More information is available at www.promote-etv.org.

References

[1] Braun J., Koschitzky H.P.: The German Research Facility for Subsurface Remediation at the Universitaet Stuttgart. In: www.cetesb.sp.gov.br/rede/documentos/oficina_europeia/vegas_2.pdf

[2] Hoppe I., Perlinska A.: Od swiatla plomyka – 140 lat Gazowni Bydgoskiej, PGNiG S.A. Bydgoszcz 2000,

[3] Irminski W., Konieczynska M.: Dokumentacja hydrogeologiczna „Stara Gazownia", Bydgoszcz, ul. Jagiellonska 42. Arch. UM Bydgoszcz WGK.VII.753/4/05, Bydgoszcz 2005,

[4] www.epa.gov/etv

[5] www.epa.gov/etv/inter-partic.html

[6] www.etvcanada.com

[7] www.im-weiss.de/modell_409i.html

[8] www.im-weiss.de/produkte.html#multilevel

[9] www.im-weiss.de/produkte.html#passiv

[10] www.promote-etv.org

[11] www.slandi.pl/lab.html

Performance of Italian zeolitic tuffs and pozzolana in 2-chlorophenol removal from contaminated groundwater: the lab-scale experience

M. R. Boni, S. Sbaffoni & L. Tuccinardi
Department of Hydraulics, Transportation and Roads, "SAPIENZA" University of Rome, Italy

Abstract

The physical and chemical properties of zeolites and the availability of localized deposits of naturally occurring zeolitized tuffs and pozzolana, make them desirable for and applicable to the remediation of contaminated groundwater. This paper documents the results of a laboratory study to test the capacity of native Italian zeolites to remove 2-chlorophenol (2-CP) from water. Italian zeolitic tuff and pozzolana were characterized in terms of their chemical and structural properties and of their adsorption capacities. Moreover, the experimental activity investigated their adsorption behaviour: time and pH dependence of the adsorption process was evaluated. The results of the time-dependence adsorption study under a constantly stirred condition showed that the adsorption increases with a longer contact time for all samples; the highest adsorption occurred at pH=8÷8.5. Due to the good removal efficiencies obtained, a column test simulating the condition of an *in situ* permeable reactive barrier was carried out, in order to estimate the removal kinetics and the long-term behaviour. The removal efficiencies reached values higher than 90%, even if some long-term performance worsening occurred, due to the progressive exhaustion of the adsorption sites. These experiments demonstrate the capacity of naturally occurring zeolites to remove 2-CP from water and the opportunity to make economic use of these native deposits for *in situ* groundwater remediation.

Keywords: natural zeolites, 2-chlorophenol, permeable reactive barriers, tuff, pozzolana, groundwater.

WIT Transactions on Ecology and the Environment, Vol 107, © 2008 WIT Press
www.witpress.com, ISSN 1743-3541 (on-line)
doi:10.2495/BF080121

1 Introduction

Chlorophenols are induced into the environment in the waste stream of several industrial operations through their use as biocides or disinfectants or as a by-product of other industrial operations; they can also appear as degradation products of other chlorinated xenobiotics [1]. Because of their toxic effects, the accumulation of chlorophenols in soil and groundwater is of concern. Several decontamination techniques are available for the removal of contaminants from water; biodegradation is a technique that could potentially degrade these contaminants to innocuous products [2, 3]. However, the majority of experiments have been conducted only under laboratory conditions and scaling-up biodegradation to field conditions is not a simple process. Applying chemical technologies for the degradation of chlorophenols may be more suitable. Of all approaches, adsorption by activated carbon appears to be most prominent [4]. As activated carbon is relatively costly, attempts have been made to utilize lower-cost and naturally present materials [5, 6]. Among these, natural zeolites, which are abundantly present in Italy in tuff and pozzolana deposits, can be potentially used as adsorbent for phenol and its derivatives [7, 8]. They are rich in chabazite and phillipsite and their physical and chemical properties make them suitable for wide applications, including the removal of pollutants from the environment. Nevertheless, few attempts have been made for taking advantage of this ability of zeolites in the case of organic pollutants.

The present work aims at widening the applications of the local materials, including their possible use in the *in situ* removal of chlorophenols from groundwater. In the experimental activity presented here the performance of the Italian native zeolitic tuff and pozzolana in 2-chlorophenol (2-CP) removal from contaminated groundwater was checked.

Both batch and column tests were carried out. The batch tests aimed at defining the influence of pH and time on the adsorption process. The results obtained during the column tests, simulating an *in situ* permeable reactive barrier, allowed estimation of the 2-CP removal kinetic.

2 Materials and methods

2.1 Materials

Tuff and pozzolana were collected at two caves near Rome; they were characterized in terms of natural pH (equal to 9.3 and 9.43, respectively), unit dry weight (equal to 0.96 and 1.26 g/cm^3, respectively), mechanical characteristics and grain size distribution. In the present experimental study only the fraction between 1 and 4 mm was used.

Additionally, the materials were analyzed by X-Ray Diffractometry, confirming the abundance of the natural zeolites chabazite and phillipsite. Both materials were characterized in terms of their environmental quality through leaching tests [9]. Tuff and pozzolana exhibited composition and contaminants release fully compatible with their use for *in situ* groundwater remediation.

2.2 Experimental apparatus: batch test

The experimental activity was scheduled as follows:
- Batch tests: to evaluate pH- and time-dependence of the adsorption process.
- Column tests: to check the long-term behaviour of the reactive media and to calculate the removal kinetics.

2.2.1 Batch tests

The batch tests were performed in a continuously mixing jar-tester at a liquid-to-solid ratio (L/S) equal to 10 l/kg for 4, 8, 24, 30 and 48 hours; the pH values investigated were those acceptable for groundwater, in the range 7–9.

Additionally, the effect of possible activation through urea and thiourea on tuff was checked. A 1.18 M thiourea solution and 1.67 M urea solution were mixed with tuff at a L/S equal to 50 l/kg for 48 h at temperatures between 50 and 60°C [7], in order to avoid damages or alteration of the zeolitic structure. At the end of the activation procedure, tuff was washed and then maintained in an oven at 50°C for 12 hours. The adsorption tests on activated tuff were performed at a natural pH with a L/S = 10 l/kg.

In all the tests, a 12.6 mg/l initial 2-CP concentration was used. The eluates obtained were characterized in terms of total phenolic compounds and 2-CP content through a spectrophotometer [10] and GC-MS, respectively.

2.2.2 Column tests

The column tests were carried out introducing zeolitic tuff and pozzolana in separate Perspex cylinders, having a height equal to 100 cm and internal diameter equal to 5 cm. The reactors were equipped with sampling ports for the collection of samples to be analyzed at 5 cm (port 1), 20 cm (port 2), 40 cm (port 3) and 80 cm (port 4) from the bottom. Each sampling port was equipped with gastight and watertight fittings (fig. 1). Sampling was made daily using Luer-Lock syringes. Samples were immediately introduced into glass vials and analysed. All tubing and connections were of VitonTM.

Prior to beginning the experimental activity with 2-CP, each column was saturated using DDW; in order to achieve a good saturation, about six pore volumes (PVs) of DDW were fed upwards to the column. The 2-CP solution was placed in a Tedlar bag (SKC) to prevent headspace as the bag empties out and it was fed upwards to the column through a multichannel peristaltic pump (ISMATEC IP, ± 0.005 cm^3/min precision). The outlet was collected in a HDPE bottle. All the results presented here relate to samples collected after five PVs were run in the column in order to reach a steady-state condition.

Four different columns were studied; their hydraulic and operational characteristics are shown in table 1.

3 Results and discussion

3.1 Batch tests

As shown in fig. 2a, 2-CP removal efficiency increased over time at a longer contact time, even if in some cases no significant differences were observed between 30 and 48 hours; probably 30 hours were sufficient to reach the equilibrium conditions in the system. As far as pH is concerned, the worst performances were observed at pH=9.5 for both pozzolana and tuff, with final removal efficiencies lower than 50%. The best performances occurred in correspondence to slightly alkaline pH, with removal equal to about 65% for both materials.

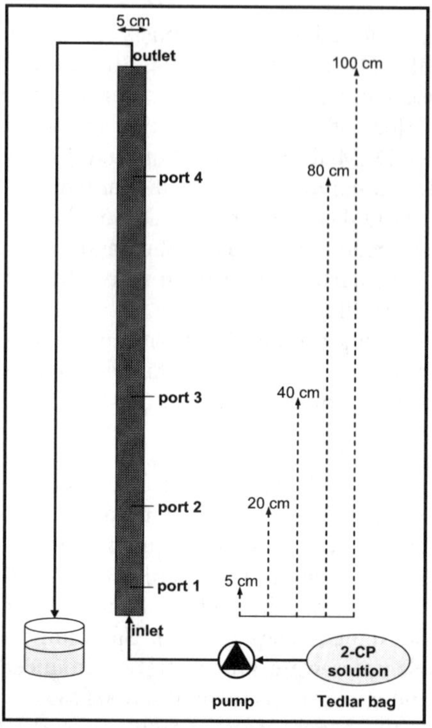

Figure 1: Scheme of the column reactor.

Table 1: Hydraulic and operational characteristics of the columns.

column	reactive medium	2-CP in the inlet (mg/l)	material weight (kg)	PV (ml)	flow rate (ml/min)	hydraulic retention time of 1 PV (h)	velocity (m/d)
P1	pozzolana	12.6	1.98	679	0.5	23	1.06
T1	tuff	12.6	1.56	809	0.5	27	0.85
P2	pozzolana	37	1.96	1129	0.5	38	0.64
T2	tuff	37	1.86	1129	0.5	38	0.64

During the tests with activated tuff, pH was periodically measured: the values detected in the batch with activated and not activated tuff were very similar during the entire period (48 h), remaining in the range 9–9.5. The results of such tests in terms of 2-CP removal efficiency are presented in fig. 2b. No increase in the efficiency occurred in the case of activation by urea. On the contrary, thiourea seemed to improve tuff performance; in fact, after 48 h, the removal efficiency of the activated tuff was equal to 20% (about 5% higher than tuff).

Nevertheless, the removal increase was considered insufficient to justify the additional costs and the operational burdens linked to the activation procedure in a real-scale application. Consequently, the experimental activity continued only on natural tuff and pozzolana as reactive media in the column tests.

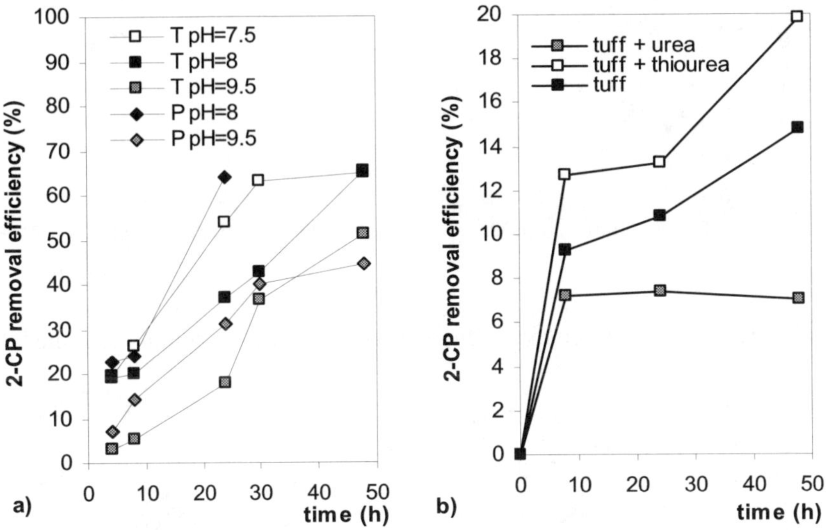

Figure 2: Results of the batch tests (T = tuff; P = pozzolana): time and pH dependence (a) and influence of tuff activation (b).

3.2 Column test

The pH and 2-CP concentrations were measured in the samples collected daily in correspondence to each sampling port of the columns during the entire experimental activity. In fig. 3 the removal efficiency obtained in the outlet of the columns T1 and P1 (initial 2-CP concentration equal to 12.6 mg/l) are shown. In the former, the 2-CP concentrations were quite high in the outlet until day 10, with removal efficiencies lower than 25%. After day 11 the performance of the system improved, with concentrations in the outlet ranging between 0.15 (below the regulation limit for groundwater, equal to 0.18 mg/l) and 5 mg/l (corresponding to a removal efficiency between 99 and 60%). The removal increase was probably due to the change in the environmental conditions in terms of pH, as presented in fig. 4 for port 1. The best performance occurred for slightly alkaline pH, ranging between 8 and 8.8, confirming the results previously obtained in the batch tests. The same behaviour was observed in the other sampling ports, not presented here.

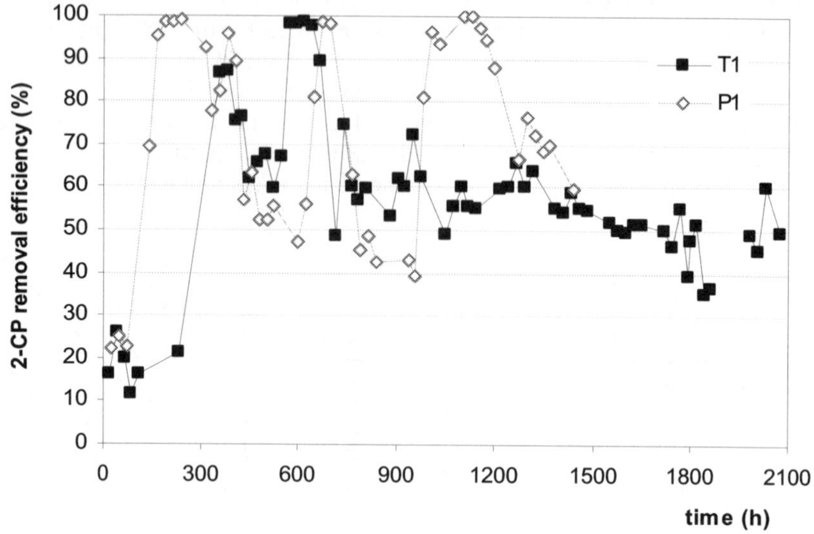

Figure 3: 2-CP removal efficiency time-profile for columns P1 and T1.

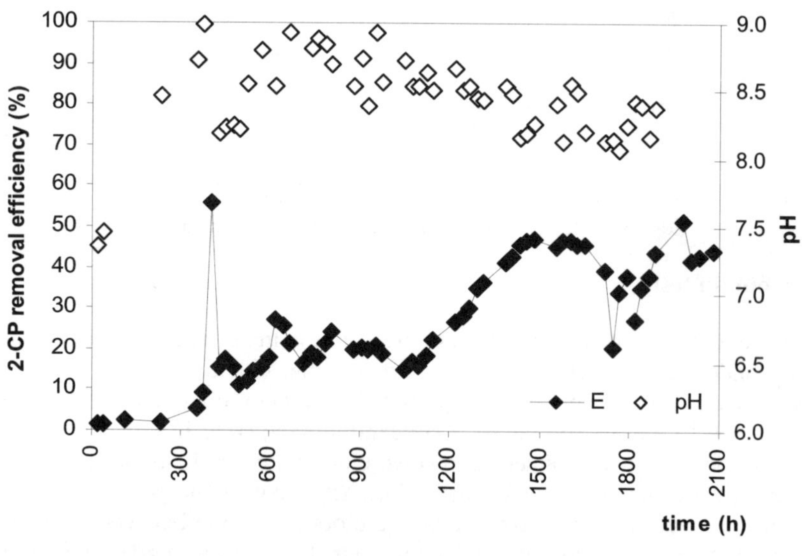

Figure 4: Removal efficiency and pH time-profiles at port 1 (column T1).

The efficiency of the column P1 decreased periodically, due to air intrusion in the column: air limiting the contact between the reactive medium and the contaminated solution, especially at the top of the column where more air was present, preventing 2-CP removal in the last few centimetres. In fact, the first three sampling ports maintained almost the same performances during the entire experimental activity. In these phases the overall removal efficiency was always lower than 50%. The re-establishment of good performances (with efficiencies near 100%) was obtained initially (on day 25) through the purge of the air present in the column, and then (on day 40) through a replacement of the feeding bag and of the gastight sampling ports, in order to avoid definitively further loss in performance. The 2-CP concentrations under the optimal operating conditions (in terms of pH) ranged between 40 μg/l (the regulation limit for groundwater is 180 μg/l) and 1.7 μg/l. In the last 10 days the removal decreased to 60–70%, probably due to the exhaustion of the material and to the progressive saturation of the active sites, since no air intrusion occurred.

In the case of column P1 the pH remained in the optimal range for the adsorption process during the entire experimental period; thus the efficiency variation was influenced mainly by the air intrusion rather than by pH.

As far as the columns T2 and P2 are concerned (initial 2-CP concentration equal to 37 mg/l), the overall removal efficiency obtained is presented in fig. 5; it was never higher than 60% with a mean value equal to about 50% during the entire experimental activity for both the columns. Such values are comparable to those obtained in T1 and P1 at the end of the monitoring period when a progressive saturation of the adsorption sites occurred. The worsening in the reactive media performances with respect to T1 and P1 was probably due to the higher 2-CP concentration in the inlet.

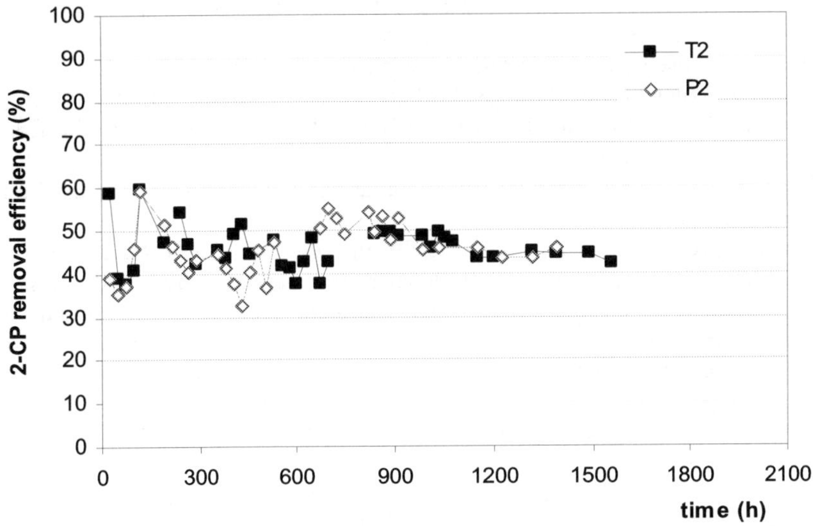

Figure 5: 2-CP removal efficiency time-profile for columns P2 and T2.

The removal efficiency did not vary significantly over time, with values always near the mean value. Such behaviour was probably due to the fact that pH assumed values almost constant in all the sampling ports, as shown in fig. 6 in correspondence to port 1 in column T2.

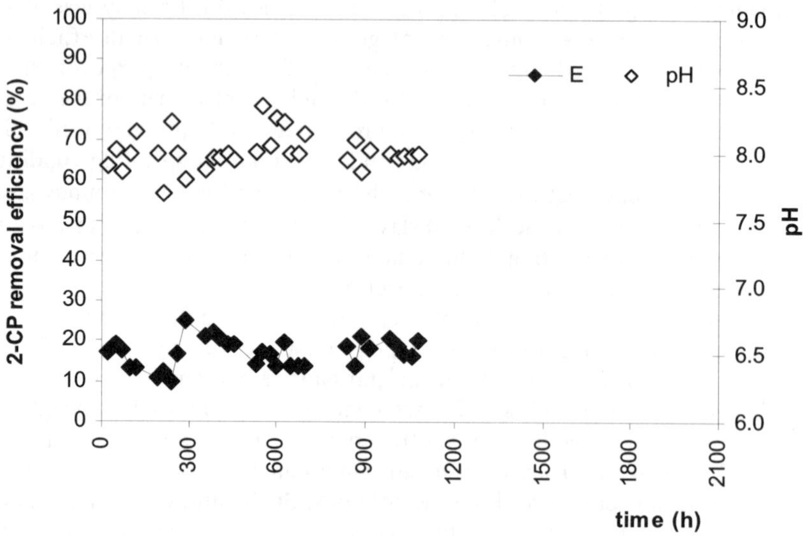

Figure 6: Removal efficiency and pH time-profiles at port 1 (column T2).

The 2-CP half-life ($t_{1/2}$) in the columns, defined as the time required for 2-CP to be reduced to half of its initial concentration, was calculated daily by using the 2-CP residual values in each sampling port of columns P1, T1, P2 and T2. To such an aim a first order reaction (exponential decay) describing the 2-CP decrease was used, with correlation coefficients higher than 0.9. In the phases characterized by significant removal efficiencies (>80%), $t_{1/2}$ varied between:

- 4 and 18 h for column T1 (mean value 8.6 h, corresponding to the first 30 cm of the column);
- 3.2 and 10 h for column P1 (mean value 5.9 h, corresponding to the first 10 cm of the column).

Table 2 presents the mean half-life for all the columns in different operating conditions in terms of removal efficiencies; the materials presented similar $t_{1/2}$ values, depending on the initial 2-CP adopted: the higher the initial 2-CP concentration, the slower the removal kinetic. Pozzolana generally showed a more rapid removal kinetic.

Table 2: Mean half-life (d) corresponding to different removal efficiency for the columns.

	Removal efficiency		
column	40–55%	55–80%	> 80%
T1	1.21	0.95	0.35
P1	1.24	0.79	0.25
T2	2.70	-	-
P2	2.59	-	-

4 Conclusions

The results obtained confirmed that natural zeolitized materials, such as Italian native tuff and pozzolana, can be successfully used as reactive media for *in situ* treatment of 2-CP contaminated groundwater.

In particular, the best performances were proven to occur at moderately alkaline pH. The behaviour of the two materials was quite similar, even if pozzolana showed a little faster removal kinetic.

Further tests are still being carried out in order to fully understand the mechanisms and the processes involved in 2-CP removal; in fact, the presence of free chlorides and of low concentrations of cathecol in the outlet suggested that along with adsorption, partial 2-CP degradation also occurred, catalyzed by the reactive media.

References

[1] Kastanek F., Meleterova Y., Kastanek P., Rott J., Jiricny V., Jiratova K., Complex treatment of wastewater and groundwater contaminated by halogenated organic compounds. *Desalination*, 211, pp. 261–271, 2007.

[2] Zilouei H., Guieysse B., Mattiasson B., Biological degradation of chlorophenols in packed-bed bioreactors using mixed bacterial consortia. *Process Biochemistry*, 41(5), pp. 1083–1089, 2006.

[3] Choi J., Kim Y., Choi S. J., Reductive dechlorination and biodegradation of 2,4,6-trichlorophenol using sequential permeable reactive barriers: laboratory studies. *Chemosphere*, 67(8), pp. 1551–1557, 2007

[4] Perrich J.R., *Activated Carbon Adsorption for Wastewater Treatment*. CRC Press, Boca Raton, FL, 1990.

[5] Calace N., Nardi E., Petronio B.M., Pietroletti M., Adsorption of phenols by papermill sludges. *Environmental Pollution*, 118, pp. 315–319, 2002.

[6] Banat F.A., Al-Bashir B., Al-Asheh S., Hayajneh O., Adsorption of phenol by bentonite. *Environmental Pollution*, 18, pp. 391–398, 2000.

[7] Yousef R.I., Tutunji M.F., G.A.W. Derwish, Musleh S.M., Chemical and structural properties of Jordanian Zeolitic Tuffs and their admixtures with urea and thiourea: potential scavengers for phenolics in aqueous medium. *Journal of Colloid and Interface Science*, 216, pp. 348–359, 1999.

[8] Syamsiah S., Hadi I.S., Adsorption cycles and effect of microbial population on phenol removal using natural zeolit. *Separation and Purification Technology*, 34, pp. 125–133, 2004.

[9] UNI, UNI-EN 12457-2:2004 Characterisation of waste, leaching: Compliance test for leaching of granular waste materials and sludge – Part 2: one stage batch test at a liquid to solid ratio of 10 l/kg with particle size below 4 mm (without o with size reduction), 2004.

[10] APHA, AWWA, WEF, *Standard methods for the examination of water and wastewater*, XX Edition. APHA, Washington, 2006.

Bioremediation of maleic anhydride contaminated soil

C. Y. Yin[1,4], H. S. Ng[2] & S. Abdul-Talib[3,4]
[1]*Faculty of Chemical Engineering, Universiti Teknologi MARA, Malaysia*
[2]*ENSR Corporation Sdn Bhd., Kuala Lumpur, Malaysia*
[3]*Faculty of Civil Engineering, Universiti Teknologi MARA, Malaysia*
[4]*Environmental Engineering Technical Division,*
The Institution of Engineers, Malaysia

Abstract

This paper presents a bench-scale study of bioremediation of soil contaminated with maleic anhydride. A quantity of 300 kg of contaminated soil was collected from a petrochemical plant in Malaysia and divided into three portions in order to investigate the effects of nutrient addition as well as mechanical aeration on the biodegradation rate of the contaminants. Online parameters measured included moisture content, redox potential, temperature and pH. The highest first-order biodegradation rate constant was determined to be 6.658 day^{-1} for soil pile with addition of nutrients and mechanical aeration.
Keywords: bioremediation, maleic anhydride, petrochemical industry.

1 Introduction

Bioremediation is an established means of treating contaminated soils especially when the contaminants are organic-based. Research in bioremediation is often focused on *ex-situ* bench-scale studies as such setups facilitate control of important experimental parameters such as temperature and pH. Previous studies on *ex-situ* bench-scale bioremediation include biodegradation of hydrocarbon petroleum contaminated soil [1], gasoline-contaminated sediments [2] and diesel-contaminated soil [3].

Maleic anhydride is used as a chemical intermediate in the synthesis of fumaric and tartaric acid, certain agricultural chemicals, resins in numerous products, dye intermediates and pharmaceuticals [4]. Its detrimental effects on

WIT Transactions on Ecology and the Environment, Vol 107, © 2008 WIT Press
www.witpress.com, ISSN 1743-3541 (on-line)
doi:10.2495/BF080131

human health include dyspnea [5] as well as acute asthmatic reactions [6]. Its presence at elevated concentrations in the soil environment as a result of industrial activities such as hydrocarbon processing presents an undesirable circumstance as humans may come into direct contact with them. In this study, soil contaminated with maleic anhydride was subjected bioremediation processes. The objective of this study was to assess the biotreatability of maleic anhydride contaminated soil via determination of biodegradation rate and half-life of the contaminant under the effect of nutrient addition and aeration.

2 Materials and methods

2.1 Soil sampling

Soil samples were taken from a petrochemical plant in Malaysia, which were contaminated with maleic anhydride due to improper storage and leakage. A total of 300 kg of contaminated soil was collected at depths between 3 to 4 m at the affected area within the petrochemical plant. The soil appeared to be coarse and dark brown in color. The pH of the soil sample was adjusted to 7 by using lime prior to treatment.

2.2 Bench-scale treatment

Due to the readily biodegradable properties of maleic anhydride as determined via a preliminary study, bioremediation was selected as the most appropriate treatment option. For the bench-scale treatment, three soil piles at 100 kg each were constructed:

i) Control soil pile (CP).
ii) Treatment pile mixed with raw nutrients and sawdust (TP1).
iii) Treatment pile mixed with raw nutrients, sawdust and equipped with mechanical aerators (TP2).

The source of the raw nutrients was chicken faeces in which the carbon and nitrogen ratio was 1:30. Sawdust layers, which acted as partition for the soil piles, were laid in three layers sandwiching two layers of soil. The sawdust and soil composition was fixed at 30% on v/v basis. The mechanical aerators for TP2 consisted of two-inch diameter slotted perforated pipes with attached mechanical blower. The three piles were subjected to a monitoring program for a period of two months in which online parameters measured included moisture content, redox potential, temperature and pH. The concentrations of maleic anhydride before and after treatment were determined via high performance liquid chromatography (HPLC).

3 Results and discussion

The initial concentration of maleic anhydride was determined to be 223,000 mg/kg soil respectively. The concentration of maleic anhydride that exceeds the U.S. Environmental Protection Agency (USEPA) preliminary remediation goal of 88,000 mg/kg indicates the need to remediate the soil. Table 1 shows the online parameters recorded during the study period. The range of temperatures in the three soil piles indicates that mesophilic microorganisms are mainly responsible for biodegradation of the contaminants. This is consistent with most of the reported studies on bioremediation in which recorded temperatures were in the mesophilic range [7,8]. In addition, redox potential ranges clearly show that degradation predominantly occurs under aerobic conditions.

Table 1: Online parameters recorded during the study period.

Soil piles	Moisture content (%)	Redox potential (mV)	Temperature (°C)	pH
CP	9.2 – 25.8	207 – 287	28 – 35	3.8 – 8.2
TP1	6.6 – 44.0	82 – 203	27 – 41	4.9 – 8.5
TP2	3.6 – 36.0	92 – 201	26 – 38	6.7 – 8.9

3.1 Biodegradation kinetics

The biodegradation kinetics are evaluated via determination of first-order degradation rate constant, k' (day^{-1}) and half-life of the chemical, $t_{1/2}$ (day). To determine the value of k', the following equation [9] is used:

$$S_t = S_0 e^{-k't} \tag{1}$$

where S_0 is the initial contaminant concentration (mg/L) and S_t the contaminant concentration at time t (day). Half-life is determined from the following equation [9]:

$$k' = \frac{0.693}{t_{1/2}} \tag{2}$$

Table 2 shows the first-order degradation rate constant and half-life of maleic anhydride in the soil piles. The addition of nutrients into the soil clearly increase the degradation rate as evident by the increase in k' value by a factor of nine. Aeration of the soil in TP2 also appears to increase the biodegradation rate constant by 12.2% as compared to TP1. This is due to increased concentration of oxygen in the TP2 as a direct result of aeration. Table 3 compares first-order degradation rate constants for maleic anhydride found in this study with other contaminants. It is obvious that biodegradation of maleic anhydride in this study is very effective as compared to degradation of other hydrocarbon contaminant such as diesel.

Table 2: First-order degradation rate constant and half-life of maleic anhydride.

Soil piles	k' (day^{-1})	$t_{1/2}$ (day)
CP	0.592	1.1
TP1	5.935	0.1
TP2	6.658	0.1

Table 3: Comparison of first-order degradation rate constants with other contaminants.

Contaminant	Addition of nutrient	k' (day^{-1})	References
Diesel-contaminated soil	Yes	0.027	[10]
Diesel-contaminated soil	No	0.010	[10]
Diesel-contaminated soil	Yes (sewage sludge)	0.272	[11]
Diesel-contaminated soil	Yes (compost)	0.182	[11]
Diesel-contaminated soil	No	0.052	[11]
Maleic anhydride-contaminated soil	No	0.592	This study
Maleic anhydride-contaminated soil	Yes (Chicken faeces)	5.935	This study

4 Conclusions

Biodegradation of maleic anhydride in the soil was carried out by mesophilic microorganisms under aerobic conditions. Results of the study indicated that bioremediation of maleic anhydride in soils was effective and feasible judging by the high biodegradation rate. The addition of nutrients into the contaminated soil significantly increased the maleic anhydride biodegradation rate as evident by the increase in k' value by a factor of nine. Aeration of the soil in TP2 increased the biodegradation rate constant by 12.2% as compared to TP1.

References

[1] Aspray, T.J., Carvalho, D.J.C. & Phillip, J.C., Application of soil slurry respirometry to optimise and subsequently monitor ex situ bioremediation of hydrocarbon-contaminated soils. *International Biodeterioration & Biodegradation,* **60(4)**, pp. 279–284, 2007.

[2] Baker, R.J., Baehr, A.L. & Lahvis, M.A., Estimation of hydrocarbon biodegradation rates in gasoline-contaminated sediment from measured respiration rates. *Journal of Contaminant Hydrology*, **41**, pp. 175–192, 2000.

[3] Cunningham, C.J. & Philp, J.C., Comparison of bioaugmentation and biostimulation in ex situ treatment of diesel contaminated soil. *Land Contamination and Reclamation*, **8(4)**, pp. 261–269, 2000.

[4] HSDB, Hazardous Substances Data Bank. *National Library of Medicine, Bethesda, MD (TOMESÒ CD-ROM Version). Denver, CO: Micromedex, Inc.*, 1995.

[5] Gannon, P.F.G., Burge, P.S., Hewlett, C. & Tee R.D., Haemolytic anaemia in a case of occupational asthma due to maleic anhydride. *British Journal of Industrial Medicine*, **49**, pp. 142–143, 1992.

[6] Lee, H.S., Wang, Y.T., Cheong, T.H., Tan, K.T., Chee B.E. & Narendran, K., Occupational asthma due to maleic anhydride. *British Journal of Industrial Medicine*, **48**, pp. 283–285, 1991.

[7] ChaoA neau, C.H., Morel, J.L. & Oudot, J., Microbial degradation in soil microcosms of fuel oil hydrocarbons from drilling cuttings. *Environment Science and Technology*, **29**, pp. 1615–1621, 1995.
[8] Fu, C., Pfanstiel, S., Gao, C., Yan, X. & Govind, R., Studies on contaminant biodegradation in slurry, water and compacted soil tube reactors. *Environment Science and Technology*, **29**, pp. 1615–1621, 1995.
[9] LaGrega, M.D., Buckingham, P.L. & Evans, J.C., *Hazardous Waste Management,* McGraw-Hill: International Edition, pp. 553–653, 2001.
[10] Taylor, C. & Viraraghavan, T., A bench-scale investigation of land treatment of soil contaminated with diesel fuel. *Chemosphere*, **39(10)**, pp. 1583–1593, 1999.
[11] Namkoong, W., Hwang, E.Y., Park, J.S. & Choi, J.Y., Bioremediation of diesel-contaminated soil with composting. *Environmental Pollution,* **119(1)**, pp. 23–31, 2002.

Section 4
Case studies

Revitalizing secondary market Brownfield sites

A. Bogen
President, Down to Earth Consulting, Environmental Planner Regional Brownfields Partnership of West Central Connecticut, USA

Abstract

Brownfield sites in secondary markets will only be revitalized through public investment. The market place has passed on these sites or never considered them in the first place because they carry multiple burdens. They are in secondary markets where land values and demographics are not strong. They can also be too small, suspected of being too contaminated, have dilapidated structures and owe too much in back taxes. These are conditions that will not be resolved without significant long term public intervention and investment. The criteria for this investment needs to be applied along with the commitment of the marketplace to rebuild the sites if they are within certain economic parameters after assessment. This is a discussion of how certain criteria are being applied in an industrial city in the USA.
Keywords: public investment, delinquent taxes, access, value, liability.

1 Introduction

There are Brownfield sites that the marketplace has already passed on that will only be restored with public financing. The burdens they carry will require significant public investment. Public leadership will need to accept and advocate nontraditional returns on that investment. The payback is in decades rather than in 15 to 20 years. For these dark sites, there is only the option of public investment to leverage them into reuse. Left alone, these sites will be a continuous cause of disinvestment, degrading the neighborhoods and negatively affecting the people who live near them. This paper lays out some of the measurements that can be used to justify the tremendous investment that is required.

It may be useful to illustrate the conditions of these sites through a case history that is unfolding in an older industrial city, Waterbury, Connecticut formerly known as the Brass City. There are difficult issues holding back the reuse of the many city Brownfields. Major industrial players on the world stage had facilities located here. Today those former titans are represented by fading painted signs and their Brownfields legacy of rusting, imploding hulks of highly specialized manufacturing facilities sitting empty. The assumption is that these sites are significantly contaminated. There is repeated documentation from environmental assessments on similar sites of the presence of polyaromatic hydrocarbons, heavy metals, ash and sludge. There are filled areas along the Naugatuck River where the ash residues are more than ten feet deep.

Waterbury, a city with a population of 107,000 people in 2000, needs to generate more taxes from this tired real estate infrastructure pervasive within its limited borders. Therefore, the first reason to invest in these sites is to allow them to return to tax generation. The burden of delinquent taxes is significant in the older industrial, secondary market cities, such as Waterbury. The city, faced with troubled tax collection rates, about 15 years ago, attempted to sell liens on some of the biggest tax debts. The lien holders want full payment. The result is that the steep old tax bill alone is often enough to discourage an investor because the properties are much inverted in value. Some of these old tax debts are carried forward as part of the analysis to balance a budget even though the likelihood of collection is open to challenge.

2 A case in point

In Waterbury, one site has been offered at tax auction 8 times without a bidder. The back tax bill on this two acre parcel is $832,000 US. If it was a clean site, it might be worth $200,000. There is a dilapidated structure that once housed a dry cleaning plant and retail outlet. Bidders have not come forward because of the unknown environmental conditions. The site is within a healthy, growing retail corridor including a revived mall and is accessible to several suburban communities as well as to the downtown. The Brownfields project has undertaken a Phase I and II assessment with an estimated cost of cleanup required in the Scope of Work. Once the assessment is complete, the site will again be offered at auction. Said assessment will cost about $20,000.

There was some debate as to whether this site should receive grant assessment funding. It is not the most blighted site within the city. Other sites owe more taxes. The building sits on a rise so the structure and the random trash piles do not have immediate street impact as this condition does on other sites. However, there have been inquiries to the City about the availability of the site. Without specific information about the environmental conditions, it will never sell at auction. The State records do not indicate any release of TCE, tetrachloroethylene, so it is possible that the cleanup could be minimal. The decision to assess this site was made as much on the basis of intervention as on any other category. Because the site is relatively small, the assessment cost is small in relation to the uncollected taxes. Turning it around can help to forestall any area decay and promote economic development.

The site also illustrates another key component of the causes of Brownfields. The owners have abandoned the site and it is owned by a corporation that has not been responsive to tax notices. Certified letters were sent to the listed person of notice. He responded that he had nothing to do with the management of the property and provided another name. That person subsequently responded that he would provide data from previous tests and would sign the access agreement. Several weeks went by without the executed access agreement being returned and follow up phone calls were not returned. Mention was made of the voice mail the owner had left, agreeing to provide access. More than five months from the first conversation and nearly nine months after the decision to assess the site, the access was granted. The earlier reports promised by the owner have not been received. Perseverance and an assertive management posture are required by the team working to overcome obstacles such as these. There has to be a willingness to take legal action to gain access to such sites. This outcome was fortunate and came about more by chance and diligence than policy or specific device.

3 The City today

The City is owed millions of uncollectible dollars on sites located all over the City. Almost no neighborhood is immune from the effect; the number of sites is stunning. Many small parcels had secondary businesses that provided services and materials and goods for the mills and factories. The tool and die makers and metal platers are largely gone but their contaminants remain. For more than 40 years there has been a diminution of the tax base making it very difficult to govern under such a burden. A major shopping mall has been built on one of the largest former industrial sites. Some of the stores in the mall are doing acceptable sales volumes but the anchor supermarket just closed leaving the core city without any such facility. The State invested monies into constructing a branch of the University of Connecticut in the downtown Central Business District. The facility replaced aging and largely vacant downtown retail buildings. The State also built a courthouse, renovated a large splendid theater across the street from the University branch and built an arts magnet school. These infusions have had some effect. The students at both the magnet school and the UCONN branch represent a positive new element to the downtown area. Several people have commented on the new faces downtown and the increased traffic on feeder routes. However, these students are commuters and for now, not spending a lot of money in the City as was anticipated prior to construction.

The historic City has also suffered the indignity and disruption of an Interstate highway slicing through its heart, uprooting the traditional patterns of commerce. The feeder roads have numerous pinch points, parking on the narrow streets is inconvenient and uncoordinated traffic signals all impede traffic flow. It is very frustrating to try to get from one area of the city to another. The contemporary commercial development is sporadic, mainly huddled together in widely distributed pockets among blocks of blighted structures.

In the past, downtown was home to numerous stores that provided services and sold fine goods to the emerging middle class, factory workers and residents of nearby communities. The factories adjacent to the downtown had three shifts of workers who were making living wages and patronizing these stores. Workers lived downtown as well as in other areas of the city. Public transportation had its major hub in the downtown, reaching out to all points of the City. Waterbury today is plagued by a high commercial vacancy rate. After the closing of the many factories and their ancillary suppliers and operations, the unemployment rate has soared, in contrast to the fact that Connecticut has the highest per capita income in the United States. Waterbury has one of the highest unemployment and poverty rates in the State.

The urban core has difficult demographics, due to it being the home to the highest density of poor residents. There is hardly a block without an abandoned building. The infrastructure is tired and in disrepair. There is gang and drug activity. The city has also been plagued by a series of corrupt and dishonored mayors. The current administration has now been reelected twice and has a reputation for integrity. The City was bankrupt and administered by the state for a number of years, emerging from that control last year. Difficult union pension obligations were contested and resolved.

Economic development efforts continue to be thwarted by the lack of virgin land and Brownfield sites ready for reuse, although there are developer inquiries made to the responsible agencies with mixed results. The shelves are bare – the Brownfields have not been prepared for reuse. Against this problematic background, the City is moving forward in its efforts to revitalize its Brownfields. Public money is providing the support.

3.1 The process and concerns

The first step taken in identifying and assessing sites was to establish a process for site selection. From the onset, it was important that a set of criteria for selection be established. The Mayor, City department heads, business and community leaders and the funding authority were involved. Sites would have to have certain attributes to be selected for assessment grants. Several of the criteria were first tier and were determined to be required in the application for a site to be assessed. These were proof of a proposed transaction, access, a beneficiary that did not cause the suspected or known contamination and a reuse that fit the City's Plan of Conservation and Development. Additional criteria were delinquent taxes, with concern for third party lien sites, community comment and regulatory review. When the consultant has developed the information on the site, a form is filled out that elaborated on data related to these criteria. Preliminary approval is sought from the State program managers. Next the Site Selection Committee reviews the proposal. Committee members are drawn from a wide community base. Their deliberation helps to assure that the public benefit is real and that the process is transparent.

There is often a lot of emotion surrounding the present site conditions. The general public is angry that the blighted and unknown and potentially dangerous conditions have been allowed to fester for so long, in some cases for half a century. They are frustrated and appalled by the corporate veil that can insulate the owners from effective enforcement action. The need to blame is met with what are seen to be a wall of rationalizations. The questions are poignant. Some individuals think the health agencies should have acted, the owners been prosecuted and that the government should have managed the problem. They feel that there should have been enforcement of regulation long before the sites were contaminated and abandoned. Issues of access and corporate insulation are further insults and obstacles to what is perceived of as a morally right resolution. For some the equation is simple - the sites are dirty; clean them up.

The site owners have their separate batch of concerns. They are wary of granting access because they often don't want to know what is on the site. They are concerned that the information could cause enforcement action, resulting in astronomical remediation costs, which could bankrupt them. Some sites are still held in personal partnerships or entities with individual exposure. The assets of those individuals and families could be built on a house of cards foundation. Prior to the establishment of remedial regulations that help to define what has to be done on a site, the regulator could act individually and arbitrarily in the eyes of the business community. Stories remain about environmental remediation without end. There was no certainty and great risk. Even if the intention was to try to do something beneficial and to make corrections, the cooperative and assertive position could be financially imprudent. That basic fear of economic ruin remains as does the very real exposure.

Waterbury has ongoing concerns about being proactive on sites. It too does not want to invoke liability exposures by discovering issues that it then must address. It could have additional liability if its agents are hurt on a site or cause damage. The risk is deemed too great to act without the listed owner granting access. There are statutes that the City will wait for others to use with the resultant established case law. Some other communities also facing significant Brownfield sites have gone to court to gain access.

3.2 Creating an entity to hold the liability

Going forward, the issue of access must be addressed in a more proactive way. Regulations allow the government to go on the site if there is a suspected significant health risk, or a release of pollutants to the State waterways. Another criterion, some benchmark of back taxes, should allow access. At a certain point the inverted value just keeps compounding beyond the capacity of any transaction to overturn while buildings and infrastructure continue to deteriorate. Municipalities must be more proactive in managing the assets that comprise their tax base. The political consequence of leaving the sites alone is worse than doing something about it.

It may be that the State needs to act as a neutral temporary repository of liability while the sites are assessed and readied for reuse. Criteria would have to be established taking into account specific factors: back taxes, health risk, and developer interest, compatibility with zoning for the proposed reuse, projected returns and quality of supporting public infrastructure. Municipalities would have to apply for the assistance based on completing an application with the site data fitting into a predetermined ranking grid. If accepted, the sites would be placed in a holding entity. The State would assess the site and define the cleanup acceptable under its regulations. There would have to be some federal signoff of the proposed remediation so that the full range of security for finance institutions would be in place. At the point that the cleanup cost is defined, a decision could be made as to whether the site is marketable. With the application of tax abatement and other assistance, the developers may be able to fund the cleanup. Other sites may require cleanup by the State.

Additional criteria could also be considered. Access to public transportation, inclusion of sustainable design components, and renewable energy capacity in the proposed reuse are some criteria to consider. It is not enough any longer to place a big box retailer on a site. It is more than a vision of tomorrow that we need to fulfill. It needs to be a requirement to build in a sustainable fashion. Fuel cells and gray water management would help the urban environment. Public money in the form of tax incentives could be in place to foster these changes. It would be attention getting to have the most blighted places become hallmarks of environmental responsibility. Brownfields represent an opportunity to incorporate on site generation where the grid is readily accessible.

Some of the parcels are too small for a viable reuse. This small size limits the return that the site can generate, making it difficult or impossible to reuse the site. Therefore, another aspect of the criteria for sites to be considered is the possibility of taking enough contiguous parcels to have a market worthy site. Perhaps a City would need to negotiate the options on the sites before presenting them to the State for review. The presence or absence of an option would be weighted in the ranking system.

There can be a lot of reasons to argue against putting the government, whether state or municipal, into an entrepreneurial role. Government is not charged with the creation of wealth. Government employees are asked to function more as processors than innovators. They can and do respond to the need for change and modification of regulations and shifting of paradigms. The taking of these Brownfields properties is a function. The administration of the assessment and cleanup are functions that the State already performs. This is a step that allows these otherwise unusable sites to be made ready for the entrepreneurs' vision and resources. Selection of the reuse plan needs to be an open and bid process so that there is community support for the final decision. Some planning and determination of acceptable reuse should go into the earliest stages of selecting which sites will be assessed. It may be that there needs to be a request for proposals on a short list of these sites to help determine which sites should receive priority. The marketplace will then have said which sites it deems valuable rather than sites selected by members of the community or professional planners.

The sites taken would have to have a proposed reuse with a demonstrable public benefit. It would be important to clarify what constitutes public benefit. Some sites will generate taxes, an obvious public benefit. Some will generate jobs in neighborhoods that desperately need them. Some will abate health risks that help not only those in the immediate area but reduce the human health exposures that can put subsequent burden on the health care system. Some sites could be used for recreation or open space, which can provide an amenity that enhances value. Cleaned sites could produce increased taxes through a rise in appraised values of adjacent parcels. Green spaces in urban areas can also reduce the heat island effects, be sites for distributed storm water infiltration and food growing plots. The decision about what is the greatest value can be local in the first place and be arrived at through extended dialogue when sites are first being selected.

4 Another case in point

In some instances the marketplace has tried to make a site work but cannot bridge the gap caused by environmental expense. In Waterbury an assessment was done on a similar site. A number of set criteria were met including proof of options held or of ownership on 18 contiguous parcels. There was a potential tenant represented by a realtor to protect their confidentiality. None of the investors had caused the site contamination and there was information on two sites in the State files indicating contamination. The back taxes were minimal and paid up before there was an agreement to fund the assessment.

The results of the assessment established a range of cleanup cost for the 18 contiguous parcels at nearly $870,000 US. One parcel alone was estimated at $500,000 and another at $240,000. The cleanup, plus the acquisition cost and demolition costs made the base cost of the land, if prepared for new construction, too high too build for the prospective tenant. The site has languished for nearly a year since the assessment. Recently the spokesman for the developer has announced that they are trying to complete plans for two mid-rise apartment buildings on a section of the site, which would give them the returns necessary with the density these market rate units would have. The issue under discussion is how to fund the $240,000 clean up of one site, which was not caused by the current owner of the factory on that parcel. The current owner is liable and wants to come out whole in any transaction. The question that sits on the table is one of undue enrichment. That is the need to be certain that an individual company does not receive extreme and unjust benefit from pubic funds used for cleanup. The seller has the liability and obligation, which the purchaser could pick up, if that is their deal.

Without intervention the deal may not work. The parcels are in back of the previously referred to Mall. The traffic count for the area is high, and the site is at one end of a blighted stretch that leads downtown to the new University building. A revitalized site could be a bookend for further redevelopment on this main City artery. These conditions spoke in favor of doing the assessment in the first place. These qualities haven't changed. The negative news regarding the cleanup costs has stalled the process. If there is to be change, some leverage has to be provided. In the context of the transaction, the cash is fungible. The assistance does not have to go directly to one party. Funding could be provided for demolition, relocation, streetscape requirements or utility upgrades. The public officials will be asked to decide if the revitalization is a worthy outcome. If the City and State do not want to provide some support, this site, with and despite its relative advantages, will pickle in the contamination.

The delays that the owners have experienced in the site process described above have left them without income and frustrated by the lack of resolution. If they weren't primarily local people who own some of the parcels and would not be able to readily sell them, they would have walked away. It does not serve the market to be in sequential crisis when dealing with Brownfield sites. The whole site must be readied for reuse. The obstacles must be defined and resolved. Timing is critical; the process must flow and the resources must be at hand. It is fatal to a deal to wait for the several months to conduct and distill the results of an assessment to find that the cleanup cost has no ready funding options. Low cost loans are of marginal value when the return from these secondary sites is as thin as it has proven to be. If we do not invest in these sites, we must accept the economic and social consequences. The contamination and liability, and therefore the risk, do not go away. These are cash flow situations. The deals don't work without intervention. We have not intervened. The sites remain unleavened.

We need to have the sites ready to be marketed rather than sit and wait for the marketplace to come around and in the end go elsewhere seeking less difficult development options. Failure to act engenders further despair and faithless views of municipal government on the part of the poor and immigrant population that live among many of Waterbury's Brownfield sites as well as in other older industrial cities across the nation. The lack of opportunity is one of the causes of crime and drug use. Reinvestment provides jobs and improves the quality of life and gives people a stake in their communities. Being proactive in the real estate redevelopment may offset the use of some of the public funds for police and counseling expenses. There is no escape from the deteriorated conditions. They will not self improve. The heart of their malaise is economic. Only government can create the leverage to breed jobs and taxes.

In the short term the investment required has limited return. The payback window will not occur in the usual financial parameters. It is possible that the capital invested in structures will have to be renovated before enough taxes have been generated to pay back the investment. That means that the horizon for returns has to be extended past usual meaningful life analysis. Even a thirty year mortgage table could be understating the time needed. However, the critical capital investment isn't in the infrastructure. It is in the land. The land has no useful life restrictions. Once cleaned, with proper operational safeguards and consistent government regulatory enforcement, the land is a renewable resource. Seen this way, the investment provides a revitalized foundation for a continuing tax base. The health risks are abated so the undocumented costs associated with contamination related illness are minimized. The willingness of investors to build on nearby parcels increases the overall tax base and may create new jobs. The effect of rescuing one site can cause positive ripples in an area.

5 The journey into tomorrow

No society has enough resources to clean every Brownfields site in a short term approach. That is why the process of how sites are selected for assessment is such an important part of the process. In order for Brownfields redevelopment to be successful, there has to be some short term returns on investment to the community. Two of the most acknowledged returns are jobs and taxes. In Connecticut, taxes can include property, equipment, sales and income varieties. The conflicting point can be raised about the need for tax abatement to lure investors. This approach has often been used in lieu of providing clean sites. If the developer will clean the site, then the market can handle that site and it is not of the variety that is being discussed here. These sites have extraordinary inversion ratios. We can't count the long term generation of a tax stream while simultaneously offering abatements. The public's capital must be reconstituted. The eligibility of sites will depend on the private reinvestment being adequate for the balance of the turnaround. The sites will be pulled out from the pit to be like other sites but with an early commitment to reuse. Many of these sites have great locations.

These sites also have available infrastructure. The public does not have to invest in new roads, sewers, sidewalks, water supply and other services as when it takes undeveloped land. If those avoided expenses are tallied, the return analysis for these blighted sites improves.

Considered this way, the issue of public investment can be seen as necessary rather than optional. The effect of continued unsustainable development is a destroyed environment. The issue of returns placed in the context of development that supports the ability to live on the planet makes moot a refined and strict analysis of the return on investment. Can there be a better place to demonstrate the functions of new technologies and planned environment than in places so difficult that commerce and government have turned away from wanting to see them? These are the places where we can and need to demonstrate our collective will toward sustainable and healthy design. The investment goes far beyond cleaning up old industrial residues. The dark places can hold the light. The rough places can be made fine. The secondary markets need to be the primary markets for public investment. The land is available. It can be made ready. It must be made ready.

Derelict building installations and infrastructures in Greek Spa Towns: the case of Kamena Vourla and Ypati

E. Beriatos & M. Papageorgiou
Department of Spatial Planning and Regional Development, University of Thessaly, Volos, Greece

Abstract

The evolution of thermal tourism in Greece has caused the construction of numerous imposing building complexes, installations of treatment (spa centers) and hotels (around important thermal springs), which formed the initial cores of future urban development.

During the last two decades, Greek thermal tourism entered a phase of decline. Consequently the above mentioned installations (built up during a long period of flourishing in the 19th and 20th centuries), and especially those found within urban areas, are abandoned and downgraded. Therefore these spa centers deserve the appropriate (architectural) restoration and (urban) renewal in order to reassemble the urban space by filling in the existing 'urban holes', modernize their infrastructure and be able to successfully compete in a more difficult international economic environment.

The Greek spa towns of Kamena Vourla and Ypati are a characteristic example of the above mentioned situation. In Kamena Vourla half of the treatment installations/buildings are completely abandoned while in Ypati the main spa center core is operating in a rather downgraded building construction and several hotels are also empty and nearly ruined.

This paper aims to investigate the possible ways for the restoration, reuse and urban integration of the abandoned installations in spa towns for the benefit of sustainable thermal tourism in Greek regions in the short and long term.

Keywords: derelict building-installations, spa town, restoration, urban renewal-redevelopment.

1 Introduction

Since ancient times, hot springs, due to their therapeutic characteristics, were a place of attraction for people as well as a place of concentration of various building constructions. For example, in ancient Greece, the Asclepeia were built around or very close to hot springs. The Asclepeia were buildings of God worship and treatment [1]. During Roman times, as proof of the importance given by the Romans to water as a means for achieving good health and vitality, we observe that magnificent bathing facilities were constructed next to hot springs. The most famous are those of the emperors Pompei, Augustus, Agrippa, Titus, Nero, Caracalla, etc [2].

With time and the emergence of the phenomenon of tourism – especially thermal tourism that appeared during the 17th century – the area around hot springs became even more developed. Many hot springs became organized facilities and we see organized bathing centers (spas and hotels). Some of those, the most important, attracted a lot of people and we observe the development of housing facilities for the residence of the permanent population and thus these centers were transformed into spa towns.

2 Greek spa towns: from prosperity to decline

Greece is a country rich in hot and cold mineral water springs. According to a survey made by the Institute of Geological and Mineral Research of Greece (in 1984), there are 822 mineral springs evenly distributed in the whole country [3]. From these, the greatest number is found close to the seashores, a small percentage is in flatlands and an even smaller one is in the mountain regions [4].

Having such a natural wealth of thermal water resources, even with some delay in comparison with the rest of Europe, Greece started, almost immediately after gaining independence from Turkish rule, to develop its hot springs, opening the first spa centers in the middle of the 19th century. Since then, thermal tourism was continuously on the rise and in the 1930s – apart from the increase of the number of spa centers – we notice the development of the first Greek bathing-spa towns – the most important of them are Aidipsos, Kamena Vourla, Ypati, Methana, Loutraki, etc [2, 4].

During the Second World War, the rise of thermal tourism in Greece was halted due to the wide destruction – among others – of the spa facilities but thermal tourism recovered relatively soon and started to rise dynamically at the end of the 1950s. Without doubt, the decades from the 1950s to the 1960s and the 1970s were the most flourishing for Greek thermal tourism and the Greek spa towns [5]. A characteristic of this development is the fact that the Greek spa towns were the favorite destination of many famous politicians, tycoons and artists of that era. Among those we can mention, the king of Libya, the king of Saudi Arabia, Aristotelis Onassis, Maria Callas, Winston Churchill, Omar Sharif, Greta Garbo, and many others [2, 6].

The prosperity of the spa towns of this period did not last for long. Since the mid 1980s (a down trend which continues to this day) Greek thermal tourism has been in a period of protracted decline [5]. The number of spa tourists decreases continuously and as a result the spa centers are gradually left without repairs and signs of serious abandonment and deterioration are starting to appear. This abandonment and decline is more evident in the spa towns where the building constructions and the infrastructure comprise a very important part of the town itself. Thus, in contrast to the common spa centers – which are usually isolated and in countryside – in the spa towns this abandonment and decline of the bathing facilities and the infrastructure creates a discontinuity of the urban tissue and destruction of the town's identity and operation/functioning.

Nowadays, the abandonment and decline of the bathing facilities and the infrastructure of the spa towns is not a solitary phenomenon but a concern for all Greek spa towns.

Figure 1: Distribution of the most important spa centers in Greece (source: processed by the authors).

3 The case of Kamena Vourla and Loutra Ypatis

3.1 The spa town of Kamena Vourla

Kamena Vourla is the second – after Aedipsos – most important spa town in Greece. It is situated in central Greece, at the Prefecture of Fthiotis, along the coast – directly on the International Road leading from Athens to Salonika. It is 175 km from the Greek capital and has a population of 3,500.

The coastal spa town of Kamena Vourla is the most recently built in Greece. The first spa building (Figure 4) was built in 1936 together with the hotel "Kallidromos". Until then there were virtually no buildings in the area, apart from some huts used by sheep and goat herders who came down from the mountains in order to spend the winter months there.

Even though the development of the area as a spa center was halted during the Second World War, Kamena Vourla soon recovered. During the 1950s in the area of the already existing spa center – approximately 60 hectares – (Figure 2), two luxury hotels were built (Figure 3) and in 1974 a second spa was constructed called "Hippocrates", since the town was starting to receive a lot of tourists [7].

Figure 2: Panoramic view of the spa center area in the 1960s.

Figure 3: Hotel "radio" in the 1960s.

Figure 4: "Asclepios" spa building in the 1960s.

In the meantime, in the broader area – and very close to the spa center –the construction of other hotels, restaurants, shops and houses began. Gradually, the area of Kamena Vourla changed from an isolated spa center in the middle of the countryside, to a small town with permanent residents having at its geometrical center the large area occupied by the spa buildings and its surrounding infrastructure (Figure 5).

Unfortunately, as happened to the rest of the spa towns in Greece, from the mid 1980s, tourism in Kamena Vourla suddenly started to decline – not only in numbers but in quality as well [5]. The number of bathers reduced sharply and

www.witpress.com, ISSN 1743-3541 (on-line)

this resulted in the appearance of the first signs of abandonment, not only inside the spa center but also in the rest of the urban tissue. Especially in the area of the spa center its bathing facilities and infrastructure started to dysfunction and to be surrounded by a downgraded environment.

Some changes started to occur in 2000, when the Greek State gave the rights of use of the spa center to private investors. The spa "Hippocrates" and the hotel "Galini" (Calmness) were largely renovated (the hotel is now operating as a luxury hotel with a wing of spa facilities). Nevertheless, the fact remains that more than half of the spa buildings of Kamena Vourla are still abandoned and surrounded by an even more downgraded environment (Figures 6–8).

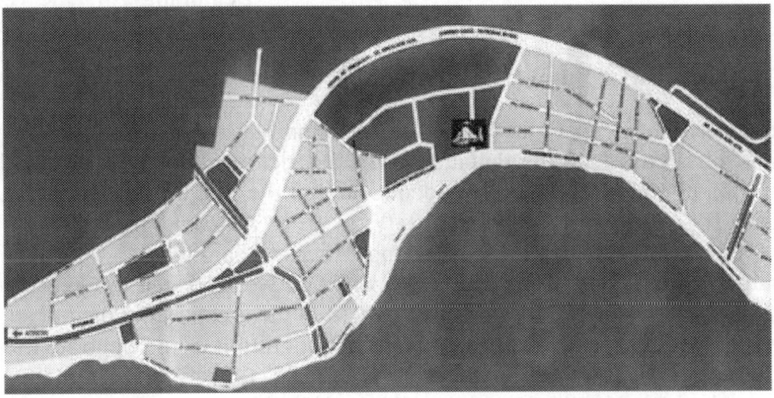

Figure 5: The town plan of Kamena Vourla with the spa center in the urban core.

Figure 6: "Asclepios" spa building today.

Figure 7: Hotel "Radio" today.

The aforementioned devaluation and abandonment of a large number of spa facilities and the infrastructure of Kamena Vourla resulted in the town: a) losing its spa identity due to the image of decline presented in the spa facilities and their infrastructure, b) having a discontinuity in the residential area since the abandoned facilities and the space surrounding them are in its urban core, c) having n non-aesthetic aspect since the abandoned facilities are in full view and centrally located and d) losing of a great number of visitors since more than half of the spa buildings are inoperative.

Figure 8: Hotel "Thronion" today.

Figure 9: Hotel "Oiti" in the beginning of the 20th century (still operating).

3.2 The spa town of Ypati ("Loutra Ypatis")

The town of Loutra Ypatis is the third most important spa town in Greece. It is also in Central Greece in the flatlands of the District of Fthiotis. It is a small spa town with a population of 1,000 residents, built at the foot of Oiti mountain, at a distance of 17 km from Lamia and 230 km from Athens. The town also has direct access to the railroad line connecting Athens to Salonika.

Loutra Ypatis is one of the first spa towns that were created in Greece at the end of the 19th century. More precisely, in 1890 the area around the hot springs received an official Town Plan as a token of recognition of the opportunities for development of the area, and two years later (1892) the first spa building was constructed next to the thermal spring (Figure 11). Until then, there were no spa buildings, nor residential development in the area. The building of the spa facilities and of a number of small and large hotels (Figures 9, 10) was the cause of tourism development in the area [8–10].

Almost from the very first day of its operation, the spa in Ypati came to be one of the main destinations for spa tourists and thus became one of the main spa destinations in Greece. Very soon, around the spa building, the first restaurants, cafés and shops were constructed and all the people working in these started to reside permanently in the area surrounding the spa building [8–10].

Figure 10: Hotel "Fthiotis" in the beginning of 20th century (destroyed during WWII).

Figure 11: The old spa building (demolished after WWII).

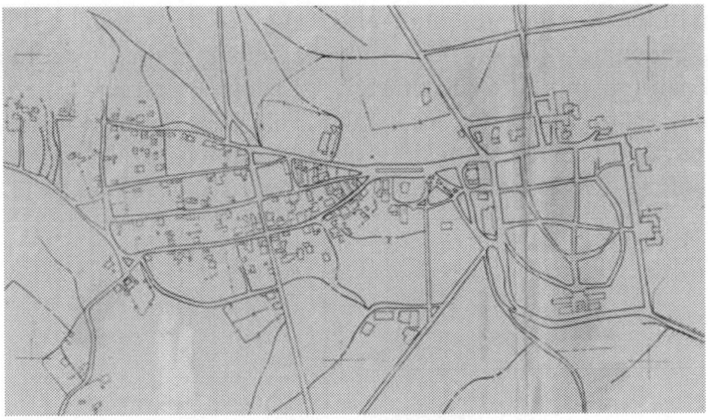

Figure 12: The plan of the spa town of Ypati.

The isolated spa center of Ypati began to be developed into a spa town (i.e. to be developed residentially on a larger scale) after the end of the Second World War. This is also a period when the spa town was entering its most important phase as tourist destination. As was the case for Kamena Vourla, the 1950s, 1960s and 1970s were a period of wealth for the spa town of Loutra Ypatis. In the beginning of the 1960s, the old spa building was demolished and a new one was constructed in order to cover the needs of a great number of people that arrived in the town for thermal treatments. The same happened to the hotel units with the renovation of the older ones and the construction of new ones. The spa town was in a constant state of development and its spa facilities became among the most famous in Greece.

Figure 13: The new spa building (built in the 1960s).

Figure 14: Historic hotel "The Springs" (still operating).

In spite of its previous growth, the fall started in the mid 1980s, which is the period during which we observe the gradual decline of spa tourism in all of Greece, and the spa town of Loutra Ypatis started to lose its splendor, following a negative course that has lasted to this day. In fact, tourism in Loutra Ypatis has decreased dramatically [5] and the spa core of the town presents evident signs of abandonment and neglect. The one – and only – spa building (Figure 13) is operating with evident signs of wear, and most of the hotels that catered to the spa tourism of the area are presenting either signs of downgrading (Figure 14) or complete abandonment (Figure 15). At the beginning of the 21st century, the spa center of Ypati (an area of approximately 90 hectares) presents the image more of a derelict area than a tourist destination. This does not help the aspect of the town nor pays respect to its history as a spa town and even more, creates negativity among investors who might be interested in developing the area.

Figure 15: The abandoned hotel "Pavillion".

4 Restoration and reuse strategies

As previously mentioned, the two spa towns of Kamena Vourla and Ypati (the second and third in importance among spa towns in Greece) are characterized by strong signs of abandonment and dereliction in the area allocated to their spa center. For this reason and with the aim of overcoming the unfavorable impacts on the urban tissue, a research was conducted in the field, with questionnaires filled in by visitors and bathers. The findings resulting from this investigation demonstrate the need for the realization of some feasible and attainable projects at the building and public space level in order to improve the given image of downgrading of such an important and vital part of these two spa towns. For instance in the case of Ypati only 15% of thermal tourists are 'very satisfied' with the offered spa facilities while in the case of Kamena Vourla the respective percentage goes up to 40%.

Taking into account the above considerations we are presenting here a series of suggestions and proposals for improving the built environment as for example, those that are described below for each one of the two spa towns (study areas).

4.1 Spa town of Kamena Vourla

The restoration and rehabilitation of the buildings of the spa center, firstly of the water spa "Asclepios" (Figures 4 and 6) and secondly of the hotels "Thronion" and "Radio" (Figures 7 and 8) with the aim of improving the offered tourist product and infrastructure.

Remodeling of the existing green spaces surrounding the spa buildings (total area of 60 hectares) with the aim of improving the quality of the environment of the spa center and the town itself.

Creating continuity with the residential areas of the town by connecting the walks inside the green space of the spa center with the urban tissue, so that people from the town may visit it.

Strengthening the spa identity of the town: Restoration and improvement of the buildings inside the town (mainly historic hotels) with the aim of redefining the identity of the town as a thermal tourist destination. It is also proposed to create landmarks and in certain places introduce town statues, mosaics etc that will have the water and thermal treatment as their main theme.

4.2 Spa town of Ypati ("Loutra Ypatis")

The restoration of the old spa building or/and the building of a new one: Restoration of the old spa building according to modern standards and needs of thermal tourism or/and the construction of a new spa building with the aim of attracting a larger number of thermal tourists.

Modernization of the hotel infrastructure surrounding the spa buildings: Restoration and improvement of the already existing hotel infrastructure, especially their facades, so that the image of the spa center and of the whole town might be aesthetically improved.

Restoration of derelict hotels with the aim of offering more – and more qualitative – hotel infrastructure to the visitors of the spa town and furthermore, to lift the image of abandonment.

Establishment of a thermal and historical museum of the town: one of the abandoned hotels in the town should be restored so that a thermal museum can be founded with the aim of strengthening the spa identity of the area and preserving its history.

Regeneration of the existing old park (total area of 90 hectares), upgrading its aesthetic image, with the aim of opening the park to visitors (tourists and local people) and improving the spatial cohesion between the spa center and the rest of the town.

Apart from the above proposed actions and interventions, a major issue that has to be addressed in such cases is the allocation of financial resources and the appropriate financial mechanisms in order to bring about the restoration and upgrading of derelict buildings. An answer to that may be a synergy between the state (central government), the local authorities and the local actors ('tripartite partnership'). Concerning the construction of infrastructures, the cooperation between public and private sectors, which was recently introduced in the Greek institutional framework, should be specifically studied in order to include the case in question. The greatest difficulty will be the maintenance and operation of this infrastructure, which should be financially viable, since this is a necessary condition in the context of a difficult international economic environment caused by the current policy of open markets and globalization.

5 Conclusions

It is a fact that in our days the sudden reduction of the number of thermal tourists in Greece has resulted in most of the Greek spa centers showing noticeable signs of decline and even – in some cases – abandonment. This unfortunate turn of events for the spa centers is even more evident in the case of the spa towns – i.e. the towns that have been developed 'ex nihilo' around a bathing center. In this case the abandonment of the bathing facilities does not only concern a remote bathing center somewhere in the countryside, but a vital part of a whole town.

In Greece, all of the spa towns – for many decades now – are suffering, if not from complete abandonment at least from a partial one. In the cases of Kamena Vourla and Loutra Ypatis, more than half of the buildings remain derelict and inactive, and the spa centers that once were full of life, are now in a state of neglect thus creating a discontinuity in the urban tissue of these two towns.

For this reason, in the cases of Kamena Vourla and Loutra Ypatis, there is an urgent need for the restoration of the aesthetic and functional character of the spa facilities as well as the reconnecting and restructuring of the urban space. These actions must be taken so that the two spa towns will not only become competitive once more as a tourist destination but also to regain the spatial cohesion and spa identity they deserve in the Greek and Mediterranean world thermal tourism.

In any case, the initiative for the realization of the proposed strategy for spatial development and the achievement of the specific aims depends on political will and is mainly a task of local authorities, which are the direct and valid conveyor of local interests, which should be mobilized with the support of the central government and the financial contribution of local private investors.

References

[1] Spathi, S., *Thermal tourism and the development of health tourism in Greece,* Centre of Economic Research and Planning (KEPE), Athens, 2000 (in Greek).

[2] Ministry of Environment, Spatial Planning and Public Works (M.E.S.P.P.W.), *Strategic Spatial Planning Study for thermal tourism development in Greece*, M.E.S.P.P.W., Athens, 2000 (in Greek).

[3] Ministry of Energy and Natural Resources (M.E.N.R.) – Institute of Geological and Mineral Research (I.G.M.R), *Mineral springs of Greece*, M.E.N.R. - I.G.M.R., Athens, 1984 (in Greek).

[4] Greek Association of Thermal Spring Municipalities (G.A.T.S.M.)- Greek Thermal Agency (G.T.A.), *Thermal Springs and Spa Towns: Greek Thermalism*, G.A.T.S.M. – G.T.A., Salonika, 2006 (in Greek).

[5] National Statistical Service of Greece, *Statistical Yearbooks* (up to 1997).

[6] Zcharopoulos C. and Barbikas M. and Christopoulos J., *Greek Spas: Tourist Guide*, Kastaniotis, Athens, 2001. (in Greek).

[7] Skouras, C., *The spa town of Kamena Vourla*, Athens, 1956 (in Greek).

[8] Evagelidis, T., *The self-shown medicinal waters of Ypati*, Cultura Publications, Athens, 1st edition 1895, republished 2005 (in Greek).

[9] Evagelopoulos, T., *The medicinal baths of Ypati*, Lamia, 1985 (in Greek).

[10] Gikas, A., *Ypati's baths*, Municipality of Ypati, 2001 (in Greek).

Case study: a brownfield site in suburban New York

Y. Hashimoto[1], J. Brooks[2], E. Conti[1], D. Averill[1], M. Beck[1] & D. Behnken[1]
[1]*Geomatrix Consultants, Inc., Oakland, California, USA*
[2]*Phillips Nizer LLP, New York, New York, USA*

Abstract

A fleet fueling facility reported a gasoline release in 1987 when impacted soils were encountered during the removal of two underground storage tanks. The subsequent remedial investigation indicated that separate-phase and dissolved-phase gasoline had migrated onto an adjacent property, consisting of a childcare facility and a wetland. Geomatrix utilized real-time-data collection methods, including the membrane interface probe, soil vapor screening, and physical analysis of soil in the field, to expedite delineation of the residual separate-phase product and impacted soil. The current property owner applied for entry into the New York State Brownfield Cleanup Program, which provides a multi-track cleanup approach to achieve closure based on land use and site-specific conditions. The program offers technical assistance grants and provides incentives to expedite cleanup, including limitations on liability and tax credits of 10–22%. Excavation was selected for removal of the residual product in the soil. Concurrent dewatering operations removed approximately 620,000 gallons of impacted groundwater. Clean backfill mixed with an oxygen release compound (ORC®) was placed in the excavation at and below the water table to increase oxygen availability in the groundwater, thereby enhancing aerobic degradation of dissolved petroleum hydrocarbons. The work was implemented on an expedited schedule, with activities commencing during the winter holiday to minimize impact to the childcare facility's operation.

Keywords: brownfield, petroleum, excavation, expedited site characterization, membrane interface probe, mobile laboratory, soil vapor, tax credits.

doi:10.2495/BF080161

1 Introduction

In the United States, the remediation and redevelopment of most brownfield sites are regulated by state (as distinct from federal) programs. The New York State Brownfield Cleanup Program (BCP), enacted in October 2003, provides legal and financial incentives to remediate and redevelop properties that are, or are perceived to be, contaminated. Most meaningful among the incentives are relief from legal liability to the state of New York, and credits against New York state income tax liability. The credits—calculated as a percentage of not only the cost of remediation but also the hard cost of redevelopment—constitute the most lucrative financial incentive of any brownfield program in the United States. The base percentage for individuals and similarly situated taxpayers is ten percent (10%); for non-pass-through corporations and similarly situated taxpayers, the base percentage is twelve percent (12%) (NYSDEC [1]). An additional two percent (2%) is added if the remediation plan achieves the most stringent standard ("unrestricted use"). If at least half of the subject property is located in an Environmental Zone (a census tract with either high poverty or high unemployment), an additional eight percent (8%) is added. Furthermore, to the extent that the credits exceed the taxpayer's New York State income tax liability, the balance is paid to the taxpayer as a refund (NYSDEC [1]).

The BCP requires that both a site and an applicant be eligible. A site is ineligible if it is already listed on the National Priority List or on the New York State Registry of Inactive Hazardous Waste Sites, or if the site is already the subject of an enforcement action under federal or state environmental law. An applicant is ineligible if, among other things, they have committed a felony in New York State or owe money to the New York State Oil Spill Fund (NYSDEC [1]).

In an effort to encourage the remediation and redevelopment of as many brownfield sites as possible, the BCP permits even "responsible parties"—those who caused or contributed to the contamination at a site—to apply. The BCP characterizes such parties as "participants," while those who are unconnected to the contamination are "volunteers."

Currently, both participants and volunteers are eligible for the same set of legal and financial incentives (amendments to the BCP recently proposed by New York Governor Spitzer would significantly reduce the tax credits available to participants). The BCP, however, does treat them differently in one very important respect: while participants are obligated to chase and clean up contamination emigrating from the subject site, volunteers are obligated to remediate only on-site contamination (NYSDEC [1]).

The BCP requires an applicant to involve the public and provide a citizen participation plan (NYSDEC [1]). The minimal requirement for involvement includes public notification via "fact sheets" describing the major issues of public concern, the site cleanup progress, and draft documents available for public review. Draft documents required of the applicant by the state are made available at a document repository for 30–45-days for public comment.

Interim remedial measures are encouraged by the state and are evaluated based on time-critical (emergency response action) or non-time-critical site cleanup needs. Time-critical remediations are expedited by waiving the public document review and extensive remedial investigations. Non-time-critical interim remedial measures are more discretionary and approval is similar to other remediations (requiring citizen participation). The state waives other processes to expedite remediation under the BCP, including the procedure for obtaining approved work permits. An applicant is required to submit all required permit applications for investigation and remediation, but an applicant may perform work prior to receipt of permit approval.

The site closure process is driven by soil concentrations. Soil cleanup levels are risk-based and multi-track, contingent upon land use. The applicant selects the appropriate cleanup track target—unrestricted or restricted (residential, commercial, or industrial)—for the site. If the applicant is a participant, off-site investigation and subsequent cleanup is required; however, off-site properties are not entered into a specific cleanup track. Each of the cleanup tracks addresses groundwater cleanup goals, easements, or restrictions. Soil vapor evaluations, such as subslab vapor sampling, are commonly incorporated into the site investigation process to assuage perceived risks from soil and groundwater contamination.

1.1 Site setting

The 2.7-acre site is currently an active fleet car rental facility located in suburban New York within a commercial/residential area. Approximately 14,000 square feet of the eastern portion of the property are occupied by an office and maintenance building (fig. 1). The remainder of the site property is used primarily for vehicle storage and is paved with asphalt and concrete, with the exception of some landscaped traffic berms. The topography of the site slopes gently downward to the south and southeast. Neighboring properties include commercial facilities to the north, east and west, and a childcare facility and wetland to the south.

The geology of the site and the adjacent property consists of silty sand overlying an intermittent peat layer and an intermittent gravel layer, with an underlying layer of silt and clay. Groundwater depths range from 4.5 to 10 feet below ground surface (bgs) at the site and between 1 to 3 feet bgs at the adjacent property to the south. Shallow groundwater flow direction has generally ranged from west to south beneath the site and from southwest to southeast beneath the adjacent property.

1.2 Background

A gasoline release at the site, a car rental facility, was reported to the New York State Department of Environmental Conservation (NYSDEC) when impacted soils were encountered during the removal of two gasoline underground storage tanks (USTs), which had been in use for approximately 21 years. Groundwater monitoring wells were installed and water samples were collected from the wells for analysis. Analytical data for groundwater samples collected from the monitoring wells indicated that the release had extended onto the adjacent property to the south, which includes a childcare facility and a wetland (fig. 1).

The monitoring wells were sampled again approximately six years after the prior groundwater sampling event, and the analytical results were similar to previous events. However, floating free product (gasoline) was found in one monitoring well near the location of the former USTs. Floating free product, other than a sheen, had not previously been reported at the site.

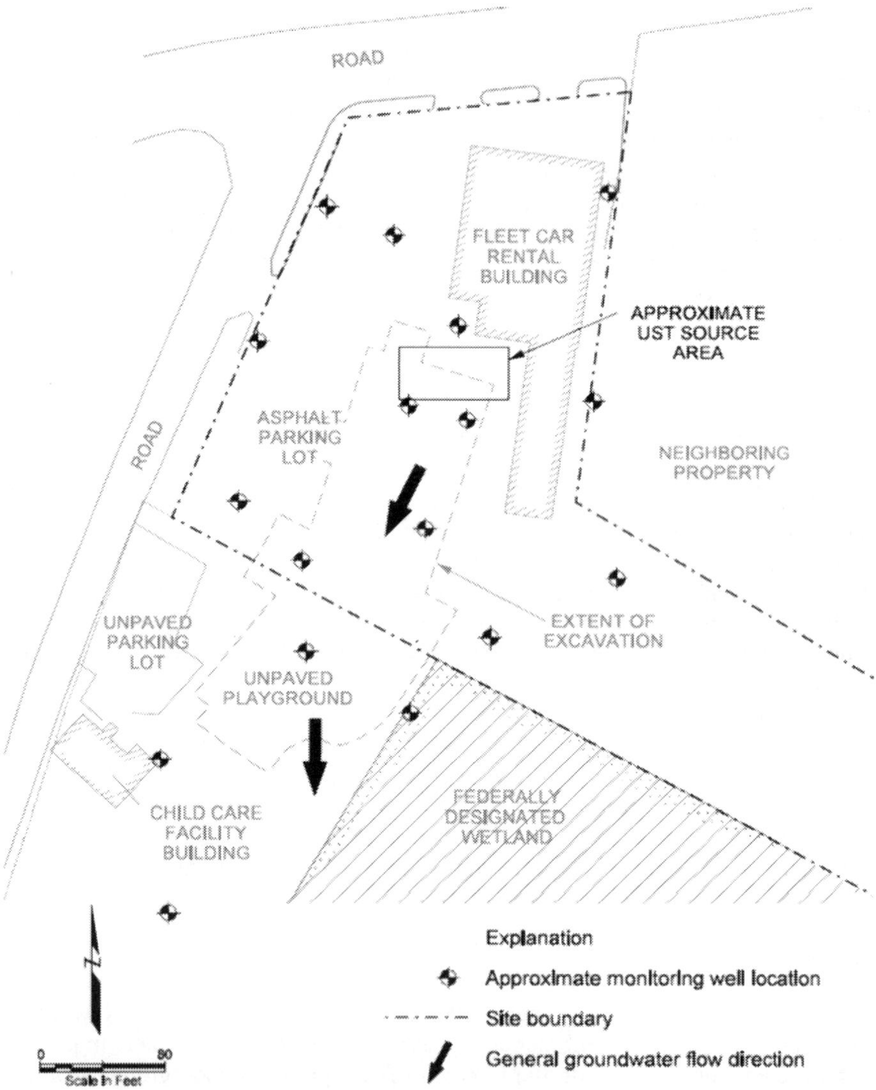

Figure 1: Site map.

Upon discovery of the floating free product, the status of the site was discussed with the NYSDEC, who concurred that the contamination was related to the release found during the UST excavation. An interim remedial measure—high-vacuum extraction—was conducted to remove the free product. Further investigations were implemented, including soil sampling near the well with floating free product, and depth-discrete groundwater sampling on the adjacent property to the south, but no floating free product was observed. Dissolved petroleum constituents were present in groundwater on the adjacent property to the south, but did not extend underneath the childcare facility building. The site property owner applied for entry to the Brownfield Cleanup Program as a volunteer and was accepted only as a participant; a Brownfield Site Cleanup Agreement was executed in 2005.

During a September 27, 2005, meeting, the NYSDEC and property owner agreed to implement a further interim remedial measure consisting of residual source removal through excavation of petroleum-impacted soils using conventional earthmoving equipment. Geomatrix developed and submitted an interim remedial measure work plan, received approval, and implemented the work in December 2005.

2 Summary of remedial investigations

Remedial investigation work, including the use of expedited site characterization techniques, defined the nature of contamination and identified the source and extent of petroleum hydrocarbons in soil and groundwater. The extent of residual hydrocarbons in soil was estimated within three days by advancing 22 borings using direct-push drilling rods equipped with a soil conductivity (SC) probe and a membrane interface probe (MIP). The SC probe provides soil lithology and the MIP provides volatile organic chemical data. The MIP contains a sensor that continuously logs volatile organic compounds that diffuse through a heated semipermeable membrane. The volatile organic compounds are brought to the surface through tubing that is connected to a detector for immediate analysis. The MIP served to qualitatively define areas with higher concentrations of petroleum constituents, both laterally and vertically. A calibration was made between the MIP logs and four companion soil borings advanced by direct push and visually logged and sampled. The extent of petroleum contamination was quantified in the visually logged soil borings with headspace readings from a portable photoionization detector (PID) and analysis of select soil samples by an off-site laboratory.

The extent of contamination in soil and groundwater was delineated and the target excavation area was defined based in part on the SC probe/MIP soil boring investigation. After defining the target excavation area, limited additional investigations were conducted to provide design information for the excavation, including advancing geotechnical borings, and to investigate potential preferential pathways, including a geophysical survey and drilling with an air knife and vacuum. Geophysical techniques utilized at the site included induced electromagnetic field and ground penetrating radar.

Soil vapor investigations were conducted prior to and following the excavation at the downgradient, off-site extent of the delineated groundwater plume. The purpose of the soil vapor investigations was to assess the risks associated with the soil vapor pathway at the downgradient extent of the groundwater plume, and to determine the effectiveness of the excavation in mitigating soil vapor migration. Because of the sensitive receptors (child care facility) downgradient of the site, subslab sampling was conducted at the child care facility building following excavation and restoration activities, as directed by the New York State Department of Health (NYSDOH). The NYSDOH works in tandem with the NYSDEC and is the lead agency for review for soil vapor investigations.

3 Interim remedial measure excavation

Regulatory requirements for approval of the interim remedial measure excavation were a hybrid of time critical and non–time critical. An interim remedial measure work plan was submitted (non-time-critical requirement), but public review was waived (time-critical waiver). The public review waiver facilitated implementation of the interim remedial measure excavation on an expedited schedule to accommodate the childcare facility's winter holiday schedule. The interim remedial measure work plan was approved within a month of submittal and excavation began three weeks later. Within those three weeks preparatory activities were conducted, including contractor selection, permit application submittal, utility clearance, survey control, site facility building natural gas service pipeline realignment, existing feature removal (i.e., playground equipment, trees, and other foliage), and site security setup (fencing).

The interim remedial measure excavation was conducted in two stages: on-site and off-site. Each stage included soil excavation, stockpiling, and loading; confirmation soil sample collection and analysis; excavation groundwater extraction, treatment, and sampling; monitoring well destruction; backfilling and paving; and excavated soil characterization and disposal. Because of the childcare facility's operating schedule, the selected approach was to excavate off site prior to excavating the on-site source area. A dewatering trench and clean buffer zone was maintained between the on- and off-site excavation areas to minimize the potential for contaminated groundwater to migrate from the site to the recently backfilled off-site area before all excavation activities could be completed.

3.1 Soil excavation

The anticipated excavation extent was delineated based on the expedited field screening and soil sampling described in Section 2. The actual horizontal and vertical extents of excavation were refined during implementation based on the results of soil confirmation samples analyzed by an on-site mobile laboratory. Final analytical confirmation was obtained using an off-site laboratory certified by the New York State Environmental Laboratory Accreditation Program

(ELAP) because the state will not accept analytical results from laboratories, including the mobile laboratory, without ELAP certification.

Soil sample analytical results were compared to recommended soil cleanup objectives known as TAGM 4046 (Technical and Administrative Guidance Memorandum 4046) during the excavation work, and in most areas the cleanup objectives were obtained. After the excavation activities, however, different track-specific soil cleanup levels (Subsection 375-6.8 Soil Cleanup Objective Tables) applicable to this site were released by the state (NYSDEC [2]). The site soil confirmation samples were compared to the unrestricted soil cleanup objectives, rather than restricted soil cleanup objectives for residential, commercial, or industrial land use. The post-excavation unrestricted cleanup objectives were similar to or more stringent than those applied during excavation.

The confirmation soil sample results were below the recommended unrestricted soil cleanup levels, with a few exceptions. These exceptions were in areas where further excavation was not feasible. The off-site excavation was not extended east into the federally designated wetlands, nor was it extended vertically beyond 12 to 14 feet bgs in the saturated silt and clay. On-site excavation could not be extended east of the shoring, which was installed near the site building to protect foundation integrity. To mitigate the potential impact to groundwater of these exceedances, Oxygen Release Compound, or ORC®, a proprietary material produced by Regenesis, Inc., was added to the backfill material in the excavation to enhance biodegradation of petroleum constituents in groundwater.

3.2 Groundwater treatment

Dewatering was performed to facilitate the soil excavation, confirmation soil sampling, backfilling and compaction, and to maximize mass removal of petroleum hydrocarbons during excavation activities. The extracted groundwater was treated by an on-site treatment system and discharged to the sanitary sewer. Approximately 620,000 gallons of groundwater were extracted, treated, and discharged. Geomatrix submitted a wastewater discharge permit application to the town and, as allowed by the BCP, commenced work without receiving an actual permit. Geomatrix complied with provisions that would typically be included in a permit and provided regular updates to the town on the status of treated water discharges to the sanitary sewer

4 Restoration

Restoration of on- and off-site properties resulted in property improvements eligible for tax credits. The off-site restoration activities included grading, installing new property boundary fencing, placing topsoil (for planting vegetation), and installing new playground equipment and other amenities. On-site property improvements included repaving the entire parking area (including the area of excavation) and replacing groundwater monitoring wells removed during the excavation activities. The effectiveness of the interim remedial measure excavation is being assessed with ongoing groundwater monitoring in on- and off-site wells.

5 Summary and current status

The site owner entered the BCP as a participant and shortly thereafter implemented an interim remedial measure excavation. The interim remedial measure excavation is intended to serve as the final remedy because it achieves the remedial goal established for the site (NYSDEC [1]). Site closure is obtained by the issuance of a "Certificate of Completion," thereby releasing the site owner of liability to the state for hazardous waste emanating from the site, and triggering eligibility for tax credits. A Certificate of Completion is issued based on determinations that remediation requirements have been achieved or will be achieved under an approved work plan and upon review and approval of a Final Engineering Report (NYSDEC [1]). These two documents will be submitted to the state in 2008.

Groundwater monitoring is the only ongoing activity following completion of restoration. Groundwater monitoring was conducted quarterly for six quarters and then was reduced to annually (every fifth quarter, to account for seasonal variations). Because dissolved petroleum constituents are present in groundwater, the state may impose a temporary environmental easement on the site until five consecutive quarters of monitoring provide analytical results that groundwater is within water quality objectives. The environmental easement serves to restrict groundwater use until natural attenuation achieves dissolved petroleum concentrations satisfactory to the state. The easement will not affect issuance of the Certificate of Completion.

Approximately \$5 million U.S. dollars in hard and soft remediation costs have been incurred. Up to 14 percent (14%), or \$700,000, will be available for tax credits upon issuance of a Certificate of Completion for an unrestricted closure track. The site is not in an Environmental Zone and is thus ineligible for additional tax credits. Those costs incurred prior to execution of the BCP agreement between the site owner and the state are not eligible for tax credits. However, the substantial available tax credits make the BCP a worthwhile cleanup pathway for this and other eligible sites.

The BCP is relatively new (2003) and continues to evolve. Specifically during this site's participation in the BCP, requirements for reports, fact sheets, and soil cleanup levels have deviated from the initial state requests and requirements. This is not unexpected, considering the numerous regulatory documents governing the BCP (NYSDEC [1–3]); participation from other agencies (NYSDOH involvement); and numerous public and regulatory steps. The BCP will become more refined as more sites, like this one, enter and complete the BCP process. Fortunately, sufficient incentives are provided to encourage participation in the program and to stimulate the cleanup and reuse of brownfields.

References

[1] New York State Department of Environmental Conservation (NYSDEC), Draft Brownfield Cleanup Program Guide, May 12, 2004.
[2] NYSDEC, 6 NYCRR Part 375 Environmental Remediation Program, December 14, 2006.
[3] NYSDEC, Draft DER-10 Technical Guidance for Site Investigation and Remediation, December 25, 2002.

References

Baton Rouge Brownfields Program in Old South Baton Rouge

T. L. Bunch, E. A. Miller, B. M. Hughes & L. J. Lyons
City of Baton Rouge-Parish of East Baton Rouge, Louisiana, USA

Abstract

In 2000, the Baton Rouge Brownfields Program (BRBP) was created as a recommendation of the Horizon Plan, the City-Parish comprehensive plan. The Plan provides the framework for all City-Parish growth-oriented decisions and initiatives including Smart Growth, In-fill Development and Environmental Planning. Funding awarded through the United States Environmental Protection Agency (EPA) will target sites impacted by petroleum and hazardous substances in the Old South Baton Rouge (OSBR) area to support the revitalization efforts of the East Baton Rouge Parish Housing Authority (EBRPHA).

According to the 2000 Census, 24% of the OSBR population is unemployed, 32% live below the poverty level and 43% lack a high school diploma. Also, the median household income is three times below the national average, and less than 40% of the homes are owner-occupied.

The BRBP identified at least 28 properties in the OSBR area that had Underground Storage Tanks (USTs), indicating that at least 104 properties in this area may be affected. Environmental assessments and mitigation of potential risks will allow the EBRPHA to continue the efforts of their Housing and Urban Development (HUD) HOPE VI Program. EBRPHA efforts thus far include the demolition of a 95-unit and 76-unit public housing development and construction of 136 units in "traditional neighborhood" design.

Partnerships with organizations and community leaders are critical to redevelopment. These relationships are vital as OSBR continues to grow and strengthen.

Keywords: historical neighborhoods, infill development, smart growth, community revitalization, non-profit, mixed-use development, low-income communities, partnerships, sprawl.

WIT Transactions on Ecology and the Environment, Vol 107, © 2008 WIT Press
www.witpress.com, ISSN 1743-3541 (on-line)
doi:10.2495/BF080171

1 Introduction

The Baton Rouge Brownfields Program (BRBP), created as a recommendation of the Horizon Plan, began as a method to encourage redevelopment while addressing issues of Environmental Planning, Smart Growth, and In-Fill Development. Baton Rouge is addressing a range of issues typical of many southern U.S. cities including sprawl, automobile reliance, and development of environmentally-sensitive areas such as wetlands. Streets that are not pedestrian-friendly contribute to the city having some of the most dangerous streets in the state of Louisiana, according to the 2004 Surface Transportation Policy Project. Automobile dominance, combined with a lack of connectivity and transportation choices have resulted in increased instances of obesity in communities. Land developers often seek clean, cheaper greenfields instead of redevelopment in urbanized areas. Additionally, environmentally-sensitive areas such as wetlands become vulnerable to encroaching development. Patterns such as these discourage economic development and investment in the central city and have adverse effects on our public and environmental health.

Since the BRBP received a Brownfields Assessment Demonstration Pilot Grant in 2000 from the United States Environmental Protection Agency (USEPA), it has established a site inventory of 155 specific properties, been awarded more than $1.3 million in assessment and cleanup funding, and conducted more than fifty (50) assessments for thirty-six (36) different sites. Additionally, it has leveraged almost $24 million in redevelopment funding.

The BRBP is now targeting specific communities in the city. In 2005 and 2006, the program received two (2) grants totaling $400,000 from the USEPA for environmental assessments. This funding specifically targets petroleum and hazardous substance-impacted sites in the Old South Baton Rouge (OSBR) area to support the revitalization efforts of the East Baton Rouge Parish Housing Authority (EBRPHA).

2 History of Old South Baton Rouge

OSBR, established in the 1800s, is one of Baton Rouge's oldest subdivisions. The earliest settlement recorded is Magnolia Mound Plantation, created by James Hillins in 1786. The OSBR land area covers about three (3) square miles in the city of Baton Rouge. OSBR was home to some of the most popular restaurants in the city, as well as successful department stores, theaters, and grocery stores. A community once thriving from a number of social and civic organizations and rich business culture, OSBR has changed significantly over time. The change can be attributed to the exodus of both Whites and African-Americans from the area after the Civil Rights Movement in the 1950s and 1960s. Seeking greater opportunities, those with the financial means left areas like OSBR seeking better homes, jobs, and schools for their children. However, those who could not afford to leave remained in the community. With such a large out-migration of people, few businesses were able to remain successful.

According to the 2000 United States Census, the Old South Baton Rouge area, located in Census Tract 21, has a 2,146 person population, with ninety-four percent (94%) being African American and five percent (5%) being White. Twenty-three and a half percent (23.5%) of the population are unemployed, thirty-two and two-fifths (32.4%) live below the poverty level, and forty-three percent (43%) are high school dropouts. In addition, the median household income is three times below the national average, and less than forty percent (40%) of the homes are owner-occupied. This Census Tract has been designated as a Difficult Development Area (DDA) by the United States Internal Revenue Service.

In addition to the historical significance of OSBR, the community is also located strategically in Baton Rouge. It is situated in close proximity to downtown Baton Rouge and Louisiana State University (LSU), the flagship university of Louisiana. Additionally, much of the community is parallel to the Mississippi River. The proximity to LSU and downtown Baton Rouge attracts some economic development interests, however, very few new businesses actually locate in the heart of OSBR

Currently, several areas in the community are in disrepair. Dilapidated properties host criminal activity and contribute to neighborhood blight. The physical appearance of these areas perpetuates the perception and fear of crime, which discourage investment in OSBR. The revitalization of the physical environment is a critical step in redeveloping the neighborhood.

3 Redeveloping Old South Baton Rouge

The Baton Rouge Brownfields Program was granted a total of $400,000 by the USEPA for petroleum and hazardous environmental assessments. This funding is eligible to sites throughout East Baton Rouge Parish, however priority will be given to sites in the OSBR area to support the revitalization efforts of the East Baton Rouge Parish Housing Authority HOPE VI office. The EBPRHA is utilizing an $18.6 million grant to demolish obsolete housing and purchase properties in the OSBR community for redevelopment.

The Baton Rouge Brownfields Program has identified at least twenty-eight (28) properties in the OSBR area that have had Underground Storage Tanks (USTs). Additionally, nineteen (19) of these sites have records indicating the USTs have been in place for more than twenty-five (25) years. Some of the oldest records suggest the USTs date back to the early 1950s. This information indicates that there are at least 104 properties in this area that may be potentially affected by these USTs. An environmental review of the project site revealed that historical past land uses more than likely contributed to the presence of these USTs. The contamination is most likely from petroleum-related products and services formerly located in the neighborhood.

3.1 Targeted sites: BR113

The BRBP has completed an assessment for the first target site, a former tire/auto repair shop, and was awarded cleanup funding. The USEPA granted

$58,696 to the EBRPHA for remediation activities involving petroleum contamination and asbestos containing materials. A Phase I Environmental Site Assessment identified environmental conditions including an UST, abandoned 55-gallon drums, hydrocarbon staining, and potential presence of lead-based paint and asbestos-containing materials. The Phase II assessment, which includes water and soil sampling, confirmed the presence of these environmental conditions.

The next step in the redevelopment process was to complete a Risk Evaluation/Corrective Action Program (RECAP) investigation. A RECAP determines the response to environmental contamination based on protection of human health and the environment, and sets minimum remediation standards for sites impacted by chemicals. The Louisiana Department of Environmental Quality (LDEQ) administers this program and oversees RECAP activities for the site. During this phase of assessments, six (6) USTs were discovered on the property. Initial site environmental review completed previously indicated that there were only two (2) USTs. The workplan created during the RECAP investigation addresses safely removing the USTs and methods to mitigate the impact of the other conditions. Additionally, brownfield sites such as BR113 can enroll in the Louisiana Voluntary Remediation Program (VRP), administered by the LDEQ. Property owners or potential owners who cleanup their sites under the guidelines indicated in the VRP can receive a release of liability and the same benefit flows to future owners of the property, Environmental assessments for this area and mitigation of potential risk will allow the EBRPHA to continue their efforts and leverage private investment in the area.

3.1.1 Targeted sites: multiple sites

In 2007, the BRBP funded environmental assessments for multiple sites in OSBR. These include approximately thirty (30) lots for redevelopment for the EBRPHA and other non-profit groups. These sites, in close proximity to BR113, will contain single-family residential homes and mixed-use developments. These lots are either on or adjacent to former heavy commercial sites including filling stations and auto repair shops.

A unique feature of these sites is that the Phase I and Phase II environmental assessments are conducted concurrently. Generally, the Phase I precedes the Phase II, however, site reconnaissance and environmental sampling and investigations will occur simultaneously due to time and access constraints. Critical to completing these assessments is coordinating a number of groups, including the USEPA, LDEQ, BRBP Steering Committee, the EBRPHA, the local community, and other non-profit groups. The BRBP facilitates meetings and active participation with these parties and will remain an integral partner throughout the redevelopment process.

4 Long-term redevelopment strategy

Essential to the redevelopment of OSBR are community involvement and establishing partnerships with various non-profit and civic organizations. While revitalization in OSBR is mostly a community initiative, there are various individuals and groups, public and private, which are catalyzing the redevelopment process. One such group is Plan Baton Rouge, a collaborative effort with EBRPHA Office of HOPE VI, the Center for Planning Excellence (C-PEX), and the Baton Rouge Area Foundation (BRAF). Each of these non-profit organizations has a vested interest in OSBR and the BRBP has assisted them in conducting environmental site assessments in the area. Additionally, through these collaborations, the City-Parish is able to fulfill goals and objectives outlined in the Horizon Plan.

A major goal in the OSBR redevelopment strategy is to prevent displacing life-long residents. Private, expensive residential developments are appearing in some areas near the community. These developments have the potential to force out families and establishments that have been a part of the long history of OSBR. Low income levels and developer disinterest in affordable housing leaves very few choices for community members. However, the EBRPHA Office of HOPE VI is leading the effort to construct quality, affordable housing in OSBR. With an $18.6 million grant from HUD, the EBRPHA is building single-family homes. The BRBP is assisting by coordinating the environmental investigations on targeted properties. Utilizing environmental assessment funding from the BRBP translates to more of the HUD funding used for redevelopment.

Ultimately, revitalization in any community is multi-party effort. The BRBP contributes not only financial resources, but also vision, knowledge, and expertise in Brownfields and redevelopment. Because the BRBP is administered by the Office of the Planning Commission, urban planners are able to provide a unique perspective on revitalization and economic redevelopment. The planners involved in the Brownfields Program introduce the planning process by facilitating redevelopment, organizing resources, and fulfilling goals outlined in the City of Baton Rouge Horizon Plan. Horizon Plan goals include the redevelopment of existing neighborhoods, affordable housing, and infill development. This community initiative has further catalyzed the redevelopment efforts in OSBR. The collaboration of organizations and community leaders has created a network of partnerships with each group contributing their own component to the shared vision of revitalization. These entities have combined to leverage funding from multiple sources, both public and private, that will improve the quality of life for residents of Old South Baton Rouge.

References

[1] Louisiana State University (LSU). LSU Office of University Relations, Baton Rouge, LA, http://www.lsu.edu/highlights/033/flower.html

[2] The Daily Reveille. "Waking Old South Baton Rouge," http://media.www.lsureveille.com/

[3] *Mean Streets 2004,* Surface Transportation Policy Project.

[4] United States Internal Revenue Service, 2008 IRS SECTION 42(d)(5)(C) QUALIFIED CENSUS TRACTS, http://www.huduser.org/Datasets/qct/qct2008m.PDF

Section 5
Risk assessment and management

Application of the "ARA-CoS$_{SSLs}$" risk analysis approach at a sub-area of a relevant Italian contaminated site

F. Tatàno, M. Giavazzi & R. Trabucchi
Science and Technology Faculty, University of Urbino "Carlo Bo", Italy

Abstract

This paper describes a significant case-study application of the "ARA-CoS$_{SSLs}$" risk analysis approach, which has been developed as a University research study and presented at the past "Brownfields 2006" Conference. Specific, procedural steps have been considered for the selection of contaminants of concern, the definition of representative concentrations, and estimation of relevant modelling factors.

Keywords: absolute risk analysis, application, case-study, contaminated sites.

1 Introduction

Management of contaminated sites represents a relevant, environmental challenge in many industrialised countries. Within an integrated plan (at a given territorial scale: provincial, regional, national) for the identification, characterisation and final remediation of contaminated sites, the application of reliable and scientifically based absolute risk analysis criteria (as a possible category within the overall soil and groundwater quality approaches [1]) is a necessary, initial step. Referring to the Italian situation, a few years ago the national technical-scientific regulation on contaminated sites was changed, with consequential effects on the regulative application conditions for the absolute risk analysis. In fact, the old Italian Ministerial Decree "No. 471/1999" on contaminated soil management (issued in 1999 [2]) enforced a particularly restricted regulative use of the health-sanitary absolute risk analysis [1]. On the contrary, the current (issued in 2006) Italian regulation on contaminated sites (as a part of the Legislative Decree "No. 152/2006" [3]) reflects (in Section IV, Title V) a "multi-tiered" approach on the quality criteria for contaminated sites,

WIT Transactions on Ecology and the Environment, Vol 107, © 2008 WIT Press
www.witpress.com, ISSN 1743-3541 (on-line)
doi:10.2495/BF080181

expressly requiring the application of a "Tier 2" absolute sanitary risk assessment to calculate contaminant site-specific target levels while the contaminant "limit values" (for soil-subsoil and groundwater) already defined by the mentioned Decree "No. 471/1999" (indeed with some minor changes) properly act as "Tier 1" screening values [1]. Consequently, as a complementary contribution within this increased (legislative and applicative) attention to the absolute risk analysis at the Italian level, the "ARA-CoS$_{SSLs}$" modelling approach for human health ("Absolute Risk Analysis for Contaminated Sites") has been recently derived (due to a University research study) in its initial, simplified version with predominant reference to the US.EPA "SSLs, Soil Screening Levels" procedure [4-6], and directly implemented on a computer worksheet basis. An original paper published in the "Brownfields III" Proceedings expressly reports on the fundamentals, calculation structure and computer implementation of the "ARA-CoS$_{SSLs}$" approach [7]. As a useful step in the approach validation and verification, this paper deals with the procedural elaborations for the "ARA-CoS$_{SSLs}$" approach exercise application at a significant potentially contaminated sub-area of a relevant Italian industrial site.

2 The case-study industrial sub-area: synthetic description

The case-study industrial sub-area refers to a power plant settlement with a complex mixture of numerous, detected contaminants exceeding (in soil-subsoil samples, small surface aquifer and primary aquifer water samples) the corresponding "contamination screening values" for soil-subsoil (commercial/industrial use) and groundwater of the mentioned Decrees "No. 471/1999" and "No. 152/2006" (see Section 1). Precisely, these detected contaminants belong to the following chemical groups: inorganic compounds (comprehensive of metals), aromatic compounds, polycyclic aromatic hydrocarbons, chlorinated aliphatic compounds, halogenated aliphatic compounds, chlorinated benzenes, PCDDs/DFs and total petroleum hydrocarbons. Referring to the available overall site investigation informative documents, the average sub-area geo-lithological and hydro-geological stratigraphy is approximately identifiable in the following order (from the top): an uppermost, heterogeneous layer of backfill soils and materials (average thickness 3.5-4.0 m), inclusive of a small and discontinuous surface aquifer with infiltration waters connected to the existing precipitation cycle; an underlying, discontinuous low permeability layer, consisting of clay, clayey silt and peat materials (average thickness 4.0-4.5 m); a primary, sandy aquifer (average thickness 5.0 m); an underlying aquitard, consisting of alternating silty clay, clayey silt and peat materials (average thickness 4.0 m); and finally, a secondary, sandy aquifer. The mentioned spatial discontinuity of the low permeability layer (underlying the upper backfill materials), precisely resulting in several areal conditions with its partial or total absence, is geologically attributable to the combined phenomena of previous natural erosions and subsequent natural and/or artificial backfilling with permeable, fine soils. Consequently, these localised situations of partial/total absence of the intermediate low permeability layer could realistically imply significant areal conditions of hydraulic connection between the small surface aquifer and the primary aquifer (see Section 3.1). According to the investigation of informative documents available for the case-study industrial sub-area, Figure 1 shows the mutual location map (derived from geo-referenced topographical co-ordinates) of the drilled subsurface soil borings, with altogether more than 890 chemical analytical determinations (in core samples) exceeding the corresponding Italian screening values (for commercial/industrial land use: see Section 1). Referring instead to the surface and the primary aquifers underlying the case-study industrial sub-area, respectively for no. 3 and no. 2 monitoring wells, it is documented that the condition of groundwater chemical analytical determinations exceeds the corresponding Italian groundwater screening levels (see Section 1).

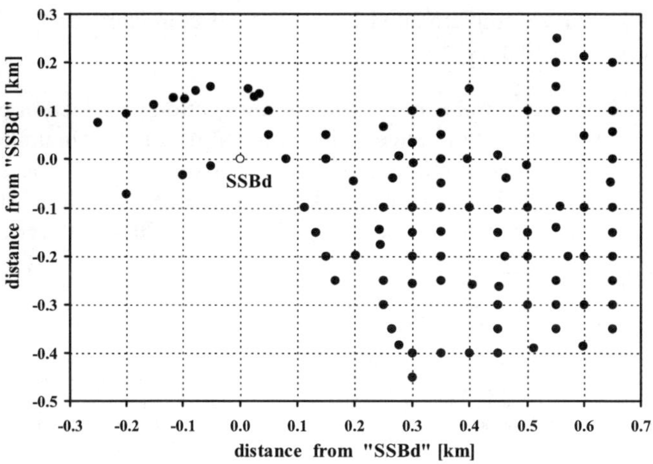

Figure 1: Case-study industrial sub-area: mutual location map of drilled “SSBs, subsurface soil borings”, as referred to the “deepest” boring (symbolically “SSBd”) topographic co-ordinates.

3 Procedural steps for the case-study application of the “ARA-CoS$_{SSLs}$” approach

3.1 Developed conceptual site model, contaminants of concern and representative concentrations

Referring to the conceptual site model for the case-study industrial sub-area (see Section 2), a non-residential (commercial-industrial) scenario has been expressly assumed, with an outdoor worker as the related human receptor. Consequently, according to the current “ARA-CoS$_{SSls}$” calculation options [7], the following, potential exposure pathways have been evaluated: for surface soil, direct ingestion, dermal contact and outdoor fugitive dust inhalation; for subsurface soil, migration to groundwater with consequential water ingestion (indeed mainly theoretical, due to the current situation of the absence of groundwater drinking use in the sub-area location territory) and outdoor volatile inhalation.

With regard to the selection of contaminants of concern (from a whole number of nearly fifty chemicals in subsoil and groundwater exceeding the mentioned "screening values" at the case-study sub-area), the application of the alternative criteria of "TS, Toxicity Score" and "normalised Comparative Hazard Index" (as described in [8]) has been carried out according to the specific assumptions (considered human exposure routes for "TS" criterion; considered generic soil screening levels for "normalised Comparative Hazard Index" criterion) and consequential results of Table 1. The final, inclusive selection of contaminants of concern for the "ARA-CoS$_{SSLs}$" case-study application is reported in the last row of Table 1: indeed, 2,3,7,8-TCDD, 1,2,3-Trichloropropane and Copper have been compulsorily excluded, as they are not in the original "US.EPA SSLs" chemical property database [6] and consequently (see Section 1) not yet implemented in the current computerised version of the "ARA-CoS$_{SSLs}$" approach [7].

Table 1: Case-study industrial sub-area: application of selection criteria for contaminants of concern. Legend: (*) resulting contaminants listed in "TS" score ranking order, comprising 99% of the total "TS" score; (**) in round brackets, max Hazard Index (100%) and normalised Hazard Indexes within at least 70% of the max value.

Applied criterion	Resulting contaminants
"TS, Toxicity Score" criterion [8]	
TS – human ingestion exposure, carcinogenic effects (max contaminant concentration in soil)	Beryllium, 1,1-Dichloroethylene, Tetrachloroethylene, 1,2-Dichloroethane, Arsenic, 1,1,2-Trichloroethane, vinyl chloride, *2,3,7,8-TCDD*, Trichloroethylene, *1,2,3-Trichloropropane* (*)
TS – human ingestion exposure, non-carcinogenic effects (max contaminant concentration in soil)	Trichloroethylene, 1,1,2-Trichloroethane, Arsenic, Mercury, Beryllium, Vanadium, Chromium, Antimony, *Copper*, Tetrachloroethylene, Vinyl chloride, Cadmium, 1,1-Dichloroethylene, cis-1,2-dichloroethylene, Hexachlorobenzene (*)
TS – human inhalation exposure, carcinogenic effects (see above)	Chromium, Beryllium, Arsenic, 1,2-Dichloroethane, 1,1,2-Trichloroethane (*)
TS – human inhalation exposure, non-carcinogenic effects (see above)	Beryllium, Chromium, Mercury (*)
TS – human ingestion exposure, carcinogenic effects (max contaminant concentration in primary aquifer water)	Vinyl chloride, Arsenic, 1,1-Dichloroethylene (*)
TS – human ingestion exposure, non-carcinogenic effects (max contaminant concentration in primary aquifer water)	cis-1,2-Dichloroethylene, Arsenic, Vinyl chloride, Trichloroethylene (*)
"normalised Comparative Hazard Index" criterion [8]	
Considering US.EPA generic SSLs for commercial/industrial scenario, outdoor worker, ingestion-dermal [6]	Tetrachloroethylene (100%), 1,2-Dichloroethane (89%), Arsenic (72%) (**)
Considering US.EPA generic SSLs for commercial/industrial scenario, outdoor worker, volatile inhalation [6]	1,2-Dichloroethane (100%) (**)
Considering US.EPA generic SSLs for commercial/industrial scenario, outdoor worker, migration to groundwater (Dilution Factor = 20) [6]	1,1,2-Trichloroethane (100%), 1,2-Dichloroethane (96%) (**)
Totally selected contaminants of concern for the "ARA-CoS$_{SSLs}$" application	
Antimony, Arsenic, Beryllium, Cadmium, Chromium, Mercury, Vanadium, Zinc, 1,2-Dichloroethane, 1,1-Dichloroethylene, cis-1,2-Dichloroethylene, Trichloroethylene, Tetrachloroethylene, 1,1,2-Trichloroethane, Vinyl chloride, Hexachlorobenzene	

The applied procedures for defining the representative concentrations for the selected contaminants of concern, in the different environmental media at the given case-study industrial sub-area, are schematised in Figure 2. Referring to subsurface soil, initially a specific, double concentration weighing criterion has been adopted, precisely consisting of a first core-length weighing step on individual soil borings according to the following eqn (1) (and related Figure 3, left-hand side), and a second weighing step for a "normalised" concentration on the whole contamination source volume based on the following eqn (2) (and related Figure 3, right-hand side):

$$c_{sb} = \frac{\sum c_i \cdot l_i}{d_{sb}} \tag{1}$$

$$c_{sb,n} = c_{sb} \cdot \left(d_{sb} / d_{sb,\max} \right) \tag{2}$$

where c_{sb} is the length-weighted contaminant soil boring concentration, $c_{sb,n}$ is the "normalised" contaminant soil boring concentration, c_i is the documented concentration available for core segment of length l_i, d_{sb} is the soil boring depth, and $d_{sb,max}$ is the max available depth of soil borings for the given contaminant. Subsequently, for the chemical groups of the selected contaminants of concern, the conclusive, statistical determination of representative subsurface soil concentrations have been carried out with the following approaches, differentiated according to the available no. (N) of $c_{sb,n}$ values for given contaminant (Figure 2): 1) for contaminants of concern belonging to the chlorinated aliphatic group (all resulting with N > 10), the maximum value, arithmetic mean and "$UCL_{95\%}$, 95% Upper Confidence Limit" on the mean have been comparatively assumed; 2) on the contrary for inorganic contaminants of concern (some instead resulting with N < 10 and others with N > 10), the maximum value and $UCL_{95\%}$ have been considered respectively for the conditions N < 10 and N > 10 (indicatively referring to a procedural rule of the methodological document on absolute risk analysis – 2005 version [9] – produced by "APAT, Italian Environmental Protection Agency and Technical Services"); 3) finally for hexachlorobenzene (precisely characterised with N < 10), the maximum value has been assumed. All $UCL_{95\%}$ determinations have been properly carried out according to the US.EPA "ProUCL" software [10]. Moreover, it should be pointed out that expressly for organic (chlorinated aliphatic) contaminants of concern, the following, alternative "hypothetical" calculation conditions (as properly implemented in the "ARA-CoS_{SSLs}" approach [7, 8]) have been simulated: 1) "real" three-phase chemical content on soil material (S), in soil water (W) and soil air (A) ("[S-W-A]r" symbol); 2) potential soil gas loss during sampling ("[S-W]r" symbol condition), and consequential, automatic derivation of "estimated" total three-phase concentration ("[S-W-A]e" symbol). Referring instead to surface soil, no direct top soil sample concentrations have been documented in the available case-study sub-area investigation documents; in this condition, surface soil concentrations have been roughly assumed as the corresponding available sample concentrations (related to drilled soil borings) of the core segment at minor depth, and consequently the similar statistical calculation procedures as for subsurface soil have been applied

(Figure 2). Finally, concerning groundwater, for the small surface aquifer the available max concentration values have been approximately considered as "measured" representative concentrations, due to the extremely limited number of monitoring wells (see Section 2). Referring instead to the more significant primary aquifer (see Section 2), apart from the same assumption for "measured" representative concentrations, additional "estimated" values have been directly generated in the "ARA-CoS_{SSLs}" approach (based on the implemented US.EPA theory of soil/water/air contaminant partition in unsaturated zone and subsequent aquifer dilution) [4-8], under the theoretical hypothesis (approximately supportable with some geological evidence: see Section 2) of a partial (at least) hydro-geological connection between the contamination source and the primary aquifer.

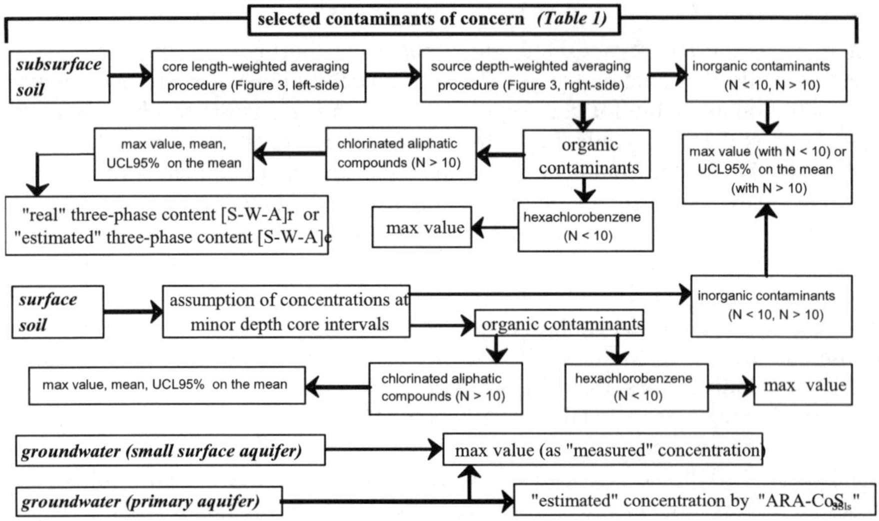

Figure 2: Case-study industrial sub-area: applied procedures for the definition of contaminant representative concentrations. Legend: N = number of boring concentrations (normalised, for subsurface soil; at minor depth, for surface soil).

3.2 Specific calculation of air dispersion and groundwater dilution factors

Referring to the "ARA-CoS_{SSLs}" modelling approach for the outdoor inhalation of particulate and volatiles [7, 8], the specific estimation (for the case-study sub-area) of the related US.EPA "SSLs" air dispersion factors "Q/C_{wind}" (for fugitive dusts emitted from surface soil [6]) and "Q/C_{vol}" (for volatiles emitted from subsurface soil [6]) has been carried out according to the sequential procedure of Figure 4. As a starting step, only contaminants showing subsurface soil boring normalised concentration sets (calculated according to eqns (1), (2)) with some values exceeding the corresponding Italian screening levels (industrial-commercial use: see Section 1) have been considered. Consequently, according to a geostatistical "Kriging" interpolation method with Surfer® 8.0 software

(Golden Software, Inc.), the corresponding concentration isopleth maps have been separately contoured for the considered contaminants. On the basis of these maps, source areal extents have been estimated (individually for each contaminant) by geostatistical integration over the perimeters defined with the proper isopleths corresponding to the mentioned Italian screening levels (see Section 1). Finally, the arithmetic mean (precisely 27.4 acres) of these resulting surface areas has been approximately assumed as the representative site areal extent A_{site} [acres], which is a specific input parameter in the US.EPA "SSLs" calculation equations (reported in Appendix D of [6]) for Q/C_{wind} and Q/C_{vol}. The resulting specific values for the case-study industrial sub-area are 49.09 (g m^{-2} s^{-1} per kg m^{-3}) (Q/C_{wind}) and 35.46 (g m^{-2} s^{-1} per kg m^{-3}) (Q/C_{vol}) respectively.

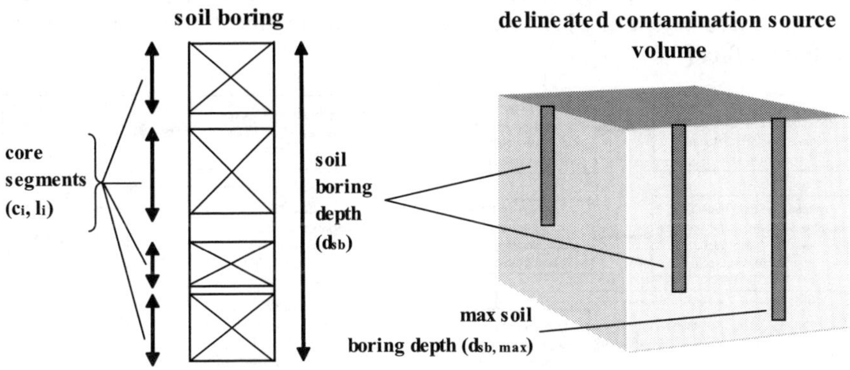

Figure 3: Contaminant representative concentrations in soil borings: assumed schematisations (for the case-study industrial sub-area) of the core length-weighted averaging procedure (left-side) and the subsequent source normalisation procedure (right-side).

Referring to the specific case-study derivation of the "DF, Dilution Factor" [4-6] in the "ARA-CoS_{SSLs}" modelling approach of migration to the primary aquifer pathway (as expressly related to the "estimation" procedure for representative groundwater concentrations: see Figure 2) [7, 8], Figure 4 additionally shows the adopted procedure. Precisely, primary aquifer hydraulic conductivity (assumed as 1,734.5 m yr^{-1}), thickness (assumed as 5 m: see Section 2), and infiltration rate (assumed as recharge of 0.20 m yr^{-1}) have been roughly estimated from available technical-scientific informative documents on the location territory of the case-study sub-area. Instead, under the assumption of a representative square contaminant source (which is consistent with the US.EPA "SSLs" procedure [4, 5]), the contamination source length has been calculated as the square root of the average site areal extent as previously defined (yielding a value of 333 m).

On the contrary, the specific determination of groundwater flow direction and consequential hydraulic gradient (properly yielding a value of 0.0013 m m^{-1}) has been carried out (as shown in Figure 5) by firstly mapping (with the above mentioned geostatistical approach) the contoured total hydraulic head equipotentials for the overall location territory of the case-study sub-area, and secondly overlapping the subsurface soil boring mutual position map of Figure 1. The relevant mixing zone depth should be theoretically estimated (using all previous hydro-geologic input parameters) with the proper adopted US.EPA "SSLs" modelling equation [5, 6]; resulting in this theoretical value above the primary aquifer thickness for the case-study sub-area, consequently this aquifer thickness has been usefully used as the upper limit for mixing zone depth [5, 6]. Conclusively, the implemented (in "ARA-CoS$_{SSLs}$" approach [7, 8]) US.EPA "SSLs" modelling equation for the Dilution Factor [4-6] has given a DF value of 1.17 for the case-study industrial sub-area. This specific condition (practically identifiable with the conservative situation of DF = 1) is indicative of little or no contaminant dilution, potentially attributable to a non-thick primary aquifer (in fact limiting the mixing zone depth) in relation to a quite large source (representative extent of 27.4 acres) causing a predominant effect of the overall infiltration flux [5,6].

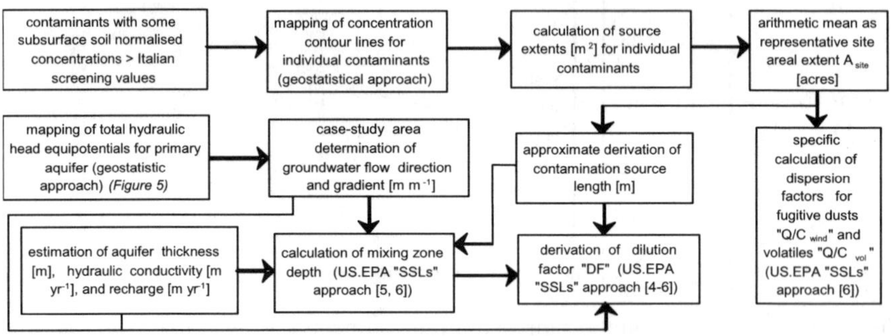

Figure 4: Case-study industrial sub-area: adopted procedures for the specific determination of air dispersion and groundwater dilution factors.

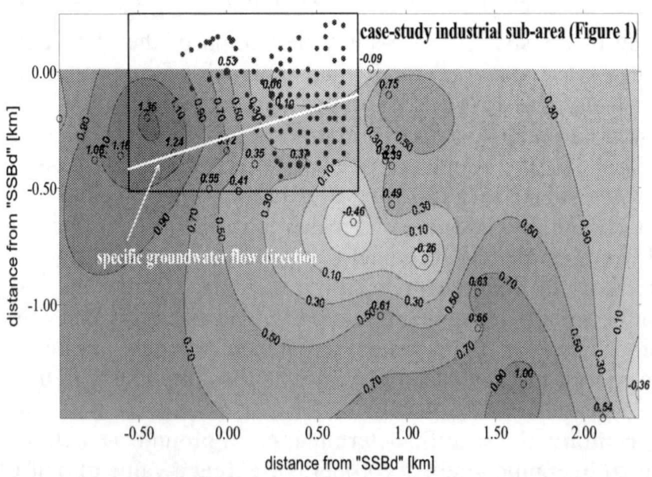

Figure 5: Case-study industrial sub-area: total hydraulic head equipotential map for primary aquifer in the location territory, and specific flow direction line for groundwater hydraulic gradient determination.

4 Summary of case-study risk analysis results and conclusions

The resulting individual risks, according to a "direct" risk assessment mode [7, 8], are summarised in: Table 2, with reference to the inorganic contaminants of concern; Table 3, related to the chlorinated benzene contaminant of concern; and finally Table 4, related to the chlorinated aliphatic contaminants of concern, indeed indicatively reporting (for synthesis reasons) only risk results based on the statistical calculation condition of "$UCL_{95\%}$" for surface and subsurface soil representative concentrations (see Section 3.1). Acceptable individual risk levels are usually adoptable as $1 \cdot 10^{-6}$ excess "CR, Cancer Risk" for carcinogenic effects and a "HQ, Hazard Quotient" of 1 for non-carcinogenic effects [4, 5].

Expressly focusing on the adopted procedural steps of Sections 3.1, 3.2 and the modelling structure of the "ARA-CoS_{SSLs}" approach, the critical analysis of Tables 2-4 conclusively allows (at least) the following, synthetic considerations: 1) apart from Cadmium and Zinc, all remaining selected contaminants in the last row of Table 1 cause at least one non-negligible individual risk level; 2) for migration to groundwater pathways, apart from the magnitude order equivalence condition on Arsenic, for considerable organic contaminants (excluding cis-1,2-

Table 2: Case-study (industrial sub-area) application of the "ARA-CoSSSLs" approach: calculated, individual risks for inorganic contaminants of concern (see Table 1). Legend: CR, HQ = see Section 4; N/D = not derivable; Cr = representative concentration; DF = Dilution Factor; * with Q/C_{wind} = 49.09 g m^{-2} s^{-1} per kg m^{-3}.

	Direct Ingestion		Dermal Absorption		Inhalation of Dusts *	
	CR	HQ	CR	HQ	CR	HQ
Antimony	N/D	1.79E-01	N/D	N/D	N/D	5.04E-05
Arsenic	5.62E-05	3.49E-01	1.11E-05	6.92E-02	1.58E-07	9.82E-05
Beryllium	2.54E-04	3.31E-01	N/D	N/D	1.40E-06	9.31E-05
Cadmium	N/D	2.45E-02	N/D	6.47E-03	1.55E-08	6.89E-06
Chromium	N/D	2.13E-01	N/D	N/D	4.49E-06	5.99E-05
Mercury	N/D	3.65E-01	N/D	N/D	N/D	3.59E-04
Vanadium	N/D	5.02E-01	N/D	N/D	N/D	1.41E-04
Zinc	N/D	1.16E-02	N/D	N/D	N/D	3.27E-06

	Inhalation of Volatiles (Q/C_{vol} = 35.46 g m^{-2} s^{-1} per kg m^{-3})	
	CR	HQ
Mercury	N/D	1.29E+00

	Migration to Groundwater			
	Measured Cr		Estimated Cr (DF = 1.17)	
	CR	HQ	CR	HQ
Antimony	N/D	N/D	N/D	7.75E+00
Arsenic	1.94E-03	1.21E+01	2.34E-03	1.46E+01
Beryllium	N/D	N/D	7.30E-03	0.95E+00
Cadmium	N/D	N/D	N/D	0.70E+00
Chromium	N/D	N/D	N/D	0.57E+00
Mercury	N/D	N/D	N/D	9.28E+00
Vanadium	N/D	N/D	N/D	1.13E+00
Zinc	N/D	N/D	N/D	0.83E+00

Table 3: Case-study (industrial sub-area) application of the "ARA-CoS$_{SSLs}$" approach: calculated, individual risks for chlorinated benzene contaminant of concern (see Table 1). Legend: see Table 2.

	Hexachlorobenzene	
	CR	HQ
Direct Ingestion	9.00E-06	1.97E-02
Inhalation of Dusts (Q/C_{wind} = 49.09 g m^{-2} s^{-1} per kg m^{-3})	2.55E-09	5.54E-06
Inhalation of Volatiles (Q/C_{vol} = 35.46 g m^{-2} s^{-1} per kg m^{-3})	2.60E-05	5.65E-02
Migration to Groundwater (DF = 1.17)	1.71E-03	3.74E+00

Table 4: Case-study (industrial sub-area) application of the "ARA-CoS$_{SSLs}$" approach: calculated, individual risks for chlorinated aliphatic contaminants of concern (see Table 1), "UCL$_{95\%}$" approach. Legend: see Table 2 ([S-W-A]r, [S-W]r, [S-W-A]e: see Section 3.1, [7, 8]).

	Direct Ingestion		Dermal Absorption		Inhalation of Dusts *	
	CR	HQ	CR	HQ	CR	HQ
1,2-Dichloroethane	1.13E-04	N/D	N/D	N/D	3.17E-08	N/D
1,1-Dichloroethylene	2.07E-04	1.08E-01	N/D	N/D	1.70E-08	3.02E-05
cis-1,2-Dichloroethylene	N/D	8.78E-03	N/D	N/D	N/D	2.47E-06
Tetrachloroethylene	5.78E-06	3.11E-02	N/D	N/D	6.34E-11	8.75E-06
1,1,2-Trichloroethane	6.79E-05	8.34E-01	N/D	N/D	1.88E-08	2.34E-04
Trichloroethylene	3.97E-07	N/D	N/D	N/D	6.03E-11	N/D
Vinyl chloride	1.45E-05	1.88E-02	N/D	N/D	8.71E-11	5.54E-07
	Inhalation of Volatiles ("IV") (Q/C_{vol} = 35.46 g m^{-2} s^{-1} per kg m^{-3})					
	[S-W-A]r *(or [S-W]r)*		*[S-W-A]e*			
			$\theta_w - f_{oc}$ *(IV modelling)*		$\theta_w - f_{oc}$ *(MGW model.)*	
	CR	HQ	*CR*	*HQ*	*CR*	*HQ*
1,2-Dichloroethane	1.78E-03	N/D	*1.85E-03*	*N/D*	*1.81E-03*	*N/D*
1,1-Dichloroethylene	7.71E-04	1.37E+00	*1.12E-03*	*1.98E+00*	*1.00E-03*	*1.78E+00*
cis-1,2-Dichloroethylene	N/D	2.11E-01	*N/D*	*2.32E-01*	*N/D*	*2.22E-01*
Tetrachloroethylene	4.51E-06	6.23E-01	*5.14E-06*	*7.09E-01*	*5.11E-06*	*7.05E-01*
1,1,2-Trichloroethane	5.54E-04	6.92E+00	*5.64E-04*	*7.05E+00*	*5.60E-04*	*7.00E+00*
Trichloroethylene	5.09E-06	N/D	*5.46E-06*	*N/D*	*5.45E-06*	*N/D*
Vinyl chloride	1.46E-05	9.30E-02	*2.91E-05*	*1.85E-01*	*2.07E-05*	*1.32E-01*
	Migration to Groundwater ("MGW")					
	Measured Cr		Estimated Cr (DF = 1.17)			
			[S-W-A]r *(or [S-W]r)*		*[S-W-A]e*	
	CR	HQ	CR	HQ	*CR*	*HQ*
1,2-Dichloroethane	8.07E-06	N/D	1.16E+00	N/D	*1.18E+00*	*N/D*
1,1-Dichloroethylene	8.53E-04	0.44E+00	3.64E-01	1.89E+02	*4.73E-01*	*2.45E+02*
cis-1,2-Dichloroethylene	N/D	1.20E+02	N/D	8.49E+01	*N/D*	*8.96E+01*
Tetrachloroethylene	N/D	N/D	2.03E-02	1.09E+02	*2.30E-02*	*1.24E+02*
1,1,2-Trichloroethane	1.08E-07	1.32E-03	4.78E-01	5.87E+03	*4.83E-01*	*5.94E+03*
Trichloroethylene	7.96E-06	N/D	2.14E-03	N/D	*2.29E-03*	*N/D*
Vinyl chloride	1.17E-02	1.52E+01	8.38E-02	1.09E+02	*1.19E-01*	*1.54E+02*

Dichloroethilene) individual risks related to the "measured" approach (certainly influenced by the extremely limited number of available groundwater determinations: see Section 2) are decreased compared with the "estimation" approach (see Section 3.1); 3) expressly according to Table 4, individual subsurface soil risks related to the "estimated" three-phase approach are increased compared with the hypothetic "real" two phase condition (see Section 3.1), but generally non-significantly (apart from the magnitude order increase registered for: 1.1-Dichloroethylene, volatile inhalation carcinogenic effect; Vinyl chloride, volatile inhalation non-carcinogenic effect and groundwater carcinogenic effect).

Acknowledgements

The authors would like to mention Dr.-Ing. Laura D'Aprile at APAT (Italian Environmental Protection Agency and Technical Services, Rome) for her availability and support concerning the site investigation and technical-scientific informative data on the case-study industrial sub-area.

References

[1] D'Aprile, L., Tatàno, F. & Musmeci, L., Development of quality objectives for contaminated sites: state of the art and new perspectives, *Int. J. Environment and Health,* Vol. 1, No. 1, pp. 120-141, 2007.

[2] Italian Ministry of Environment, *Technical Regulation D.M. No. 471/1999 on containment, remediation and environmental restoration of contaminated soils,* Annex of the Italian Official Gazette No. 293, 15.12.1999 (in Italian).

[3] Legislative Decree No. 152, *Environmental Framework Regulation,* Annex of the Italian Official Gazette No. 88, April 14, 2006 (in Italian).

[4] United States Environmental Protection Agency (US.EPA), *Soil Screening Guidance: User's Guide,* Publication 9355.4-23, 1996.

[5] US.EPA, *Soil Screening Guidance: Technical Background Document,* Office of Emergency and Remedial Response, EPA/540/R95/128, 1996.

[6] US.EPA, *Supplemental Guidance for Developing Soil Screening Levels for Superfund Sites,* OSWER 9355.4-24, 2002.

[7] Giavazzi, M. & Tatàno, F., "ARA-CoS_{SSLs}" risk analysis approach (on a computer worksheet basis) for contaminated sites: implementation and case study application, *Brownfields III* (C.A Brebbia & Ü. Mander Editors), WIT (Wessex Institute of Technology) Press, pp.63-73, 2006.

[8] Giavazzi, M. & Tatàno, F., A possible sanitary risk analysis approach for contaminated sites, *Int. J. Environment and Health,* Vol. 1, No. 2, pp. 199-220, 2007.

[9] Italian Environmental Protection Agency and Technical Services (APAT), *Methodological criteria for absolute risk analysis application at contaminated sites, Version* June 2005 (L. D'Aprile, R. Baciocchi & G. Marella Editors), available at www.apat.it (in Italian).

[10] US.EPA, *ProUCL Version 3.0,* User Guide, EPA/600/R04/079, April 2004.

World Heritage Inscription for naval heritage brownfields?

C. Clark
Fellow, Wessex Institute of Technology, UK

Abstract

Inscription onto UNESCO's list of World Heritage sites is an important way of drawing international attention to the legacy left by centuries of military and naval activity – brownfields par excellence. Three dockyards (government shipyards) are already so designated – in Karlskrona in Sweden, Suomenlinna in Finland and Venice – as part of the broader inscription of the city. Rochefort in southwest France and Chatham in southeast England are candidates, and Portsmouth Harbour, the Isle of Wight and Spithead might be the first 'cultural seascape' to be so inscribed.

Each country maintains a tentative list of candidates for world heritage status, usually controlled by the ministry of culture. One entry per year is put forward by member countries for ICOMOS, UNESCO's advisory body to consider for inscription. To be accepted sites have to meet tests of authenticity, prepare a justification and supporting nomination dossier and ultimately have a management plan for safeguarding their future.

The process of application requires considerable local commitment: viable management plans over a ten year period must be drawn up by local authorities, site owners and other stakeholders. These requirements reflect increasing concern that inscription is not enough in itself to guarantee protection of these very specialised brownfields from decay or overdevelopment. World Heritage Sites may be placed on the list of sites in danger if there is damaging change. This paper examines the extent to which inscription safeguards these unusual brownfields.

Keywords: dockyards, ICOMOS, inscription, World Heritage sites, conservation, maintenance.

WIT Transactions on Ecology and the Environment, Vol 107, © 2008 WIT Press
www.witpress.com, ISSN 1743-3541 (on-line)
doi:10.2495/BF080191

"A European colonial ensemble in the Caribbean of outstanding value and integrity, which illustrates the organic growth of a multicultural community over three centuries and preserves to a high degree significant elements of the many strands that came together to create it. The modern town consists of several distinct historic districts whose architecture reflects not only European urban-planning concepts but also styles from the Netherlands and from the Spanish and Portuguese colonial towns with which Willemstad engaged in trade". [1]

1 Introduction - defence cuts

Inscription onto UNESCO's list of World Heritage sites is an important way of drawing international attention to the legacy left by centuries of military and naval activity – including colonial survivals. As armed forces in different countries are reduced and regrouped, significant historic sites associated with national defence are on the closure list in many countries. In 2008 the United States federal government pledged to purge military bases of 50 million unused square feet in the next five years. The Department of Defense's edict has put pressure on many of the country's military bases—including the United States Naval Base at Pearl Harbor—to tear down rather than reuse their historic buildings [2]. Military and naval sites are brownfield sites par excellence. Historic defence sites may have significant architectural and engineering legacies, as well as problems such as contamination, decay from lack of maintenance, absence of documentation, isolation, difficult transport access, depressed local economies, unemployed workforces.... This rapidly moving and widespread process is still not much studied. There is little interchange between sites, or indeed between countries undergoing similar experiences, yet the importance of historic defence sites to their local communities is cultural and social as well as economic. More needs to be done to share good practice in this most symbolic of transitions.

2 Lack of research or exchange of experience

There is little research into this profoundly important and symbolic land use exchange. Literature on post-defence reconstruction, its economic, social, spatial and physical impacts, and the implications for the historic defence estate is rare, though more common in the United States. Although base conversion may be intermittently highly visible in land use and development policy debates, administrative and academic interest is not sustained because of the long timescales involved. Since 1994 the Bonn International Center for Conversion (BICC) does pioneering work on decontamination and the economic effects of closure upon defence dominated communities in many countries including Germany. It has been actively tracking all aspects of the conversion processes in central and eastern European countries; military expenditure, surplus weapons, demobilisation, conversion of military research and development, conversion of defence industry and base conversion. But, as in the BICC case, the effect of conversion on the defence industry has dominated conversion research, while conversion of military properties and lands such as airfields, depots, barracks, dockyards, training centres has received far less attention. This absence in social scientific research has left significant gaps in our knowledge about the effects of base closures and the prospects for civilian reuse in many parts of the world.

3 Development opportunities

Brownfields par excellence, military and naval sites offer unprecedented development opportunities. Sites large and small – contaminated, built over with utilitarian or historic structures or protected for wildlife value – all offer a challenge to the achievement of creative, sustainable reuse. Job creation and technical innovation may or may not result, but land values and local tax bases are considerably affected as these sites emerge into the property market. Marine, maritime, commercial, leisure/shopping, educational, cultural, heritage tourism, residential and industrial uses are emerging in this enormous transition.

What happens when the navy leaves? As long-term industrial sites, significant industrial archaeology may survive: cranes and hoists; objects: anchors, chains, figureheads; railway and tram lines; below ground archaeology; water pumping systems; power stations; specialist buildings: roperies, drydocks, wet docks, workshops, storehouses, foundries, electrical shops, covered slips, airplane shelters; specialist machinery; bridges, mast towers; air raid shelters; preserved ships, submarines; textural details: paving, mooring rings, signage; 'intangible heritage'- cultural tradition, folklore….One mechanism for protecting them is inscription on the World Heritage List maintained by UNESCO.

4 The World Heritage Inscription process

Each country maintains a tentative list of potential World Heritage sites, usually controlled by the ministry of culture. One entry per year is put forward by member countries for ICOMOS, UNESCO's advisory body to consider for inscription. In 1999 Chatham dockyard was nominated onto the UK list, which is managed, by the Department of Culture, Media and Sport. To be accepted sites have to meet certain tests of authenticity, prepare a justification and supporting dossier and ultimately to have a management plan for safeguarding their future.

The case for inscription has to make a claim of the universal human value to mankind of the site. There are two broad categories: natural sites and sites of cultural value. There are ten selection criteria. Sites must fulfil one or more categories. They are:

- to represent a masterpiece of human creative genius;
- to exhibit an important interchange of human values, over a span of time or within a cultural area of the world, on developments in architecture or technology, monumental arts, town-planning or landscape design;
- to bear a unique or at least exceptional testimony to a cultural tradition or to a civilization which is living or which has disappeared;

- to be an outstanding example of a type of building, architectural or technological ensemble or landscape which illustrates (a) significant stage(s) in human history;
- to be an outstanding example of a traditional human settlement, land-use, or sea-use which is representative of a culture (or cultures), or human interaction with the environment especially when it has become vulnerable under the impact of irreversible change;
- to be directly or tangibly associated with events or living traditions, with ideas, or with beliefs, with artistic and literary works of outstanding universal significance. (The Committee considers that this criterion should preferably be used in conjunction with other criteria);
- to contain superlative natural phenomena or areas of exceptional natural beauty and aesthetic importance;
- to be outstanding examples representing major stages of earth's history, including the record of life, significant on-going geological processes in the development of landforms, or significant geomorphic or physiographic features;
- to be outstanding examples representing significant on-going ecological and biological processes in the evolution and development of terrestrial, fresh water, coastal and marine ecosystems and communities of plants and animals;
- to contain the most important and significant natural habitats for in-situ conservation of biological diversity, including those containing threatened species of outstanding universal value from the point of view of science or conservation.

The protection, management, authenticity and integrity of properties are also important considerations. Since 1992 significant interactions between people and the natural environment have been recognized as cultural landscapes.

5 Naval sites on the World Heritage list – and applicants

Three dockyards (government shipyards) – Karlskrona in Sweden, Suomenlinna in Finland and Venice – as part of the broader inscription of the city – are already so designated. Rochefort in southwest France and Chatham in southeast England are candidates, and in 2008 a group from around Portsmouth Harbour and the Isle of Wight was preparing the case to be the first 'cultural seascape' – the harbour and the sheltered anchorage of Spithead – to be inscribed in the list. The only other harbour already on it is the Dutch trading settlement founded in 1634 in Willemstad in the Netherlands Antilles on the Caribbean Island Territory of Curaçao.

Chatham dockyard's statement makes reference to other dockyards in Europe and to its unique contribution to world heritage. Its justification emphasises the dockyard's national role and include the associated military functions:
"Britain's naval power is exemplified at home by three great Royal dockyards – Chatham, Portsmouth and Devonport. Chatham is now the most complete

example of a home dockyard from the age of the sail powered navy, which reached its zenith in the 18th and early 19th centuries. It is this completeness that sets it apart from either Portsmouth or Devonport. [Its] importance is enhanced by its close association with contemporary military establishments, notably the Brompton Lines and Brompton Barracks. This combination of a substantially intact 18th century dockyard with its contemporary massive landward defences is unique. The importance of Chatham is further enhanced by earlier associated structures like Upnor Castle, which functioned as part of the 18th century military presence in the Medway. Internationally only the existing World Heritage Site of Karlskrona, Sweden, is comparable to Chatham for its surviving dockyard buildings and associated fortifications. Of the dockyards belonging to the other major 18th century naval powers very little has survived the subsequent centuries or the ravages of war. The best preserved French dockyard is Rochefort but here survival is partial. The dockyard of the Arsenal of Venice retains many structures but, as with Dutch historic naval installations, was on a comparatively small scale. The German navy was essentially a creation of the 20th century and hence there are no comparable dockyards to Chatham. Overseas the British created a string of dockyards and supply bases to keep the fleet operable anywhere within the expanding empire. These, however, were never intended to build ships in the same way as the home dockyards and are not comparable in terms of scale or complexity. Many suffered war time destruction. Alongside Karlskrona, Chatham is outstanding amongst the surviving historic dockyards"

"Chatham was instrumental in securing and maintaining Britain's worldwide influence. The completeness and survival of the dockyard and its defences – Fort Amherst, Upnor Castle and the Great Lines – is unique. In addition, a series of historic barracks and military installations help make Chatham one of the greatest British garrison towns." [3]

In June 2007 Chatham's World Heritage site bid, supported by Chatham Historic Dockyard Trust, English Heritage, The South East England Development Agency (SEEDA) and Medway Council was launched, with the aim of being the UK's nomination in 2010 or 2011.

Greenwich on the River Thames in London – celebrated for its cultural heritage: its naval and sea-faring history and its grandiloquent formal planning – is already a World Heritage site. The Royal Naval College was built as a hospital for veteran sailors; Admiral Lord Nelson lay in state in its Painted Hall prior to his funeral. The National Maritime Museum and the preserved ship the *Cutty Sark* are also within the boundaries. The splendid classical townscape set in and around the oldest Royal Park in London and bordered to the north by the River Thames were designed by Sir Christopher Wren, Inigo Jones, Sir John Vanbrugh, Nicholas Hawksmoor and Joseph Kay. Together the ensemble constitutes the World Heritage Site. Key scientific developments: Greenwich Mean Time, and Longitude 0° – making Greenwich the centre of time and space – are also a key to its value in world terms.

6 Scientific and technological innovation as justifications for inscription

Scientific advance and technological innovation are current themes for World Heritage sites. Following the failure of ICOMOS to recommend inscription of Charles Darwin's Down House in Kent in southeast England in 2007, the British Department of Culture, Media and Sport and the UK National Commission for UNESCO hosted an expert international workshop on behalf of the World Heritage Committee in January 2008 on 'World Heritage: Science and Technology'. It was designed to develop guidelines to identify future World Heritage Sites that represent advances in science and technology of global significance. Experts from 15 countries, representing the physical sciences and technology as well as those with detailed knowledge of the operation of the UNESCO World Heritage Convention discussed ways to create a scientific framework, to help identify and recognise sites that represent the heritage of science and technology that could potentially become World Heritage Sites. The conclusions of the expert meeting will be presented to the World Heritage Committee for consideration at their next meeting in July 2008 in Quebec, Canada [4].

In 2007 no less than fourteen of the citadels, fortresses, town walls and towns designed by the great French engineer, strategist, town planner, philosopher, political theorist and designer of more than 150 fortresses as well as extensive civil engineering works Sébastien Le Prestre maréchal de Vauban (1633-1707) were chosen by a network of major Vauban areas to be put onto the UNESCO list of World Heritage sites, with the support of the French government (Casemate 2007) and the European-funded project Septentrion which united 20 or so fortified cities in Northern Europe [5] Interestingly, the areas chosen did not include Vauban's work in Cherbourg dockyard. Its case, by the Syndicat Mixte Du Pays Rochfortais: Charte Patrimoniale de l'Arsenal Maritime du Rochefort: Paysage Culturel Évolutif" dated September 2005 is available on the web. Rochefort's bid, bringing together fourteen local councils, may not succeed on its own, because western Europe is already so well represented on the list, compared with the rest of the world. It may be necessary to join with similar dockyard sites – as was the case with the fortresses designed by Vauban.

Making the case for unique universal value is a challenge. Technological innovation is an unsung characteristic of government establishments.

'The English royal dockyards, victualling yards and hospitals formed what are arguably the largest industrial centres in Britain before the Industrial Revolution, while their economic impact was out of all proportion to their size' [6]

'...Given the way the dockyards, drawing on public funds, were able to influence private sector enterprise is a somewhat under-researched area.' [7]

7 The Portsmouth Harbour, Isle of Wight and Spithead case for inscription

Examples of outstanding innovation in dockyards perhaps reached a peak in Portsmouth dockyard in the UK. Block Mills is the site of a world first: the first steam powered mass production factory using metal machine tools to make the hundreds of thousands of pulley blocks required by sailing ships. It was developed by a constellation of brilliant engineers led by Marc Isambard Brunel, a French émigré. Brunel had experimented with block making equipment in America. When he returned to Britain he took out a patent and had models made of his first design by the engineer Henry Maudslay when he got the contract. The brilliant team of engineers included Simon Goodrich who developed the factory. Block Mills was built over a small basin of 1791-8 used as a reservoir for the dockyard pumping system. In 1799 a 12 horsepower steam engine invented by Sadler was installed, which powered the woodworking machinery by day and pumped water from a borehole into the reservoir by night. The block-making machines were the earliest machine tools of substantial size (except clock-making tools) to be constructed entirely of metal a major advance in the history of mass production. Ten men could produce the same number of pulley blocks - 130,000 – as 100 men working by hand. By 1806 45 machines and 10 men were producing 140,000 blocks a year.

Other key innovations in the area include the first working caisson to close dry docks, the first circular saws, key developments in wrought iron in response to the demand for quality iron by dockyards the base metal of the industrial revolution, the first clinical trials for treatment of scurvy, the first steam powered dredger, early large scale ship testing tanks, ship-borne radar and the invention of freeze drying…. How are these brownfields sites of innovation to be preserved and celebrated?

These inventions, together with the successive layers of defences including the 1860s ring of forts commissioned to defend Portsmouth dockyard by Lord Palmerston, four of them in the sea, and the 'submerged landscape' showing human occupation over 5,000 years make the Portsmouth Harbour, the Isle of Wight and Spithead bid for World Heritage status a new concept: the world's first 'cultural seascape'. The public launch of the project in January 2008 was in an appropriate venue – the modern auditorium of the converted Boathouse 6 in the Historic Dockyard. It followed closely on the good news of the Heritage Lottery Fund's massive grant for a new museum for the Mary Rose, Henry VIII's sixteenth century flagship.

The first speaker at the launch in January 2008 was David Michelmore of ICOMOS – the international advisory body that advises UNESCO on the list. He has successfully inscribed 11 sites onto the World Heritage List, and is preparing several others. After a year of preparatory work, the Portsmouth Harbour bid was ready for its promoters to ask for public support. As he said, creative, forward looking cities regularly reinvent themselves, and the process towards achieving this project would help the harbour and Island communities to establish new roles.

Another speaker, John Rodger, spoke eloquently about the difference World Heritage status has made to Blaenavon Industrial site in South Wales, a ruined and contaminated historic brownfield of worldwide significance. Local people's perception of the area's key history as a cradle of the Industrial Revolution had been totally changed by a continuous programme of events and activities. Physical repairs and new buildings had raised property values and encouraged considerable inward investment, and tourist figures to the Big Pit and other industrial sites have tripled.

ICOMOS recommends that World Heritage sites anticipate the effect of climate change – reminding us all of how vulnerable the area is to rising sea levels. This is particularly true of Portsmouth, where the whole low lying-city could be flooded. Unlike Chatham where the naval base closed in 1985, Portsmouth is one of three surviving dockyards for the British navy. The leader of Portsmouth City Council, Gerald Vernon-Jackson, said that nothing should jeopardise the navy's freedom of operation. The Ministry of Defence is already subject to civilian planning law on land and to the myriad of marine consents, and Defence Estates are to commission a study of the effect of World Heritage designation on the navy's operations, taking advice from the Swedish navy about Karkskrona – already on the list.

8 Another layer of bureaucracy? Maintenance – development versus conservation

An obvious question is whether World Heritage Status would frustrate economic progress and just become another layer of bureaucracy. All the research undertaken suggests that the reverse is true; it positively encourages inward investment, is good for tourism and unlocks grants and it may demand that new design is appropriate and of good quality.

Maintenance – or lack of it – affects potential for future brownfield use. Poorly maintained buildings cost more to repair and convert. Even pioneering buildings are not always valued. The Gunner's Mate School, also known as Building 521, located on Naval Station Great Lakes in Lake County Illinois, designed by the famed firm of Skidmore, Owings & Merrill in 1954, was the office's first "curtain wall" structure. With its massive volume, the building exemplifies Mies van der Rohe's concept of universal space, which promotes Cathedral-like interiors that are unobstructed and therefore flexible. "You could almost do anything in it. That's what it was designed for; it was designed to adapt," but it is under threat of demolition. The firm's July 2006 study says it would cost $34 million to retrofit the building as a double-walled cafeteria and club facility: "in the same price range" as the Navy's estimate for a new building [1]. Things are not any better on the other side of the Atlantic. The UK MOD at best only keeps historic buildings for which it has no use wind-and weather-tight. The Stewardship Report on the Defence Estate 2005 acknowledged the need to take into account the wider interests of society – in particular sustainability and the environment – in defence historic buildings at risk. In 2001 there were 43 defence buildings at risk: 6.1% of the total; this has now been reduced to 32. However, 33% of the 9000 Scheduled Ancient Monuments on MOD land were in fair condition, while 21% were in poor or unknown condition. The same problems occur with subsequent private owners who have no use for historic buildings on their sites.

The Gibraltar government was apparently willing in 2006 to forsake the opportunity of applying for World Heritage status by granting permission for the destruction of the six huge brick water tanks built in Rosia Bay between 1799 and 1804 to supply the Royal Navy with 5,000 tons of water. At that time the Royal Navy had no allies in the Mediterranean, and Tetuan and Ceuta could not be relied on. Rosia Bay is a tiny bay with a harbour only about 300 yards wide which has Parsons Battery (Moorish/Spanish/British), Dutch Battery, the Grand Magazine, Victualling Yard, Agent's houses, Cold Meat Store and Naval Hospital above – once a complete naval enclave. The tanks were supplied with water collected from the roof of the adjacent Victualling Storehouse, and were in continuous use by the Royal Navy until 2004 when they were transferred to the Gibraltar Government. An Irish development company OEM proposed to build a block of 200 flats of 'affordable housing' and car parking on the site of the water tanks, even though there were other brownfield MOD sites available [8]. The Bay is a key site for maritime heritage, and Gibraltar aims to build up its tourism. But despite protests from the Council of Europe, ICOMOS-UK, Europa Nostra and MEPs, the Prince's Foundation, SAVE Britain's Heritage, the Society for Nautical Research and the Naval Dockyards Society, protests signed by 10% of Gibraltar's population, considerable press coverage in British and Gibraltarian newspapers and following visits from historians from Britain, France and Spain gathered in Rosia Bay in 2005 to commemorate the Battle of Trafalgar, the tanks were demolished after court hearings in January 2006.

The Gibraltar Heritage Trust had to withdraw from the case because it could not risk the costs of judicial review – as mentioned above, often the greatest deterrent to small organisations or individuals who want to challenge government actions. The British government said it was a domestic matter and that they could only intervene if the Gibraltar government acted unconstitutionally or illegally. Gibraltar has listed very few historic sites in recent years and it is not complying with EU guidelines for historic areas. It is not clear whether the government has signed the Venice Charter, but as a member of the European Union it must comply with the Grenada Convention (1985), and should have protected the site. Historians and heritage experts in several countries were sympathetic to the campaign, but there seemed to be no mechanism to call in any outside agency to intervene and prevent demolition [9]. Clearly there are serious limitations on the extent of protection when a government is determined to allow redevelopment, and there are also temptations to put economic development before heritage protection in rapidly developing countries such as Estonia, where tall hotel and offices blocks close to the Old Town prompted a threat to remove World Heritage status.

9 Conclusion – is inscription as a World Heritage Site and tourism a panacea?

The process of application requires considerable local commitment: viable and renewable management plans over a ten year period must be drawn up by local authorities, site owners and other stakeholders in conjunction with the Nomination dossier, in accordance with the *Operational Guidelines for the Implementation of the World Heritage Convention* and the *Vienna Memorandum*. These requirements reflect increasing concern that inscription is not enough in itself to guarantee protection of sites from decay or overdevelopment. World Heritage sites may be placed on the list of sites in danger if there is damaging change, and IOCOMOS works with those responsible for the site to ensure its long term future.

This paper has not examined the complex and sometimes damaging relationship between tourism and world heritage sites which is often the dominant new land use for naval sites such as Greenwich and Chatham. Arguably Venice with its shrinking population is being destroyed by tourists, although the mangnificent buildings of the Arsenale are occasionally beneficially reused for cultural events such as the Biennales of Art and Architecture. In view of the importance of this relationship, a significant 18 month long project is to start in March 2008 organised by UNESCO World Heritage Centre and the UN World Tourism Organisation in conjunction with ICOMOS and IUCN. It will examine the whole relationship between world heritage sites and tourism. All World Heritage Sites will be involved, including Natural Sites and Natural Protected Areas, Cultural Landscapes of mixed values, Cultural Sites including archaeological and underwater, vernacular, industrial and military heritage,and Uban places including historic cities, towns and villages. Key questions to be discussed were : how can tourism benefit heritage places and enhance the livelihoods of the local communities who live and work near them? What actions are necessary to protect heritage sites in the context of tourism activity? What are the main issues which should be raised and examined? [10]

Other stakeholders in international cultural heritage, tourism and development will also be consulted, and tangible as well as intengible values and relations will be examined. This is the first time that all four agencies have combined to examine this relationship in a holistic manner, so it is an opportunity for all interested parties to contribute.

Inscription of historic naval and military brownfields onto the list of World Heritage sites is valuable in focusing world attention on these specialised but difficult to reuse brownfields. Their history of technological innovation as well as their architectural and engineering legacy make the case for their inclusion, but it is the physical remains that visitors come to see. There are gains from the process, whether or not the application for World Heritage Inscription succeeds. While not a panacea, this rare privilege, joining the 851 sites on the List, helps to preserve and sustain these unique brownfields – built, underwater, archaeological, cultural, natural – by committing their owners to longterm, sustainable management as well as emphasising their importance to local people and to the local economy, holding them in trust for future generations.

References

[1] http://whc.unesco.org/en/list/
[2] http://www.nationaltrust.org/Magazine/story/ January 2008
[3] Department of Culture, Media and Sport UK 1999)
[4] http://www.xpressdigest.org.uk/2008/01/18/dcms-and-uk-national-commission-for-unesco- hosts-world-heritage-science-and-technology-an-expert-workshop/?=xpdmail
[5] www.septentrion- we.org/index.php/septentrion_en/content/view/full/129
[6] Coad JG (1989) *Royal Dockyards* Studies in Naval History no. I
[7] Ray Riley 'Henry Cort and the Development of Wrought Iron Manufacture in the 1780s: the Naval Collection' in *Transactions of the Naval Dockyards Society Volume 3 November 2007*
[8] Marcus Binney 2006 Binney Marcus 2006 'Nelson caves to be turned into car park' *The Times* 30 January 2006 p.31
[9] Coats Ann 2006 'Gibraltar: Rosia Bay Water Tanks Update' *Dockyards* Newsletter of the Naval Dockyards Society Volume 11 Issue I pp 1–4 Portsmouth UK
[10] G & C Brooks: brooks@bigpond.net.au email to members of ICOFORT 3 February 2008

A unique approach to addressing brownfield sites

V. Pitruzzello
US Environmental Protection Agency, Region 2 - New York, USA

Abstract

The purpose of this paper is to describe the unique approach used by EPA Region 2 in providing expertise at the federal and state government levels to communities with brownfield sites. This approach can serve as a "model" for such programs elsewhere by illustrating how EPA Region 2's program has fostered and encouraged brownfields re-use by utilizing and combining various funding, administrative and technical resources available at the "state" and "national" level to address local brownfields issues. The U.S. Environmental Protection Agency's (EPA) Brownfields program began in 1993 with a small number of grants to municipalities. A report by the General Accountability Office estimated that there are nearly 450,000 brownfield sites in the United States. These grants were "pilots" at the time – the purpose of which was to test the process for getting brownfields identified, characterized, remediated and eventually redeveloped. In January 2001 the "Small Business Liability Relief and Brownfields Revitalization Act" was signed establishing the Brownfields legislation and moving the pilot/initiative program into a fully recognized self-standing program. Initial funding for the program had been $400,000 and rose steadily during the pilot phase. With the enactment of legislation, the funding level rose to over $165 million. Grants are provided to communities for the purpose of identifying brownfield sites and for site remediation. Funds are provided to states to develop state programs.

EPA Region 2 includes the States of New York and New Jersey, seven tribal nations, the Commonwealth of Puerto Rico and the U.S. Virgin Islands. The challenges to the Brownfields program are varied across the wide range of regional municipalities, from densely populated cities, to small hamlets, to tribal lands and to tropical communities. To address this variety, the Region 2 Brownfields program has developed a unique partnership with a number of Federal and State government agencies. We have formed an Interagency Workgroup (IAWG) that has over 40 partner agencies that bring member resources to assist individual communities. We have brought such assistance to over 140 communities. This presentation will illustrate some of the challenges and successes experienced by EPA Region 2 throughout this unique process and offer a model for brownfields programs throughout the world.
Keywords: brownfields, Environmental Protection Agency, Interagency Workgroup, hazardous waste sites, hazardous cleanup, redevelopment, United States.

WIT Transactions on Ecology and the Environment, Vol 107, © 2008 WIT Press
www.witpress.com, ISSN 1743-3541 (on-line)
doi:10.2495/BF080201

1 Introduction

Over the past several decades, the United States has undergone significant changes in its industrial and manufacturing economy. Businesses have changed locations moving to different geographic sections of the country and some industries have closed entirely. The result of this, in many cases, is hundreds of thousands of properties that were left contaminated or at least perceived to be contaminated. Many contamination problems associated with these blighted properties are being addressed by the U.S.E.P.A.'s brownfields program.

In addition to the stigma associated with such sites, brownfields has increased pressure on developing 'greenfields'. Developers became wary of tackling environmental problems, which could be expensive and potentially involve liability to the owners. Thus, commercial, industrial and residential developers opted for greenfields development, leaving brownfields vacant. In many cases, brownfield sites are located in the urban /inner city environment. Their vacant status left eyesores in the community and an overall negative impact on the community at large. Vacant tracts of land resulted in deleterious effects to "main street America" as businesses closed shop and moved on to non-contaminated areas. Urban areas suffered from decay and rural/suburban areas expanded with sprawling growth which was often unchecked or done in a haphazard fashion. The additional effect of air contamination from clogged rural roads became a reality and an unwanted result of suburban sprawl.

Local communities and some state governments realized early on that the issue needed to be addressed. They developed some creative funding programs and contamination cleanup programs to encourage cleanup and re-use of properties. However, it soon became apparent that there was a need for the Federal government to become a participant in addressing the overall problem of such contaminated sites. That role fell to EPA, which began their current Brownfields program in 1993 with a few grants designed to provide technical and funding assistance to "pilot communities".

The program has since expanded to over 1200 grants and funds are now provided for assessment and cleanup of sites. EPA also instituted a job training grant program, which provides funding for select local organizations to train a cadre of environmental technicians to conduct cleanup work. Many of these technicians work with environmental companies addressing sites local to their area (i.e. in their own "backyard"). There are currently over 90 job training grants.

The EPA brownfields program has resulted in leveraging over $8 billion in cleanup and redevelopment funding and has helped create over 25,000 jobs associated with redevelopment.

2 History and organization of region 2's brownfields Interagency Workgroup (IAWG)

EPA Region 2 includes the States of New York and New Jersey, the Commonwealth of Puerto Rico and the Virgin Islands Territories. We realized early on that an effective brownfields program requires partnerships not only at the local level but also at the state and regional levels. This paper describes our Regional initiative to partner with local, state and federal agencies to address the brownfields problems within our area of jurisdiction. Through the IAWG, we have developed strong working relationships with many agencies to bring financial, administrative and technical assistance to brownfields communities.

2.1 History of IAWG

In 1998, EPA, at the national level, initiated a program known as "Showcase Communities". Through this program a partnership of federal agencies with interests in brownfields redevelopment was formed to offer special technical, financial and other assistance to selected communities. Brownfields Showcase Communities have three main goals: to promote environmental protection, economic redevelopment and community revitalization through the assessment, cleanup and sustainable re-use of brownfields; to link Federal, State, local and non-governmental action supporting community efforts to restore and re-use brownfields; and to develop national models demonstrating the positive results of public and private collaboration addressing brownfields challenges.

As a result of the Showcase Communities program, EPA 2 created the IAWG to marshal the resources available throughout the Federal and State governments in support of brownfields redevelopment. The initial focus of the IAWG was to support the two EPA 2 Brownfields Showcase Communities located in Glen Cove, New York and Trenton, New Jersey. The successes and partnerships developed through these initial actions were further expanded to other communities who received brownfields grants from the Federal government. To date, over 140 communities in Region II have experienced the benefits of working with the IAWG.

2.2 Primary member agencies and summary role in IAWG process

The primary federal and state agencies and organizations that participate in the IAWG process with EPA-2 are identified below

2.2.1 Federal Government agencies

- U.S. Department of Commerce Economic Development Administration (EDA)

The EDA's purpose is to generate new jobs; help retain existing jobs; and stimulate industrial and commercial growth in economically distressed areas

- Department of Defense: U.S. Army Corps of Engineers (USACE)

USACE investigates, designs, constructs, and maintains a variety of projects for national economic and environmental security.

- Department of Health and Human Services: Agency for Toxic Substances and Disease Registry (ATSDR)

ATSDR was created by the Superfund legislation of 1980 to prevent or mitigate adverse human health effects and diminished quality of life resulting from exposure to hazardous substances in the environment.

- Department of Housing and Urban Development (HUD)

The Brownfields Redevelopment Initiative brings together different types of existing HUD assistance that communities can use to clean up and revitalize potentially contaminated sites.

- Department of the Interior, National Park Service

The National Park Service enables states and local governments to establish park and recreation areas and adapt historic buildings for public use.

- Department of Transportation: Federal Highway Administration (FHWA)

The Federal Highway Administration's (FHWA) mission is to help fund the construction, reconstruction and improvement of Interstate highways and other roads on the federal-aid interstate, primary, secondary and urban systems.

- U.S. Environmental Protection Agency: Brownfields Program (EPA)

The goal of EPA's Brownfields Program is to empower localities to work with public and private stakeholders to develop locally appropriate approaches to prevent, assess, safely cleanup and sustainably re-use brownfields.

- General Services Administration (GSA)

GSA reviews and identifies underutilized federal properties through its Brownfields Redevelopment Initiative.

- Small Business Administration (SBA

The SBA's mission is to provide prospective, new or established persons in the small business community with financial, procurement, management and technical assistance.

2.2.2 State of New Jersey agencies

- New Jersey Department of Environmental Protection (NJDEP)

The New Jersey Department of Environmental Protection includes a variety of resources, incentives and programs administered by various state agencies in order to provide a comprehensive tool box to support private and public brownfields revitalization. It administers a voluntary cleanup program.

- New Jersey Department of Transportation (NJDOT)

The New Jersey Department of Transportation (NJDOT) is committed to advancing projects that enhance safety, renew the aging infrastructure and support new transportation opportunities.

- New Jersey Economic Development Authority (NJEDA)

The NJEDA is a self-supporting, independent state agency whose mission is to stimulate business development, job creation and community revitalization throughout the State.

- New Jersey Redevelopment Authority (NJRA)

The NJRA is a state financing authority committed to the redevelopment of urban New Jersey areas and is a comprehensive resource center that customizes project financing for redevelopment projects.

- New Jersey Environmental Infrastructure Trust

This trust provides financing for environmental infrastructure projects and open space acquisitions.

2.2.3 State of New York agencies

- State of New York Department of Environmental Conservation (NYSDEC)

The New York State Department of Environmental Conservation has three main functions: natural resource management, environmental quality protection and the promotion of public health, safety and recreation. It administers a voluntary cleanup program.

- New York State Department of Health (NYSDOH)

NYSDOH oversees the Drinking Water State Revolving Fund, which provides financial incentives for public and private water system infrastructure improvement.

- New York State Department of Transportation (NYSDOT)

NYSDOT oversees the Industrial Access Program, which is designed to complement economic development projects where transportation access poses a problem. The Transportation and Community and System Preservation Program provides funding for surface transportation projects (such as access to brownfield sites).

- New York State Division of Housing and Community Renewal (NYSDHCR)

NYSDHCR administers the Housing Development Fund to provide loans to non-profits organizations for low income housing projects.

- Empire State Development (ESD)

ESD provides loans, loan guarantees and grants that can help companies reduce the costs of undertaking a job creation or retention project.

- New York State Environmental Facilities Corporation (NYSEFC)

NYSEFC administers the Clean Water Revolving Fund where applicants can obtain interest free short term or low interest long term loans for facilities that reduce or prevent water pollution. Water quality portions of brownfields projects generally are eligible for such financing.

- Governor's Office for Small Cities

The Federal Housing and Urban Development (HUD) community development block grant program provides annual grants to states and eligible cities and urban counties for community improvement. The New York State Small Cities program utilizes the federal grants provided to New York.

- New York State Office of Park Recreation and Historic Preservation

This office provides for the acquisition of permanent easement for land and water properties (recreational access). It also oversees a Historic Preservation Program for the acquisition and rehabilitation of historic properties.

- New York Department of State, Division of Coastal Resources and Waterfront Revitalization

The Division of Coastal Resources is responsible for administering New York State's Coastal Management Program while advancing economic development opportunities and protecting natural coastal resources.

2.2.4 Puerto Rico and the U.S. Virgin Islands

In addition to working with the above agencies and entities, EPA 2 has initiated a very aggressive campaign to bring IAWG resources to the Commonwealth of Puerto Rico and the Virgin Island Territories. To date, over 60 communities in these locales have met through the IAWG process. The key agencies for the Caribbean initiative are listed below:

- Puerto Rico Department of Health
- Puerto Rico Department of Agriculture
- Puerto Rico Department of Natural and Environmental Resources
- Puerto Rico Department of Transportation and Public Works – Highway Authority
- Puerto Rico Department of Housing
- Puerto Rico Environmental Quality Board
- Puerto Rico Office of the Commissioner for Municipal Affairs.
- Puerto Rico Economic Development Bank
- Puerto Rico Department of Recreation and Sports
- Puerto Rico Aqueduct and Sewers Authority (PRASA)
- Puerto Rico Industrial Development Company (PRIDCO)
- Puerto Rico Department of Labor

3 IAWG process

The IAWG process is straightforward:

- We inform communities which have received brownfields grants or have an interest in redeveloping brownfield sites that the IAWG is a standing group ready and able to assist them.
- Communities contact EPA expressing their interest in participating in the process.
- EPA then meets or has a teleconference with the community to discuss the issues of concern and to how the community can best prepare for and present to the IAWG the issues of concern. This '"prep" approach came though a trial and error process from our initial meetings. It greatly assists the community to focus their needs rather than present a general review of their community.
- Communities are strongly encouraged to identify and request participation of local agencies (such as environmental department, health department, economic development, etc.). This helps develop strong ties with "sister" agencies at the state and federal levels.
- The IAWG meetings typically cover 3-4 community presentations over the course of a day. Whenever possible the IAWG meetings are held in a location close to the communities. This allows participating members to get a better sense of the affected community needs. All communities who present are strongly encouraged to attend the full day session to hear and learn from their co-presenting communities. Often, community needs are somewhat similar and so "lessons learned" is an excellent way to illustrate practical approaches to problem solving. What works in one community often will work in another.
- All meetings are facilitated by an independent non-government entity. This results in greater participation by both the community and the member

agencies since the facilitator can quickly identify or expand upon community needs and draw in the resources to address the issue.

- Minutes are provided after the meetings to capture the issues, highlight follow up actions needed and identify the agency responsible for the follow up. Communities often receive financial assistance (in the form of competitive grants or low interest loans), technical assistance (engineering suggestions for assessing or cleaning up a brownfields site) and administrative assistance (such as expediting a permit or making contact with an appropriate agency person that can assist in resolving the issue).

3.1 Success stories

A number of redevelopment projects have been accomplished as a result of the coordination among the various Federal and State agencies. A few examples are provided below.

Trenton, New Jersey has been very aggressive in its use of the IAWG in support of its redevelopment projects. The Crane site was a former cook pottery company in the 1800s/early 1900s. The city acquired the property and used an EPA Brownfields grant to assess the site's environmental conditions. It then used funds provided by the NJ Department of Environmental Protection to remediate the site. Lastly, funds from the Urban Enterprise Zone (a HUD funded program) were utilized to convert the property to a commercial park. The Magic Marker site was a former battery manufacturing facility and later a felt pen (marker) production site. The city used an EPA grant to assess the site and then an EPA revolving loan fund grant for site remediation. Funds were also accessed from the NJ Economic Development Administration and the NJ DEP Watershed grant. The site will eventually be developed for affordable housing units and a contaminated drainage problem will be addressed to allow for public open space. In Kearny, New Jersey a former tool and dye manufacturing site was converted into a much needed local playground. Funds were provided by the EPA (assessment grant), NJ Economic Development Administration and HUD's Community Block Grant program.

In New York, the City of Glen Cove is undertaking a massive redevelopment of its waterfront district. The area was home to many industries including leather belting, tinwear manufacturing, tungsten ore refining and photographic film manufacturing. The planned future uses include a marina, ferry terminal, hotel, conference center, residential units and a pedestrian/cycle esplanade. Funding has been derived from five federal agencies, seven state agencies and seven local government entities. In addition, 11 local area agencies/businesses have provided funding or technical assistance for the project. In Yonkers, New York, the city used funding or technical assistance from the EPA and HUD, New York State Department of Environmental Conservation, the New York State Department of Health and local city and private sector entities to convert a former manufactured gas plant into the location for a new bakery, parking and green space. The bakery hired a number of local residents for its operation.

Through the IAWG efforts in Puerto Rico, the US Department of Agriculture - Rural Development was able to provide funding to the municipality of Aguas

Buenas to rehabilitate an abandoned building into a youth center. HUD worked with the Municipality of Carolina on an affordable housing project for low income families. The Small Business administration provided technical assistance to the Municipality of Jayuya on ways to enhance business improvements (new hotel, restaurants and a panoramic cable car attraction).

4 Conclusions

These examples illustrate that through partnerships with and between communities, government agencies at the local, state and federal level it is possible to marshal the critical resources from diverse sources to successfully address the financial, technical, legal, and environmental challenges posed by brownfield sites. The IWAG process has provided an essential vehicle to facilitate such partnering, communications and cooperation among all three levels of government and other major brownfield stakeholders.

References

[1] New York State Department of Environmental Conservation-Brownfields Financial Resources Manual, Albany NY, 2003
[2] Hudson County Economic Development Corporation (New Jersey)
[3] Hudson County, NJ, November 2007
[4] City of Trenton, New Jersey, November 2007
[5] The United States Brownfields Program-Sven-Eric Kaiser, USEPA, Washington, DC, 2005
[6] United States Environmental Protection Agency, Office of Brownfields Cleanup and Redevelopment

Risk assessment and occupational safety and health protection in construction work on brownfields

A. P. Feige-Munzig
Berufsgenossenschaft der Bauwirtschaft, BG BAU, Germany

Abstract

Working on brownfields, the workers, who have to carry out these jobs, may be exposed to hazardous substances (chemicals and/or micro-organisms). This paper proposes a method of risk assessment and specification of measures for occupational safety and health protection, consisting of two steps: danger analysis and exposure assessment. Danger analysis means the investigation of the hazardous substances, of their physical, chemical and hazardous properties and the states of matter, being responsible for their mobility and emission behaviour. Exposure assessment starts with the so-called "working area analysis" – the investigation of the jobs that have to be carried out and of the working area conditions, which have a serious influence on the chance and level of exposure. Taking into account the possible absorption routes and limiting values used in occupational safety and health protection, the combination of the danger analysis data with the results of the exposure assessment leads to the risk assessment, the assessment of the possible health risk, and finally to the specification of safety measures. Risk assessment saves money: the less you know about the hazardous properties of a contaminated site, the higher the level of safety measures has to be, and the higher the costs of safety and health protection become.
Keywords: brownfields, contaminated sites, risk assessment, occupational safety and health protection, construction work, danger analysis, exposure assessment, safety measures, safety and health plan.

1 Introduction

During the remediation of contaminated sites hazardous substances are released causing a high risk to the health of the workers involved in these activities. To

WIT Transactions on Ecology and the Environment, Vol 107, © 2008 WIT Press
www.witpress.com, ISSN 1743-3541 (on-line)
doi:10.2495/BF080211

minimise this risk, safety measures need to be provided that match up to the risk potential of each individual project such that, on the one hand, the employees suffer no injury to their health and, on the other hand, the reclamation of a site of this nature remains economically viable.

In 1994, a concept for safety and health protection during work on contaminated sites was worked out in the Federal Republic of Germany, called *Rules for Safety and Health Protection for Working on Contaminated Sites – BGR 128*. Following the European Building Site Directive 92/57/EEC, a single directive on the basis of Article 118a of the EEC Treaty, those rules require that whenever construction work is to start on a brownfield site, the owner and the owner's coordinator for safety and health matters have to draw up a safety and health plan.

In particular as the basis for the call for tenders the safety and health plan needs to list the hazardous substances on the future building site, it needs to evaluate the safety and health risks for the workers and, on the basis of this evaluation, it needs to determine the special protection measures required for handling these substances. In this sense risk assessment is the most important tool to achieve this aim (Figure 1).

Figure 1: *The owner's tasks:* safety and health plan and risk assessment.

Risk assessment for construction work on brownfields requires occupational safety and health protection in relation to hazardous substances and micro-organisms depending on the following steps (Figure 2):

- *investigation for hazardous substances* such as chemicals and micro-organisms;
- *danger analysis* to investigate the chemical, physical, toxic and other hazardous properties (e.g. infection) of the hazardous substances;
- *exposure assessment* to assess the levels of emission exposure combining the results of the *working area analysis* with the mobility properties of the substances;
- *risk assessment* to assess for each separate activity (→ working area analysis) the dimension of the safety and health risk combining the results of the exposure assessment with the hazardous properties of the contaminants (→ danger analysis).

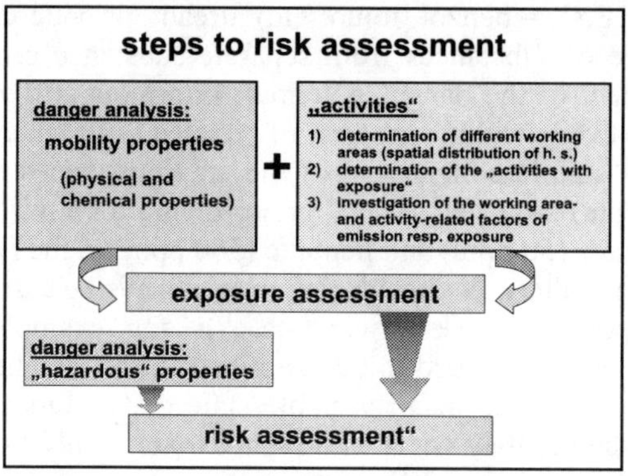

Figure 2: Steps to risk assessment.

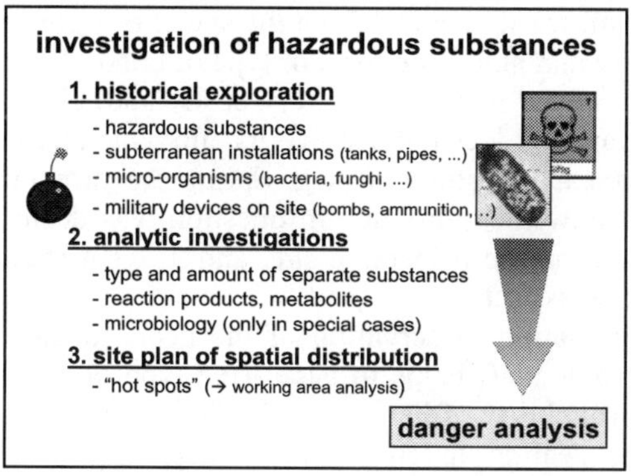

Figure 3: Investigation of hazardous substances.

2 Investigation for hazardous substances

As the first step to risk assessment those hazardous substances that are *suspected* of being on the site have to be investigated by means of the so-called Historical Investigation into the past, historical use(s) of the brownfields site. This data is required not only for establishing the testing parameters for further substance investigation, for example, by means of a chemical analysis of the substances, but also for the safety planning of the subsequent site work necessary to investigate a suspected area. The Historical Investigation also covers the investigation of "inherited military devices", i.e. whether unexploded bombs or similar objects are to be expected on the site (Figure 3).

Based on the results of the Historical Investigation the type, quantity and spatial distribution of the *existing* hazardous substances need to be determined by means of exploratory measures (prospecting, drilling, sampling, analysis etc.). Within the framework of the analyses it is always necessary to look for separate substances. Although simple data from summation parameters (“HC-(IR)” = all hydrocarbons, “BTEX” = benzol, toluol etc) already provide useful information about the existence of substances from separate substance groups, they do not permit an assessment of the danger potential. Enormous differences in the risk may be present even within groups of related substances. This can be demonstrated by a simple comparison of the air limit values of benzol (1ppm) and toluene (50 ppm) from the BTEX group or the air limit value of pentane (1000 ppm), n-hexane (50 ppm) and heptane (500 ppm) in the HC-group.

With ambivalent values, the health risk must always be assessed on the basis of the highest potential risk (“worst-case”): for example, with cyanide contamination, the cyanides need to be examined to see whether they occur in a complex bound form, i.e. in a fairly stable state that is bioavailable only to a trivial extent, or whether they occur in a highly toxic, easily liberated form. The sole indication of the “cyanide” summation parameter inevitably leads to higher-level protection measures and hence to greater costs.

In the case of heavy metals, the concentrations of individual metals are given, containing limited informative value about the actual risk present, which depends on the bioavailability and hence the form or type of bond of the heavy metal.

An investigation of the bond type is very costly and, given the large number of possibilities, ultimately does not achieve its aim. One possible way, however, is to use the Historical Investigation, e.g. during the dismantling of industrial plants, to establish how the substance in question was dealt with and in what form or combination, on the respective site, and in what reactors and pipelines these materials can be expected.

With soil contamination, observation of the geochemical or hydrochemical milieu (e.g. E_h-pH potential) helps to assess the type of chemical combination and hence the bioavailability of heavy metals. For example, under conditions of reduction, hermetic sealing in soils with a high organic content, mercuric chlorides used to impregnate wood may be reduced to metallic mercury. In particular account should be taken of the products of the change, sometimes even entire series of degradations, such as the degradation of certain chlorinated hydrocarbons to vinylchloride (VC) or the denitrification of TNT via DNT to aromatic amines by microbial activity. All reaction products or even “metabolites” possess different chemical-physical and/or toxicological properties from the original, initial products that were processed or produced on the site, a factor that may have an effect on safety planning.

Further key factors in the investigation for hazardous substances are

a) the establishment of the existing concentration of hazardous substances, and
b) the spatial distribution of the substances in the contaminated zone.

In conjunction with its properties (see Section 3 on “Danger Analysis”) the concentration of a substance in the soil, in masonry, groundwater etc. is a measure of the extent to which safety planning must allow for this. Ascertaining the spatial distribution of the substances helps to establish different “working areas” with different graduated measures, e.g., the excavation depth at which contaminated material can be expected and from what point in time or from what depth special safety measures are necessary.

It is not only the risks arising from "chemistry" that have to be accounted for, but also the biological hazard caused by pathogenic germs (bacteria, fungi, viruses) or human endoparasites (cf. European Directive on Biological Working Materials EEC 90/679/EEC). An investigation into biological hazards should always be carried out if

- biological agents were used on the site;
- certain materials or other local conditions favour the survival, growth or possibly the propagation of germs;
- the presence of germs or parasites can be expected in certain areas, for example, in remediation of suspected areas used by the leather industry (anthrax pathogens), or from sewage ditches, drains etc.; or
- microbiological remediation of the soil is required, for which our firm has prepared a set of instructions on the action to be taken in determining safety measures.

3 Danger analysis

The task of danger analysis is required to determine the properties of the assumed or analytically determined substances (Figure 4) with regard to mobility and hazards; to use these properties for the assessment as to whether dangerous quantities of the hazardous substances may be released during or even because of the work; and to assess what the chances or risks are of intake or exposure via the different absorption routes – inhalation, ingestion, and/or dermal contact. Table 1 shows the most important danger characteristic and the corresponding evaluation parameters.

In principle, the danger analysis has to be done for every substance assumed or analytically determined on the site. However, a broad mixture of different substances and their microbial metabolism products are often found at brownfield sites. Therefore, the most practical method would be to select those individual substances as indicator substances from the existing spectrum of hazardous substances having the most critical assessment parameters with regard to the respective danger characteristics:

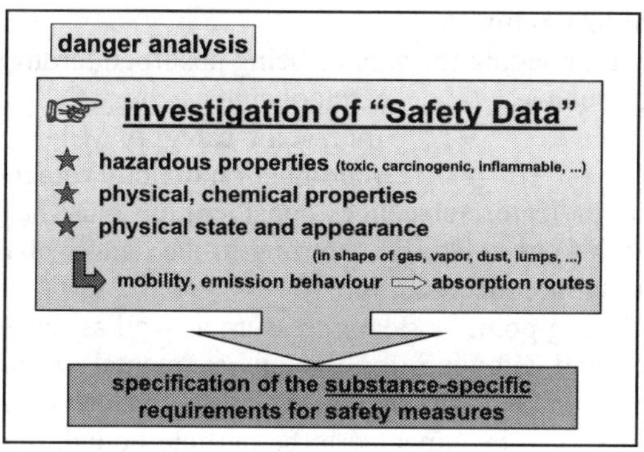

Figure 4: Danger analysis.

Table 1: Assignment of danger characteristics to characteristic groups and evaluation parameters.

Characteristic group	**Danger characteristics**	**Typical evaluation parameters (hazards, mobility)**
Inflammable substances	explosive possibly explosive highly inflammable easily inflammable inflammable	explosion limit values flashpoint vapour pressure [mbar (20°C)] firing power
Explosive substances	explosive	chemical reactivity
Combustible substances	combustible	available oxygen
Toxic substances	highly toxic toxic injurious to health	atmospheric limit value LC / LD 50 absorption route skin contact boiling point vapour pressure [mbar (20°C)] ability of sublimation aqueous solubility
Substances damaging the skin/mucous membrane	caustic irritant	atmospheric limit value vapour pressure [mbar (20°C)] pH value skin contact aqueous solubility
Substances with special danger potential	carcinogenic mutagenic teratogenic or toxic to reproductive cells	atmospheric limit value boiling point vapour pressure [mbar (20°C)] ability of sublimation absorption route carcinogenic category C 1-3 mutagenic category M 1-3 reproduction toxicity categories R_F and R_E 1-3
Allergens	sensitising	atmospheric limit value vapour pressure [mbar (20°C)] ability of sublimation absorption route
Micro-organisms	infectious, toxic or sensitising properties	Risk group Colony forming unit [CFU/m³]

- the lowest atmospheric limit value
- the lowest explosion limit value
- the property of damaging the skin or being absorbed through the skin,
- classifications such as
  - carcinogenic category C 1-3
  - mutagenic category M 1-3
  - reproduction toxicity categories R_F/R_E 1-3

In selecting the indicator substances consideration must be given to whether the substance that is to be selected according to the danger characteristics exists in a relevant quantity or concentration.

By using the boiling point or steam pressure as well as the aqueous solubility of the substances and allowing for the environmental conditions during the construction phase, an assessment can be made of the extent to which the individual substances can be expected to be particle-bound, in aqueous solution, in fluid form or in vaporous or gaseous form.

To avoid having to assign every single danger characteristic to the assessment parameters, it is possible to combine "related" characteristics into a characteristic group. Table 1 contains a suggestion for this method of assignment.

Other assessment parameters are the physical-chemical properties of the substances: explosion limit values (LELV, UELV), flashpoint, firing power, boiling temperature, steam pressure, aqueous solubility, volatility (sublimation tendency).

In addition, the volatility has to be allowed for, because some substances, for example, from PAH, HCH, dioxin, have a high sublimation tendency, i.e. the transition from the solid state of aggregation to the vapour phase and vice versa. Benzo(a)pyrene has a high boiling point (495.5°C) and a correspondingly low steam pressure ($7.3x10^{-9}$mbar at 20°C), but it has a tendency to sublimate in an air current when powered filtering devices are used so a composite filter for particles *and* organic gases and vapours should be employed.

The evaluation of the form or type of hazardous substances and their mobility (for example, behaviour as air-borne dust) is a major factor in the danger analysis. It is not only the analytically determined concentration of a substance that is the decisive evaluation criterion for protective measures but also the exact description of the material that is highly important. The comparison of two samples will shed light on these problems: within a sandy matrix we find lumps of tar (sample 1) or filter-dusts containing PAH (sample 2) (Figure 5). The chemical analysis of sample 1 shows far higher benzo-a-pyrene contents than in the other case, because small pieces of tar were included in the sample. All other things being equal, the comparably lower level of soot contamination in the sand nevertheless constitutes a higher risk, because the soot becomes airborne much more easily than the particles in the lumps of tar.

At the same time attention must be paid to changes arising during the actual work in the states of aggregation or the form of appearance, or even through the protective measures themselves creating new dangers, for example by dissolving water-soluble hazardous substances when using water to dampen down dust.

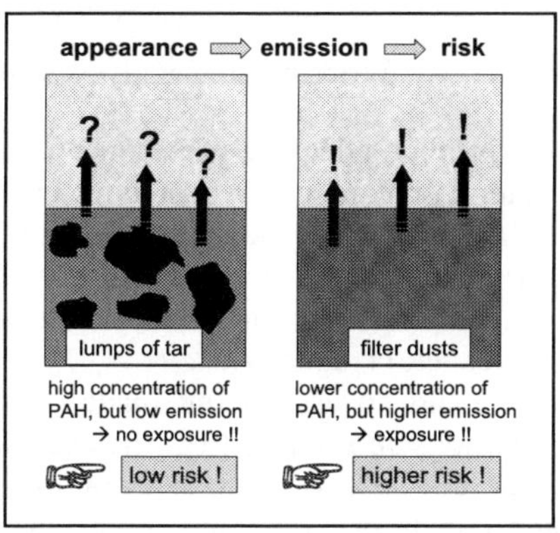

Figure 5: The form of appearance determines the risk.

Danger analysis is the basis for the determination of *substance-related* protective measures (Figure 4), because it is the properties of the substances that decide what type of protective clothing or breathing equipment is to be selected. The presence of substances that can be absorbed by the skin is a basic factor in the choice of protective clothing (coated or uncoated), just as the water-solubility of combustible substances also influences the choice and provision of suitable extinguishing agents.

With insufficient knowledge of the separate substances, their properties and the forms in which they occur, the "worst case" must always be assumed, i.e. they must be assigned for health-protection purposes to the most critical category (volatile, bioavailable, toxic) of the compound or form.

4 Exposure assessment – working area analysis

The first step of the working area analysis is to divide the construction site "brownfield" into different "working areas", corresponding either to the spatial distribution of the hazardous substances, to the spatial division found on the site (e.g. industrial site with different plants and facilities), or to the different types of jobs which have to be performed on the site (Figure 6).

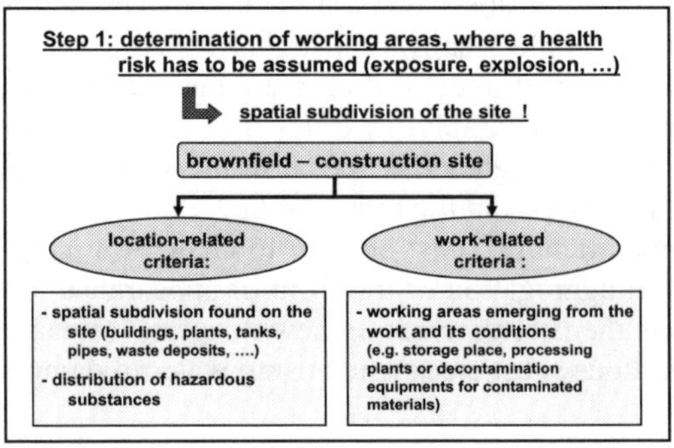

Figure 6: Working area analysis step 1.

Safety measures must provide adequate protection for each separate activity. Therefore an important step in risk assessment is to provide a detailed analysis of the planned work procedure as regards the steps necessary for its execution, the jobs arising from this (machine operator, truck driver, etc) and the types of activities (manual work, cleaning, servicing and maintenance of machines and plants, supervisory activities, etc) (Figure 7).

A record must be kept and an assessment made of all activities that may involve contact with hazardous substances (e.g. the excavator operator does not only operate the excavator, but he also has to carry out maintenance work on the equipment that has been contaminated during the course of his work, and the appropriate decontamination and other safety measures must be specified for this).

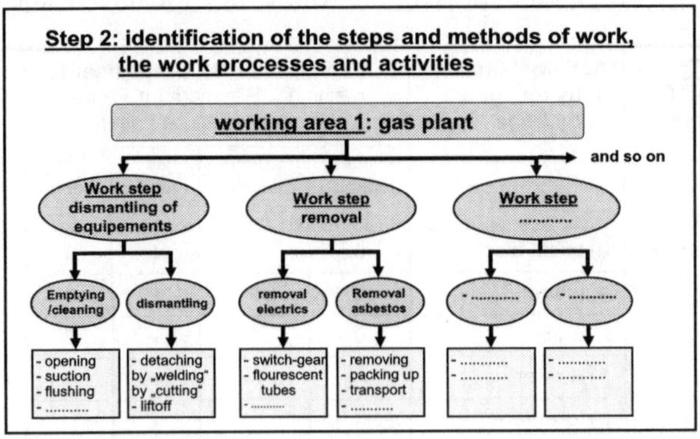

Figure 7: Working area analysis step 2.

So far we have collected the data to assess whether an exposure or dangerous situation could occur or not. But for risk assessment and the specification of appropriate safety measures we need further work- and location-related data in order to estimate the magnitude of the "event" or danger. In this phase of "planning", the results of measurements are not available and therefore it is necessary to use "soft" criteria:

- weather conditions to be assumed during the execution of the work
- the source of the emission (e.g., at a certain point or over a certain area
- one might expect low or high emission rates)
- working method with high or low emission potential
- environmental conditions (e.g., working in a closed room or on top of a hill would result in higher or lower concentrations of dust or vapours)
- proximity of the activity to the point of the source of the emission
- frequency and period of activity in the emission's danger zone, which might lead to a range of potential risks of exposure.

The investigation of this data may be called "step 3 of the working area analysis".

Combining the data of the mobility of the substances and their exposure-routes, according to their state of aggregation, with the results of the working area analysis it is possible to estimate the magnitude of an exposure and the probability that unacceptable hazards may be encountered on site

5 Risk assessment

Combining the hazards of the substances (see "danger analysis", Table 1) with the data of the exposure assessment it is possible to provide a qualitative assessment of the risk in terms of a minimum or maximum likelihood of risk. For instance:

- High exposure to a "harmless" substance may lead to low health risk.
- Low exposure to a serious toxic substance may cause a high health risk.
- Cold temperatures in winter time may decrease the vaporisation of highly volatile, inflammable organic carbons and consequently the risk that such

Table 2: Proposal to present the results of exposure/risk assessment.

PROJECT: GAS PLANT working area: **tar pit** work step:	Activity / Staff a) by machine b) by hand	Exposure / Risk assessment (+ = high, , +- = medium, - = low, 0 = no exposure / risk)				Explosion risk
		contam. materials	contam. liquids	gas / vapour	dust / aerosol	
excavation "tar pit"	a) excavator	0	0	+	0	-
	a) loader	0	0	+	0	
	a) truck	0	0	-	0	
	b) worker	+-	+-	+	+	
	b) foreman	-	-	-	-	
	b) surveyor	0	0	-	-	
cleaning of excavator loader	b) outside (steam)	-	+	0	0	
	b) inside dry (vac cleaner)	0	0	0	+-	
	b) inside, wet	0	+-	0	0	

compounds will reach inflammable concentrations in the air, especially on top of a hill!

A suggestion for the presentation of this assessment is shown in Table 2.

6 Specification of protective measures

On the basis of a risk assessment similar to that presented above, it is possible to define the appropriate protective equipment for each activity. Whenever this method of risk-based specification of protective measures is applied, it may be that two people, while working in the same working area, may be required to wear different protective equipment. Utilizing different protective gear within the same working area may not be readily understood by the workers; however, with proper instruction about the different risks of different "jobs", they will better understand and accept that such safety measures will reduce the risk and cost to all.

Exploratory drilling in a special waste dump as an example. The worker, who works longest and closest to the source of emission, places the pipework and screws on the new rod assemblies, removes the core from the central column, and is generally always proximate to the point of the emission is given a complete protective suit with breathing apparatus that is independent of the ambient air. On the other hand, the foreman driller, who normally only operates the controls of the drilling equipment, and comes into the working area five times a day to help his colleagues with certain jobs, could manage with a disposable protection suit and a filter mask, depending on the substances present (Figure 8). While this is only an example, the selection of protective measures must always be made according to the premise that effective technical measures (ventilation, equipment for air supply on earth-moving machinery) must necessarily take precedence over the use of personal protective equipment (PPE).

PPE always means an additional strain on the human body, e.g. through heat accumulation in protective clothing or the extra weight of breathing equipment, which leads in turn to reduced performance, and not only because of the associated regulations governing limits on wearing periods and work intervals.

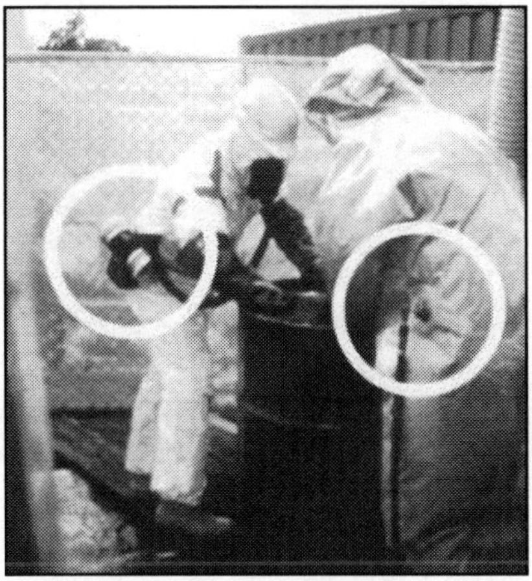

Figure 8: Different risks require different protective equipment.

7 Conclusions

Qualitative risk assessment of whether high or low exposure or other dangerous situations related to hazardous substances are to be expected during work on brownfields is a suitable method for ensuring that:

a) appropriate measures are taken at each workplace that conform to the project-specific risks utilizing state-of-the-art knowledge,

b) the acceptance of the protective measures by all participants is increased by avoiding exaggerated measures, and

c) the costs remain within an acceptable framework.

Risk assessment is not only a part of any safety and health protection scheme for employees but also an important component in ascertaining the optimum, most cost-effective working method, which makes it an integral part of any remediation project.

References

[1] Council Directive 92/57/EEC of 24 June 1992 on the implementation of minimum safety and health requirements at temporary or mobile construction sites

[2] BGR 128 – Rules for Safety and Health Protection for Working on Contaminated Sites; Germany, 1997 (updated 2006);

[3] Andreas P. Feige-Munzig, Gefährdungsbeurteilung bei Arbeiten in kontaminierten Bereichen, Tiefbau 2/2005, S. 71–77

The design evaluation and reuse recommendation for Japanese naval facilities located at Fongshan Wireless Telecommunication Station in Taiwan

C.-K. Ku
Department of Architecture and Interior Design, Cheng-Shiu University, Taiwan

Abstract

Fongshan Wireless Telecommunication Station (FongshanWTS) used to be listed as one of the three biggest wireless telecommunication stations in Japan. The buildings in the FongshanWTS offer a great deal of information related to the histories of construction technology, military installation and telecommunication equipment for precious historical assets in Taiwan. According to the official record, FongshanWTS was constructed from 1917–1919, and the design technology was originated from Germany. The reason why and how it was constructed in Taiwan, and also the evaluation of design technology and reuse recommendation are discussed in this paper. Since the history of FongshanWTS involves four countries, e.g. Taiwan, Japan, China and Germany, it is the purpose of this paper to get correlated information from this international conference, especially from those countries in Europe.
Keywords: wireless telecommunication station, telecommunication, reuse.

1 Introduction

There are many Japanese vestiges of military facilities in the southern part of Taiwan, particularly at Kaohsiung. Some of these facilities have been demolished not only because of the reconstruction project for the military housing community, but also because of the disarmament plan in Taiwan. The land area used for military affairs is actually considerably large in Kaohsiung. The popularization of martial culture has led to the desire to witness the history

WIT Transactions on Ecology and the Environment, Vol 107, © 2008 WIT Press
www.witpress.com, ISSN 1743-3541 (on-line)
doi:10.2495/BF080221

of military affairs in this region. It has been more than 60 years since the end of WWII. The conservation of military facilities needs to be taken into consideration.

2 Historical background

The historical background can be traced from the end of the 19th century. After winning the Sino-Japanese war of 1895, it was approved that the Japanese had developed the navy force successfully in the past. Consequently, this made Japan expand the navy force more confidently and more actively. The Japanese parliament originally had widespread comment about too great an expenditure on the navy; however, the expansion action of the navy was accepted at this time [1]. In addition, at the beginning of the 20th century, Japan became the only country in Asia that stood side by side with American–European big powers by defeating Russian. From the Shimonoseki Treaty in 1895 to the Japan–Russia war in 1905, the Japanese navy had been developed very quickly within this decade. Taiwan was incorporated into the domain of Japan in this military expansion and became the first colony of Japan.

The key point that allowed the Japanese navy to conduct a military operation successfully at that time depended on the newly developed weapon in the battlefield, the wireless telecommunication machine (which was developed at the beginning of the 20th century). Therefore, in 1915, the first wireless telecommunication station on a large scale was completed at Funabasi in Japan. Then the second one, Fongshan located in Taiwan, was chosen as the second wireless telecommunication station and finished in 1919. The last one was completed at Hario in 1922 [2]. With three large-scale wireless telecommunication stations finished within nine years, the geographical distribution should be considered as a whole. Namely, Funabasi was near the capital Tokyo, it was the heartland of the political center in Japan; Hario in Sasebo is the location of the naval port in the west-coastal end of Japan, and can monitor Korea or even China; Fongshan was near the naval base at Kaohsiung which is in the southern territorial end of Japan, and from here it was easy to get in touch with the archipelago of the south Pacific Ocean.

After WWII, a lot of people and military forces from Mainland China moved to Taiwan, especially after 1949. At that time, besides the wireless telecommunication function, FongshanWTS was also used as a prison for political offenders. Some of them were taken as the suspects of Chinese Communist agents and died there [3]. Therefore, FongshanWTS is not only the technical place for wireless telecommunication, but also the memorial place for those people who died there for political reasons.

Among these three wireless telecommunication stations, the Funabasi Wireless Telecommunication Station (FunabasiWTS) was originally constructed by Germany and no longer exists now. Hario Wireless Telecommunication Station has nothing left now but three wireless towers made of reinforced concrete. It seems more important for FongshanWTS to keep the related cultural assets. The preservation and reuse of FongshanWTS are under consideration at this moment in time.

3 Landscape of surrounding environment

3.1 Funabasi Wireless Telecommunication Station in Japan

Funabasi Wireless Telecommunication Station was located near Tokyo. The disposition of FunabasiWTS is shown in Figure 1. The diameter of the outer circle is 800m. The major steel tower with a height of 200m was situated at the center of the circle. The wireless telecommunication room was located beside the major tower. There were also 18 secondary steel towers around the outer circle with equal distance between each other [4].

FunabasiWTS was constructed by technicians from Germany. The construction began in October 1913 until the beginning of WWI. The related design drawings were burned before the technicians hastily returned to Germany in August 1914. At that time, only the foundations of the major steel tower were finished. The big wireless telecommunication machines were not yet assembled. However, the remaining parts of FunabasiWTS were finally completed by Japanese technicians on their own in April 1915 [5]. Nevertheless, it was demolished in 1971.

It could be more interesting if similar wireless telecommunication stations can be found in Germany or other countries in Europe. The correlations of wireless telecommunication stations among Taiwan, Japan and European countries can be connected.

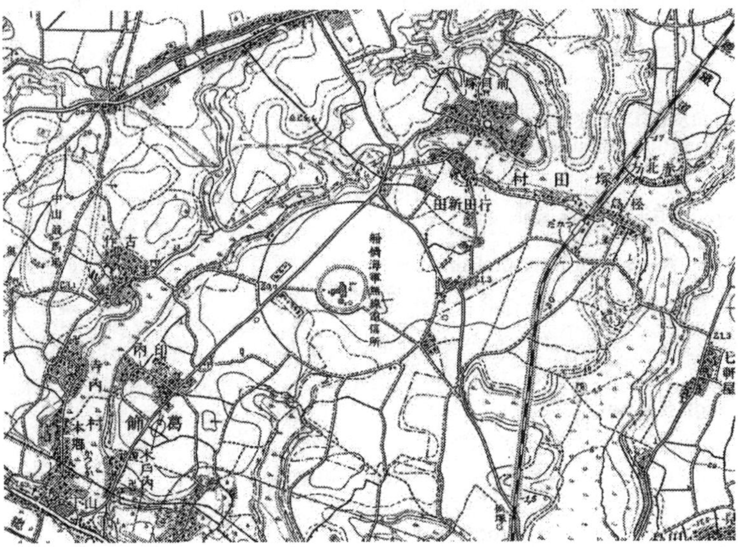

Figure 1: The disposition of FunabasiWTS.

3.2 Fongshan Wireless Telecommunication Station in Taiwan

The surrounding configuration for FongshanWTS is illustrated in Figure 2. Farmland originally surrounded the FongshanWTS when it was constructed.

However, only the eastern side is farmland now. The remaining foundations for fixing 60m high antennas are kept in this area. The oncoming urban planning for this area is residential district. How to preserve these foundations becomes an intricate issue now.

There is a primary school on the south side. The western part has several buildings with different functions, e.g. traditional market, military dependants' remodelling residences, veterans' service center, military welfare supply center, junior high school, etc. The military dependants' remodelling residences will be constructed this summer. The military dependants' housing located in the northern part was constructed 43 years ago and will be demolished after the remodelling residences are finished.

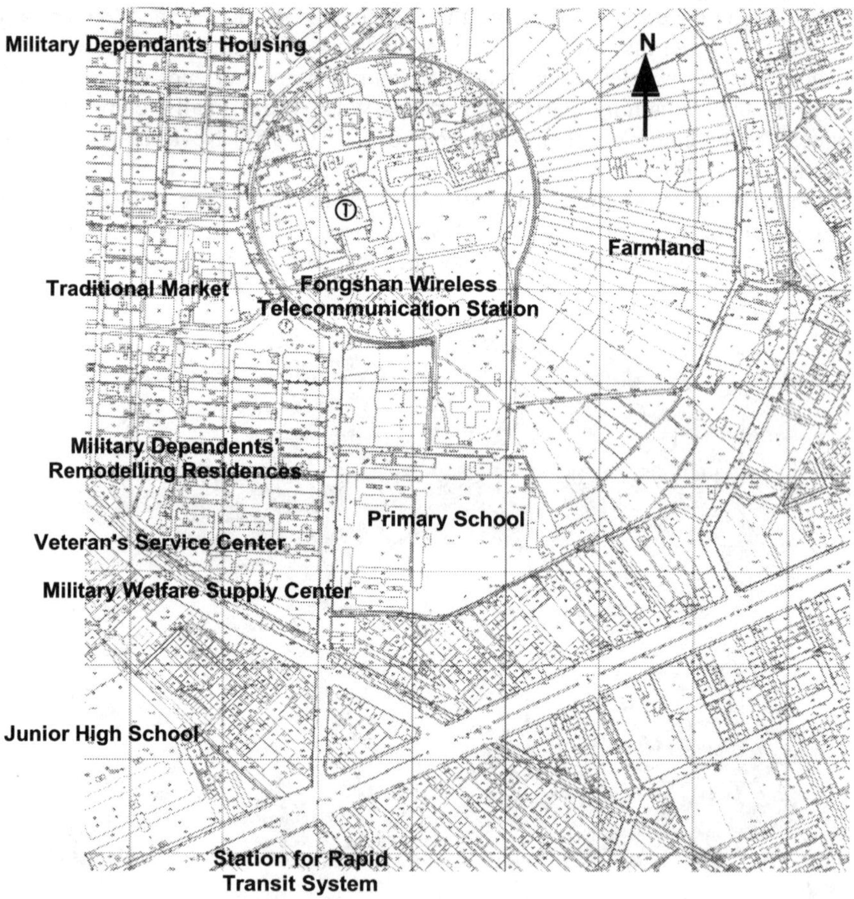

Figure 2: The surrounding configuration for FongshanWTS.

The construction of FongshanWTS began in the summer of 1917, and finished in May 1919. The aerial view of FongshanWTS and the related foundations for fixing antennas are displayed in Figure 3. The design conception was the same as that for FunabasiWTS. There was also a steel tower with a height of 200m situated at the center of the circle, and 18 secondary steel towers, where were the same as FunabasiWTS, with a height of 60m, surrounded the outer circle. The small circles, marked as A, B, and C circles as shown in Figure 3, were the foundations to fix the antennas. The diameter of circle A is 800m, while the diameters of circles B and C are 680m and 260m respectively as shown in Figure 4.

There were 36 foundations situated in circle A, but only six remain, they are marked as A5, A6, A7, A11, A14 and A19 in Figure 3. The A11 foundation is displayed in Figure 5. There were 18 foundations in circle B, only B2 to B7 are left now. All these foundations in circles A and B are the same size, namely length 400cm×width 250cm×height 112cm. The biggest foundations for fixing antenna were C1 to C3 with length 10m×width 7m×height 2.6m. The C2 foundation is shown in Figure 6.

Figure 3: The aerial view of former FongshanWTS with the small circles marking the locations of foundations.

Figure 4: The black lines mark the diameters of the foundations for fixing antennas.

Figure 5: The A11 foundation for fixing antenna.

Figure 6: The C2 foundation for fixing antenna.

4 The design configuration of telecommunication room

There are 15 historical buildings in FongshanWTS, they are the telecommunication room, office buildings, water tower, ammunition installation, infirmary, dormitories for officers and soldiers, etc. The representative building in this station is the telecommunication room marked as number ① in Figure 2. The plan is approximately rectangular with slopes stepping from both sides and covered with soil. The roof is covered with quite deep soil in order to prevent bombing from the air. The height of the telecommunication room is 12.3m. There are 13 blast-resistant windows and six blast-resistant doors as illustrated in Figure 7. The blast-resistant doors and windows are made from reinforced concrete with a steel frame attached to the outside. The whole structure is made from reinforced concrete, especially in the north–south direction, while the partition walls in the east–west direction are made from bricks.

Figure 7: South elevation of the telecommunication room.

There are three long tube shaped spaces inside the telecommunication room as shown in Figure 8. The circles on top of the right hand side and left hand side arches are installations of electric lines for the power supply. The circle on the central top of the arch is a big fan for ventilation. The right hand tube has two stories. The second floor is a wooden structure with cryptomeria girders. The timbers were transported from Japan. The central tube also has two stories, but the second floor is made of reinforced concrete and fire-resistant bricks. The left hand side tube is a machinery room with a travelling hoist on the top of the columns.

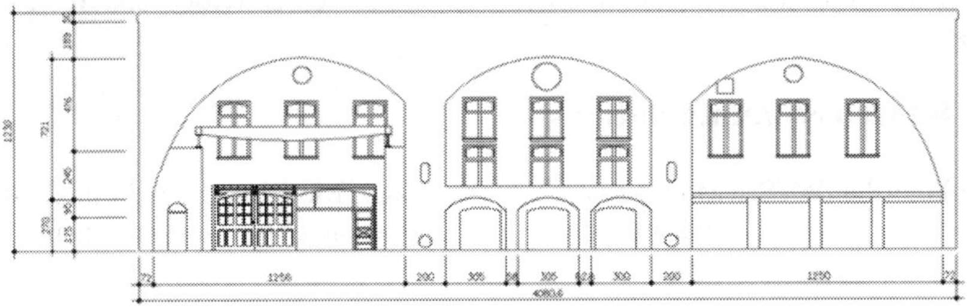

Figure 8: Cross-section of the telecommunication room.

5 Reuse significances

The reuse significances for FongshanWTS are listed as follows [6]:

1. Continuity of native culture
The FongshanWTS is like the long lane of history, from a Japanese telecommunication station to a Taiwanese anti-communism base. Every scene, every thing, even a copy of the precise loyal sentiment, aspiration and spirit that were dedicated to the service of the country resulted in some touching stories and anecdotes that should be preserved.

2. Extension of education on martial culture
There are several military bases in Fongshan that are known around the whole country. Before 1945, the Japanese managed battlefields in southern Taiwan. The Ministry of National Defence in Taiwan still continues to use the peripheral military installations in Fongshan. The land area used for military affairs is actually considerably large. The popularization of martial culture has led to the desire to witness the history of military affairs.

3. Manifestation of historical framework, activation of historical district
The government of the Republic of China moved from the mainland to Taiwan in 1950. In order to prepare for counterattack, the housing for military dependants was established near the military camps. The landscape of the military housing community and agricultural society nearby showed simple and honest humanity. Based on social values and cultural changes, it is the historical mission to activate the district if combining FongshanWTS with the traditional market, military dependents' remodelling residences, military welfare supply center, veterans' service center, junior high school, primary school, shopping street and the station for rapid transit system, and so on.

4. Recollection of local emotion and utilization of spare space
The existence of the FongshanWTS is in the memory of the military housing community and local neighborhood. It is all closely related to the education network in this area from primary school to junior high school, even to college. As military dependants' housing is reconstructed, an extensive population will move into this area. It can offer enough space for activities and recreation usages.

6 Reuse recommendations

The FongshanWTS was constructed 90 years ago. Most buildings in this station should be repaired. The short-term and long-term objectives of reusing this station are listed below [6].

6.1 Short-term objectives

1. Planning and design
The damage level of the buildings should be assessed and the planning of work for space, safety devices, maintenance and repair technology should be undertaken.

2. Applying trusteeship
The related documents are assembled, including trusteeship planning, authentications of official departments and the institutional framework of trusteeship. FongshanWTS is now managed by the organization, "Cultural Developmental Confraternity for Kaohsiung Military Housing Community".

3. Introducing civic organizations
There are some organizations in the nearby area. Relevant organizations can be introduced to adopt this district, and the co-management organizations can be taken as the basic administrative units in the future.

4. Volunteer training
Through volunteer training, the culture assets can be realized, the environment can be known, the mission can be understood, and the area of responsibility can be adopted.

5. Space opening
The space will be opened for residents' recreation activities. The interior spaces of the buildings can be taken as the classroom for local organizations and folks. The surrounding environment can be realized through opening the space. The function of managing the space; therefore, can be fulfilled by users' maintenance.

6.2 Long-term objectives

1. Establishment of a cultural recreation center
After successively finishing the construction and repair work of the FongWTS in the relevant stages in accordance with the plan, the goal of constructing a cultural recreation center can be implemented. This district can be moulded as the space for local recreation, performing art and historical cultural continuity.

The name "Martial History Station for Fongshan Wireless Telecommunication" was proposed for the former FongshanWTS this year. It is expected that this historical station will be kept and utilized properly, enriching the cultivation of the community, allowing the preservation of cultural assets and the improvement of local economy to bring out the best in each other.

2. Introducing business activities
Many public places in Fongshan are managed through conducting commercial activities at present, and these activities have developed the local characteristics of the city. The traditional delicate food in the military dependants' community was originated from northern China and having its special flavour. In addition, coffee and table delicacies are introduced through proper commercial activities, thus the local economy can be activated. The income from commercial activities can be taken as the funds for managing and safeguarding this station.

3. Experiencing environmental adventure
A sustainable base for local organizations can be provided, and the multifunctional study space and its high additional value can be offered; for instance, as an environmental education base for nearby schools, social activities for local organizations and construction practice place, etc.

4. Touring local characteristics
After finishing the relevant software and hardware improvements in this district in the future, it cannot only be used as the living space for residents, but the local distinguishing features can also be established. In addition, local sightseeing through performing arts and festival celebration activities can be improved, and so on.

7 Conclusion

FongshanWTS was one of the three biggest Japanese wireless telecommunication stations before WWII. It represents the developmental history of wireless telecommunication, having an historical value that cannot be replaced. In addition, after the navy of the Republic of China took over this station, it was divided into military dependent's housing and a training base for offenders in the navy. It has its own special historical background that has many stories.

It is more interesting if similar design schemes of wireless telecommunication stations can be found in Germany or other countries in Europe. The international correlations of such wireless telecommunication stations among Taiwan, Japan and European countries can be achieved.

References

[1] The conservation of navy history foundation, *Japanese navy history*, volume I, Tokyo. The first regulation publish corporation, p.245, 1995.
[2] The conservation of navy history foundation, *Japanese navy history*, volume V, Tokyo. The first regulation publish corporation, p.464, 1995.
[3] Ku, C.K., Chen, C.C. & Han, S.S., *The Investigation and Repair Report for Former Telecommunication Base of Japanese Navy at Kaohsiung County (Ming-Der Navy Training Base)*, Kaohsiung County Government, pp.2-8~2-10, 2006.
[4] Committee for Electric Wave Supervision, *The History of Japanese Wireless Telecommunication*, volume X, p.440~441, 1951.
[5] Committee for Electric Wave Supervision, *The History of Japanese Wireless Telecommunication,* volume X, p.49, 1951.
[6] Ku, C.K., The history and reuse of Fongshan wireless telecommunication station. *Proceedings of International Conference on the Installation, Design and Reuse of Japanese Military Facilities in Taiwan*, National Center for Research and Preservation of Cultural Properties, Taiwan, pp.4-15~4-19, 2006.

Section 6
Community and public involvement

Public participation in the brownfield redevelopment process: lessons learned in two case studies in Michigan, USA

A. P. Fontaine
Senior Urban Designer, JJR, LLC, USA

Abstract

This paper documents a defined approach for successfully engaging public participation in brownfield redevelopment projects. The two case studies vary by community size (140,000 to 870,000 residents) and by project area (17 acres to 3.5 miles of riverfront), but the basic approach stays the same. By comparing the two case studies, a list of lessons learned is generated and demonstrates how this basic approach can be applied to almost any brownfield redevelopment effort.
Keywords: participation, brownfields, Michigan, credible champion.

1 Challenge of public participation

The challenge in involving the general public in any development project is determining the optimum level of input the community should have in the process. Too little input and the project runs the risk of not gaining crucial community support – necessary for public funding, changes to adopted plans, and acceptance in the neighborhoods where change will take place. Too much input and the project will become unmanageable, responding to every nuance, local issue, and parochial concern.

Brownfield development projects add an additional layer of complexity in the public participation process. Brownfields often create many questions: What is a brownfield? How long has it been like this? What are the public health considerations? These are just a few of the more basic questions the public will have. The vast majority of residents will not understand the basic science involved in repairing the site, nor will they comprehend the complex regulatory conditions that must be met or the amount of effort that will be needed for a successful project to be created.

www.witpress.com, ISSN 1743-3541 (on-line)
doi:10.2495/BF080231

All of these issues along with others create the largest obstacle for successful community involvement: the time it takes to redevelop a brownfield. To sustain interest and have meaningful input over the many years it takes for even the simplest of brownfield sites to be developed requires a detailed strategy designed to manage expectations. Share too much technical information early on and the community is either scared off, intimidated, or just tunes out. Print a colorful rendering of how the project may look in a decade in the newspapers and people expect changes immediately, will organize to fight it, or land speculation will run rampant – or all of the above.

2 Public participation approach

Working on brownfields in the United States' Midwest for the past 30 years, JJR, a land planning, landscape architecture, and civil engineering firm, has developed a basic approach for community involvement that applies to brownfields for communities of all sizes. The five fundamentals of the approach for creating successful public participation in brownfield redevelopment projects are as follows.

2.1 The project narrative

The community needs the technical information woven into an overall project narrative that gives context and translates the many details into a compelling reason why the brownfield redevelopment makes sense and is the right thing to do. Creation of this narrative, its refinement, timing, delivery, and manifestation in a design solution is at the very core of a successful public participation effort.

Why a project narrative? Because people remember stories and the larger arc, and can relate its meaning to their everyday lives. The language is more user-friendly and more detailed than a slogan or speaking points. No idea, bit of information, or news should be released to the public before it can be aligned with the larger project narrative. A small group (not more than 10-12 members) of key stakeholders (technical experts, civic leaders, key residents, institutional leaders) should preside over the considerable effort of managing the evolution of the project narrative.

The project narrative explains what the project is, and the benefits and reasons for undertaking it while framing the issues and setting the table for public support. Most importantly, the narrative manages expectations. By actively managing the narrative, the community's expectations are in line with the reality of the site, the market, and the overall project vision.

Managing expectations is especially important in communities that have been suffering great economic, cultural, and social losses. Even larger communities only get so many chances to turn the tide of disinvestment, and no one project can by itself transform a community's fortunes. Residents often expect too much from a single project, or they fear that if it isn't successful, the town is doomed. The reality is always somewhere in the middle, and it is the job of the narrative to find that middle ground of realistic optimism while encouraging active and meaningful community participation. Once a community understands the value of a project narrative, the approach for managing public participation becomes a much simpler affair.

2.2 Support a credible champion

Consultants play a key role in the process: organizing meetings, developing technical plans, designing solutions, and managing the development process, but they can not be seen as leading the effort. The community needs to hear the vision and its issues from an elected or at least a widely acknowledged public figure. The leader needs to have the trust of the community, be able to communicate at the community level, and have strong ties to both the public and private sector. For a transformative project that will affect an entire city, the mayor, city manager, or leader of a larger non-profit will need to step up to the role for the project to attract the level of attention it deserves. The leader must champion the project through the entire process for success to be achieved.

2.3 Take small, connected steps, and stick to a simple schedule

The shortest brownfield redevelopment projects have a timeline of at least three years, and these are the exception. A typical timeline can stretch more than six to eight years depending on the size of the project, the authorities involved, and the level of remediation needed (necessary repairs to the site).

Few projects have the ability to sustain public interest over an extended period of time (two years is usually the maximum time any one resident can be expected to follow in detail a specific aspect of the project). Therefore, it is important to establish larger project goals and then break the project into smaller, two-year phases that respond and relate to the larger goals. Here is an idealized example:

- Phase 1: Understanding remediation issues – what will it take to repair/fix the site? Years 1-2. Phase 1 covers technical issues and determines project limits, jurisdictions and roles, and possible approaches to repairing the site.
- Phase 2: What is possible – defining the vision! Years 3-4. Topics include overall project goals and standards, ways of measuring success, understanding market and site conditions, and crafting a defined solution.
- Phase 3: Getting the vision built. Years 4-6. The focus of phase 3 is finding private and public sector partners to build the vision – marketing the project beyond the confines of the community.
- Phase 4: Expanding the vision. Year 7-onward.

Each phase builds on the previous one, creating further refinement on issues and the overall design while building support for the project in a way the public can follow and understand. A strict and simple schedule must be maintained throughout, linking the phases. Quarterly community workshops and monthly updates on a website and through the local newspapers are standard and effective methods of making sure everyone is on the same page.

2.4 Manage the project narrative

One constant in brownfield projects is that things change: consultants change, leaders change, and issues change, but the underlying narrative of why the brownfield project is important must remain the same. Narratives are user-friendly ways of communicating complicated technical data so that while people may not understand all of the details, they are able to follow the broader issues.

Specific issues that arise need to be integrated into the project narrative. By doing so, the narrative keeps up with current events and responds to specific topics (e.g., how traffic in a particular neighborhood is going to be impacted).

Support is quickly lost when the community starts to hear different views on the same topic. The more muddled the narrative, the less people will understand it and believe in it, eroding support and the overall feasibility of the project. Larger projects need to develop a public relations strategy that includes recruitment of key media players to foster a healthy relationship with newspapers, internet sources, radio programs, and television stations.

When the revised narrative has been determined, it needs to be continuously released through many kinds of media through one media contact person. When people don't hear about a project, rumors begin to circulate. By being proactive, the brownfield redevelopment team can frame the issues and minimize any disruptive rumors or damage done by uninformed critics. The credible leader should be the one delivering any major breaking news.

2.5 Design flexible solutions

Brownfields are like house renovations – there is no knowledge of what might be encountered until the job has started. Until the construction equipment is at the site, and digging and debris removal has begun, there cannot be 100% certainty as to what will be found and how it may influence the final design. The public needs to understand that changes can occur at any stage of the process and that deadlines may need to be extended – all part of aligning and managing expectations.

3 Case studies

Both case studies are located in Michigan. Michigan is experiencing a profound transition, moving rapidly from an industrial manufacturing base to a knowledge-based economy. While home to an outstanding collection of public universities, protected natural environments, and an established transportation network, the transition has been an extremely difficult one for the local population. Michigan is one of two states that have lost population since 2000 (2005 U.S. Census) and has witnessed seven consecutive years of net job losses – more than 300,000 manufacturing jobs alone have been lost since 2000.

This transition is most evident in the city of Detroit. Detroit is the home of the American automobile industry and Michigan's largest city. The city is less than 50% of its peak population and continues to lose more than 1,000 residents a month. Detroit has among the highest rates of poverty, unemployment, and crime in the nation. In short, it is a city in a state that is in need of transformative projects.

Taken together, the two case studies represent communities looking to proactively shape their future. Not content with letting the market determine their future, the two communities decided to use civic facilities as a way of leading by example in an attempt to encourage future economic development. Because each of the case studies centers on civic facilities (a city hall and a riverfront park) and the general anxiety about the future of the region, effective public participation was essential.

Population: 140,000
Project site: 17 acres, located in city's civic center
Brownfield issues: Existing city hall; vacant county building; parking lots
Project timeline: 1998–2007
Major project players: City of Warren Mayor's Office and Departmental Staff, JJR, Neumann/Smith Architecture, Skanska USA, Hubbell, Roth & Clark, Inc.
Project program: 112,000 sf city hall/library, 632-space parking structure, 2-acre city square, and 14 blocks of streetscape

Figure 1: City of Warren.

3.1 City of Warren

3.1.1 The project narrative

Founded in 1957, Warren was built around the 900-acre General Motors Technical Center, home to more than 21,000 employees working on automobile engineering and styling for all General Motors products. Additional manufacturing plants and automobile factories soon called Warren home, and the town quickly grew with vast neighborhoods of single-family homes and strip commercial corridors. What was envisioned to be the town's downtown evolved into a series of disconnected buildings surrounded by acres of parking lots further separated by wide boulevards.

By the mid 1980s, population growth stopped, housing values stagnated, and industry began leaving the city for cheaper locations. By 1998, the beginning of a comprehensive visioning effort, the city was slowly losing population, blight was developing on the edges of the community, and there was talk that General Motors would soon leave. Mayor Steenbergh knew that the city needed to act quickly and make a significant investment in its future.

The comprehensive visioning effort focused on what areas needed to be revitalized to appeal to younger workers while offering new retail and housing opportunities to existing residents. Of the six corridors and districts identified, the highest priority was assigned to the city's failed downtown. Through a series of workshops and public meetings, it was determined that a new downtown, complete with a new city hall and library, would be built. The project was completed in 2007, in time for the city's 50th birthday celebration that attracted more than 25,000 residents to the new city center.

While it was an expensive undertaking ($75,000,000 through bonding covered by tax increment financing), more than 80% of the residents who attended workshops favored the project. In one setting, the attendees saw maps that outlined the growth of blighted areas, saw examples of other communities that revitalized themselves through the creation of a new civic center, and heard of the need to create an environment that would appeal to a younger generation. Of particular interest were the 21,000 employees of the General Motors Technical Center – more than half are under the age of 40, and of those, less than 2% live within a 5-mile radius. The average income of a General Motors Technical Center employee is more than $80,000, and very little of that money was staying within the community.

The narrative that guided the project from day one was the need for Warren to be competitive and attract the next generation of workers and employers to the community – things could not stay the same. Residents could see the devastating effects of blight, being so close to Detroit, and it began to creep into their neighborhoods. Waiting wasn't an option. The narrative spoke directly to what the residents were experiencing and addressed their fears/concerns in a positive manner. The ultimate message of the narrative was hopeful and positive – this is the dawn of Warren's next great era.

One aspect that could have been improved upon in the narrative was to better explain how a healthy community center helps all neighborhoods. The few vocal complaints of the project have been that existing residential neighborhoods have been neglected in favor of building a downtown for newcomers. While the idea of the center helping improve the quality of life for all residents was stressed in later phases, it did not fully take root with those nearest to and in blighted areas.

3.1.2 Support a credible champion

The project could not have had a better credible champion. Mayor Steenbergh was an extremely popular mayor who saw the need for his community to change with the times. He put the success of the project on his shoulders and made sure every detail was looked after, and that it represented the values and beliefs of the residents. Mayor Steenbergh made the new city center a focal point of all of his speeches, was completely available to the media, and took an active role in recruiting private sector partners. The mayor was also active in selecting the artist for the monument in the new city square and participated in design charrettes. The project would not have been completed on time, at such a high level of execution without the mayor's ongoing support and drive, or the complete support he had from City of Warren staff.

3.1.3 Take small, connected steps, and stick to a simple schedule

It is essential for transformative projects to have a separate and dedicated group of individuals whose main task is to ensure a successful effort. Hiring a separate project management firm ensured that all parties were on the same page, and knew of meetings and internal deadlines, and that issues were comprehensively covered. Having a defined goal of completing the project in time for Warren's 50th birthday gave everyone a clear target. By starting the planning for a new downtown in 1998 for a phase 1 completion in 2007, no steps were rushed or overlooked, and details were carefully and meticulously addressed.

3.1.4 Manage the project narrative

A quarterly newsletter updated residents on the project's progress. It was made available in print at the existing city hall and online on the City of Warren's website. All meetings held in connection with the project were shown on the community's television access channel, and input from residents was welcomed via the Internet. A day-to-day point person was chosen to handle inquiries and feedback from residents and interested development parties, and to handle media requests.

The point person, Gina Cavaliere, the Downtown Development Authority director, was an integral part of the project's success. She not only wrote the newsletter, but also met with dozens of contractors, assisted in scheduling events to announce the project, and found additional funds to complete the public art in the city square. A valuable lesson learned was recognizing the importance of the point person. There are hundreds of day-to-day items that need to be prioritized and addressed. All of the steps of a carefully thought out plan can be in place, but without an organized and highly effective point person on the community's side, the project will not succeed.

3.1.5 Design flexible solutions

Warren is currently in the process of selling the 17 acres that surround its new city hall, library, and city square. The land for sale is governed by newly adopted urban design guidelines that allow many different land uses, design approaches, and exterior materials. The importance of the city hall and related civic uses are protected through massing, restrictions on entrances, and the shielding of loading docks, parking areas, and HVAC systems. Warren understands that great cities grow over time and require a flexible approach to allow for new ideas and technology. They are entering year 11 of their transformation and are continuing to manage the narrative while visible results are being built every year.

3.2 City of Detroit

3.2.1 The project narrative

The city of Detroit has been losing population and jobs for the last 40 years. Almost 50% of newborns are born into poverty – by far the highest rate for an American city. In 2000, according to the City of Detroit's records, less than 1,000 hew housing units had been created in the last two decades, while more than 10,000 vacant homes were removed in that same time period, with an additional 8,000 on the list to be removed as well. The one bright spot has been the city's downtown. With the announcement and construction of two new

Population: 871,121

Project site: City of Detroit's East RiverWalk, from Hart Plaza to Belle Isle, a distance of 3.5 miles

Brownfield issues: Heavy metals; PCBs; obsolete/abandoned structures; landfills; rotting structural supports adjacent to river; other related industrial issues

Project timeline: 2000–2007

Major Project players: Detroit Riverfront Conservancy, City of Detroit, JJR, SmithGroup, Hines, White/Olson

Project program: 3.5 miles of continuous pathway along the Detroit River, punctuated by six plazas offering a variety of recreational activities

Figure 2: City of Detroit.

stadiums and the renovation of the Renaissance Center – an office complex of more than 3 million square feet of office space converted into the General Motors (GM) World Headquarters – things started looking up.

Hart Plaza was the one public space in downtown that offered access to the Detroit River. It was designed to hold large festivals. Cut off from the rest of the city by an 8-lane road, a 12-lane entrance into the Detroit-Windsor Tunnel, and a private office building, most of the time the plaza felt empty and did not offer any amenities other than views, a large fountain that didn't work, and sun.

The rest of the riverfront was either inaccessible because of private ownership or offered no safe place to sit or walk. If the emerging success of the downtown could be stretched to other parts of the city, it would be along the Detroit River. Many other former industrial cities in the region have converted their waterfronts into park land and successful new neighborhoods to complement their downtown. Detroit firmly believed in this model and started planning for a major riverfront park in 2000.

The project had to be positioned carefully. Many residents thought too much attention and civic resources had already been given to the downtown. Therefore, the announcement of the RiverWalk – the project's official name – was positioned as bringing the river back to the people of Detroit. It was a project for everyone – in the most racially segregated major city in North America, that can be a very difficult sell. The RiverWalk was envisioned to be the place to stroll along the river for many miles, next to cafés, new apartments and town homes, and revitalized neighborhoods. Nowhere in Detroit could a person walk next to the river and be near a café, town home, or even an office.

3.2.2 Support a credible champion:

Detroiters have become weary of large projects. Many major revitalization projects had been promised over the last 40 years. Most never happened, and the few that did very rarely delivered what was promised, with the most famous example being the original Renaissance Center (Ren Cen). The Ren Cen was billed as the rebirth of the entire city of Detroit when it was opened in 1977. Instead, its size and location emptied many existing office buildings into what had been called a suburban bunker. Once in the Ren Cen, few workers ventured out into the city. The city was not saved.

For this project to receive the community backing it needed, a champion with a track record was mandatory. In fact, two champions working together were needed. Matthew Cullen (General Manager, Economic Development and Enterprise Services, General Motors Corporation, and Co-Chair of the Detroit Riverfront Conservancy) and Derrick Miller (Chief Information Officer with the Mayor's Office) worked together from land assemblage to ribbon cutting. Together, they formed a credible champion team that was able to handle issues of race, present a proven track record, and have the experience in communicating both public policy and real estate goals.

3.2.3 Take small, connected steps, and stick to a simple schedule

The completion goal for the RiverWalk was easy to communicate once Detroit was chosen to host the 2006 Super Bowl – the largest single-day sporting event in North America. While January is not the ideal time to enjoy a walk along the Detroit River, it became a matter of pride. When the world was in town for the Super Bowl, the RiverWalk had to be ready. With that goal firmly set and Detroit wanting to demonstrate that it was on its way back, the schedule fell into place with all stakeholders involved.

3.2.4 Manage the project narrative

The fundamental narrative of giving the river back to the community has proven to be a durable and successful message. Over the two-year planning period, there were more than 12 community workshops to ensure that the final plan represented a place that reflected the values and needs of the local residents. The phasing of the workshops allowed residents to offer input on different levels of detail, from master planning to final programming and site details. The workshops even helped shape the characters on the extremely successful carousel ride. Strategically timed press releases, feature articles in the major newspapers, and a special on the coming attractions of the RiverWalk ran on television.

The creation of the Detroit Riverfront Conservancy (DRC) has created a one-stop shop for all things RiverWalk. The DRC gives the citizens of Detroit a way of not only learning more about the project as it grows towards the east side of the city, but also a chance to get involved and even learn about the local ecology. It is another example of giving the river back to the community – an extremely active way to manage the narrative.

3.2.5 Design flexible solutions

There were more than 10 different ownership groups to negotiate in creating the RiverWalk. Getting everyone to agree within the timeline of the Super Bowl became one of the most challenging aspects of the project. As the deadline approached, it became clear that a few temporary solutions would need to be in place in order to meet the larger goal of having a continuous pedestrian experience. At times, the path needed to head inland, more than 200 feet away from the Detroit River's edge. There were, and are, ongoing lawsuits, and there are still brownfield issues not completely resolved, but the larger goal of having a place to take a stroll along the river, complete with cafés, carnival rides, nature, and places to sit quietly was accomplished. In the year that it has been completed, a new 80-unit apartment complex has been constructed and three additional mixed use projects have been approved.

4 Conclusion

Of the five fundamentals outlined in this paper (The Project Narrative; Support a Credible Champion; Take Small, Connected Steps, and Stick to a Strict Schedule; Manage the Narrative; and Design Flexible Solutions), the most important for achieving success is having a credible champion. None of the case study projects would have gone on to become award-winning developments or held up as Best Practices without a well-received credible champion. The case studies show that a proven track record is an essential ingredient for a credible champion along with being highly visible and managing the other three components.

One final lesson is the need to celebrate small successes and to have fun along the way. Brownfield redevelopment requires patience, but it also needs inspiration. The payoff cannot only come at the ribbon cutting – 5 to 10 years after the start of the process. Using the site for a marathon, a county fair, or for holiday decorations (all actual events within the case studies) can help to keep people engaged and hopeful that positive things can happen. Successful public participation in the brownfield redevelopment process maintains a positive outlook and gets things done through active management and alignment of the project's credible champion, narrative, schedule, and ongoing communications.

References

[1] Cavaliere, Gina, Personal Communications, September–December 2007, Downtown Development Authority Director, City of Warren, Michigan
[2] Miller, Derrick, Personal Communications, September–December 2007, Chief Information Officer, City of Detroit Mayor's Office, Detroit, Michigan
[3] Ford School of Public Policy, Personal Communications, September–December 2007, University of Michigan, Ann Arbor, Michigan
[4] Editorial Board, Personal Communications, September–December 2007, The Detroit News, Detroit, Michigan
[5] Office of the Governor, Governor Jennifer M. Granholm, Personal Communications, September–December 2007, State of Michigan, Lansing, Michigan

Choosing a competence based governance role in brownfield redevelopment processes

E. G. J. Blokhuis, W. F. Schaefer, N. van Gogh & A. J. Kleine
Department of Architecture, Building and Planning,
Chair Construction Management and Urban Development,
Eindhoven University of Technology, the Netherlands

Abstract

The redevelopment of brownfields in the Netherlands stagnates. The fact that the central directing role of municipalities is abandoned is often considered as a cause of the stagnation occurring within these processes. Currently, municipalities can only manage brownfield developments in strategic alliances with different public and private actors. The precise role of municipalities as governor within these alliances is still very indistinct. This paper describes a software model that enables municipalities to determine a suitable governance role in brownfield redevelopment processes. This is realised by distinguishing four types of governance roles and four factors determining the necessity of involving actors in the process. Depending on the presence of these factors in a brownfield redevelopment project, the suitability of the several governance roles can be specified. The method also offers municipalities the possibility of developing their capabilities and related levels of competences based on the predefined governance role they want to practice.

Keywords: brownfield redevelopment, municipal governance, roles and competences, stakeholder involvement, process guidance model.

1 Introduction

The Dutch government is facing a constantly growing need for redevelopment of ageing brownfields [3]. The arising redevelopment projects are very complex because of the network of economical, political, administrative and legal concerns, physical restrictions and diverging social influences [1]. Current redevelopment projects stagnate because of a lack of insight in the guiding role

www.witpress.com, ISSN 1743-3541 (on-line)
doi:10.2495/BF080241

of municipalities [1]. This municipal guiding role has undergone a number of important changes in the previous decades.

The changed positions of market parties and their bigger influence on land exploitation made the exertion of governmental process control increasingly weak [5]. To a great extent municipalities have abandoned their central directing role and are therefore only able to manage redevelopment projects through strategic alliances with different public and private actors each having their own specific interests. The precise role of municipalities as governor within these alliances is still very indistinct.

The research focuses on the determination and development of governance roles and their contributing characteristics related to the ambitions and competencies of the municipalities combined with relevant project and process characteristics. This research resulted in a supportive management method to determine the governance role for municipalities involved in brownfield redevelopments.

2 Problem elucidation

In the late nineties, Dutch municipalities could operate fairly autonomous in brownfield development projects, and were able to draw up a plan on the basis of their own insights [4]. Municipalities had several financial instruments at their disposal to secure their position and role, and market parties were mostly not interested in land exploitation because of the market conditions. Because of the changed market conditions, e.g. the bigger influence of market parties on land exploitation, municipal control in these projects decreased.

Brownfields are no longer (re)developed by top down governmental steering [8]. In the growingly complex society, pluricentric network steering – in which several public and private parties play a role – seems more suitable [6]. In current brownfield (re)development processes, the municipality is largely dependent on the behavior and interests of other parties, mostly of landowners and other parties with formal positions in the plan area. The municipality must integrally assess these interests, taking into account the public interest, and integrate the result of this assessment into a plan with a firm social basis [9].

While respecting the responsibilities and relative independence of the parties involved in brownfield redevelopments, the parties usually need stable governance, in which the main direction is monitored, the tempo is raised, the most important decisions are coordinated and the relation with laws and legislation and the public responsibilities are always monitored. Without governance, brownfield redevelopments come to a standstill and implementations gaps or – even worse – contradictions between urban strategy and actual implementation arise [6]. This is the main problem treated in this paper. To prevent the occurrence thereof, municipalities must make a choice regarding their governing role depending on their resources. This has been elaborated in section 3 of this paper. Section 4 describes the development of a decision support model.

2.1 Governing brownfield redevelopment processes

This research handles governance as a particular form of steering: exercising guided influence in a process. Moreover, governance refers to combining separate components into one plan. Thus, governance encloses steering as well as coordinating activities. In this research, we define governance as 'the way in which the municipality gives direction to a brownfield redevelopment, thereby taking into account the interests of all public and private parties involved and the common interest, aimed at guaranteeing a certain result'.

The aim of the municipal governance within brownfield redevelopment projects is to establish cooperation between relevant parties, in order to realize a number of functions and purposes from a public, social importance. The reason to adopt a governance role in a redevelopment project is mostly aimed at controlling a number of aspects. The most important are (1) quality of the project, in relation to other policy fields; (2) relation with the program and the market; (3) financial dimension and feasibility; and (4) time dimension [4].

3 Assumptions and findings

The goal of this research is to develop a method that enables municipalities to select the governance role and the related competences in order to successfully guide brownfield redevelopment processes. To reach this goal, several research steps are necessary. These research steps concern roughly the specification of governance roles, relating the governance roles to current cooperation-forms, and specifying the criteria determining these roles. These steps will be treated below.

3.1.1 Specification of governance roles

The governance role can be designed in different ways. We distinguish four types of governance roles by means of two variables [7]: (1) Does the governor have perseverance? In other words: can the governor imply his will on other relevant involved parties? (2) Does the governor write his own script or policy, or is the governor dependent on other actors?

Putting these two variables into a matrix (see figure 2) leads to the identification of four types of governance roles: (1) *Independent governance role*: governor derives his strong position from a high level of perseverance and a low level of dependency on other actors in writing policy; (2) *Outsourcing governance role*: governor has a high level of perseverance, but is dependent on other actors when writing policy; (3) *Co-operating governance role*: governor has the privilege to write his own policy, but lacks the required power sources to force other actors to cooperate in executing this policy, whereas the governor is dependent on these actors. In the quest for agreement, the cooperating director is willing to accept compromises on his own policy; and (4) *Regulating governance role*: governor has a servicing role in the negotiation. Regulating governors are not able to put their policy first, but regulates to partly control the policy of other actors, and to check the proposed policies to the appointed project scope.

3.1.2 Relating governance roles to cooperation-forms

In the Netherlands, five cooperation-forms can be distinguished that are regularly applied in brownfield (re)development projects. Figure 1 represents these five forms on a scale of required interaction. The joint venture has the greatest level of public-private interaction.

- (I) Public development with private execution
- Public-private partnerships, encompassing
    - (II) building-claims relationships
    - (III) joint venture relationships
    - (IV) concession-based relationships
- (V) Private development and execution in accordance with public law

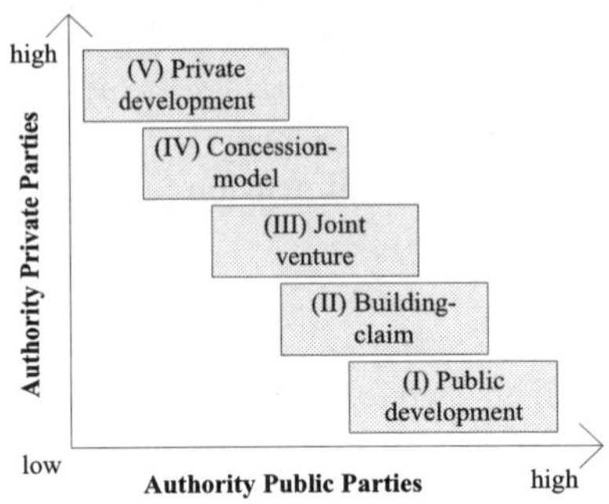

Figure 1: Level of interaction between parties in different cooperation-forms.

		Level of dependency in script-writing	
		Low	High
Level of perseverance	High	(1) Independent governor (I) Public development	(2) Outsourcing governor (III) Concession model
	Low	(3) Cooperating governor (II) Building claim (IV) Concession model	(4) Regulating Governor (V) Private development

Figure 2: Governance roles related to forms of cooperation.

The above mentioned findings resulted in a matrix showing the relation between the governance roles and current cooperation-forms (see figure 2).

3.1.3 Criteria determining the appropriateness of governance roles

The appropriateness of a certain governance role in a given situation is determined by several factors. In this research we limit this to four factors [4]:

- Competencies: internal municipal organization, capacity and quality, harmonization and decision-making, presence of process memory and continuity, knowledge of procedures in public and private law;
- Landownership: municipal ownership, level of fragmentation in the property situation, number of stakeholders;
- Uncertainties and risks: market developments, demographic developments, soil pollution, behavior of residents and other actors, uncertainty concerning the competencies of the municipality and the way in which the project is dependent on these uncertainties;
- Complexity: the scale of the project, the program that must be realized, the number of players.

These factors determine the necessity to involve actors in the governance process related to the positions they possess and the objectives they pursuit. This means that the level of knowledge regarding these factors determines the quality of governance according a selected role by the municipality.

4 Supportive management model

In this research, the four factors – as mentioned above – determine the necessity of involving actors in the process, and what position they possess. Depending on the presence of these factors and on the mutual relation, the suitability of the several governance roles can be specified. To determine the level of presence of these factors in a brownfield redevelopment project, we conducted literature research, which led to the determination of the most important level qualifying variables per factor. These level qualifying variables formed the basis of the composition a software tool with four questionnaires. A project can be objectively assessed by weighing the several variables in the questionnaires.

4.1.1 Factor 1: municipal competences and capacity

The seven aspects are grouped in three areas: internal municipal organisation, knowledge about procedures related to public and private law, as well as municipal capacity. For each aspect a weigh factor is indicated (table 1).

The total qualification score represents the level of municipal competency and capacity. In table 2, an arbitrary partition of the level scores is shown.

The third step is to relate the qualification score to the five possible cooperation-forms to indicate the most suitable role of the municipality regarding this factor. A graphical representation of the total results in a perspective regarding the extent to which the municipality is able to fulfil its role along the scale of possible forms of cooperation is shown in figure 3.

Table 1: Variables composing the level of municipal competence and capacity.

Level qualifying variables		**Weigh factor**
	Internal municipal organisation	
1	Internal coordination	… (0 to 20)
2	Decision making	… (0 to 20)
3	Process memory	… (0 to 15)
4	Continuity	… (0 to 5)
	Knowledge about private and public law procedures	
5	Contracts	… (0 to 20)
6	Rules	… (0 to 20)
	Municipal capacity	
7	Capacity	… (-100 (no) or 0)
Total qualification score (sum of weigh factors of all variables)		**…**

Table 2: Qualification levels of municipal competency and capacity.

Qualification table of competency- and capacity-level		
-	Low level of competencies / capacity	<0 to 33 points
+/-	Moderate level of competencies / capacity	34 to 66 points
+	High level of competencies / capacity	67 to 100 points

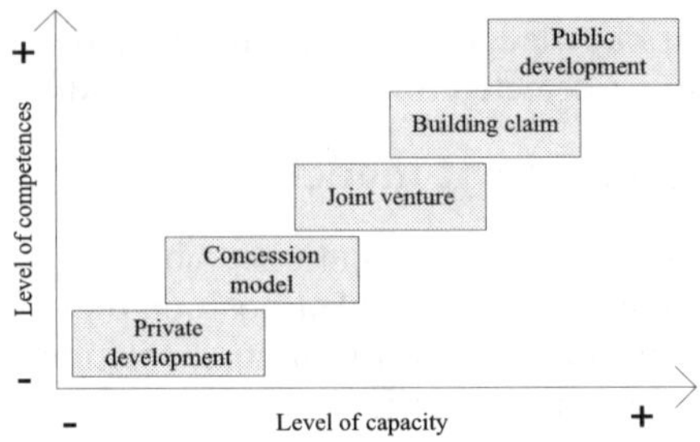

Figure 3: Levels of competencies and capacities related to cooperation-forms.

4.1.2 Factor 2: project risks

The estimated magnitude of a risk can be estimated by multiplying the expected level of the chance of its occurrence with the level of expected consequences. Table 3 lists twenty-seven important project risks categorized in six groups. Applicants have to validate the risks by attributing a weigh factor to the estimated occurrence and the estimated consequences.

The total qualification score represents the level of project risk magnitude. In table 4, an arbitrary partition of the level scores is showed.

The effectiveness of managing risks within different governance roles is attributed to the relation between an estimated risk level and the level of authority of the governor to influence the chance on occurrence of the risk. The higher his authority, the more likely it is that the effect of his influence will contribute to a reduction of the estimated risk magnitude. The relation between the total estimated risk magnitude and the determined level of authority gives an indication in which cooperation form the governor has the biggest influence on risk reduction. A graphical representation of the total results in a perspective regarding the extent to which the municipality is able to fulfil its role along the scale of possible forms of cooperation is shown in figure 4.

4.1.3 Factor 3: project complexity

Complexity of a project is the third factor contributing to dependency on other actors. The questionnaire to validate the level of complexity is described below (table 5).

The total qualification score represents the level of project complexity. In table 6, an arbitrary partition of the level scores is showed.

The controllability of projects depends not only on the level of complexity but also on the number of parties involved. A graphical representation of the total results in a perspective regarding the extent to which the municipality is able to fulfil its role along the scale of possible cooperation-forms is shown in figure 5.

4.1.4 Factor 4: division of landownership

The factor landownership is the fourth origin that plays a role in the reciprocal dependency of actors. Two variables are presumed to be of high importance: (1) the percentage of public landownership; and (2) the number of private landowners. It is clear that having a high percentage of landownership and a low

Table 3: Variables composing the level of project risk magnitude.

Level qualifying variables		Occurrence (a)	Consequence (b)	Magnitude
Risks in the plan area				
1	Ownerships	… (1 to 4)	… (1 to 4)	… (a * b)
2	Soil research	… (1 to 4)	… (1 to 4)	… (a * b)
3	Buildings	… (1 to 4)	… (1 to 4)	… (a * b)
4	Flora en Fauna	… (1 to 4)	… (1 to 4)	… (a * b)
5	Existing greenery	… (1 to 4)	… (1 to 4)	… (a * b)
6	Connection to ext. roads	… (1 to 4)	… (1 to 4)	… (a * b)
7	Land surveying	… (1 to 4)	… (1 to 4)	… (a * b)
8	Image	… (1 to 4)	… (1 to 4)	… (a * b)
Risks in the environment (surroundings)				
9	Stakeholders	… (1 to 4)	… (1 to 4)	… (a * b)
10	Positioning	… (1 to 4)	… (1 to 4)	… (a * b)
11	Environmental aspects	… (1 to 4)	… (1 to 4)	… (a * b)
12	Infrastructure	… (1 to 4)	… (1 to 4)	… (a * b)
13	Surrounding buildings	… (1 to 4)	… (1 to 4)	… (a * b)
14	Damage caused by planning	… (1 to 4)	… (1 to 4)	… (a * b)
15	Business rights	… (1 to 4)	… (1 to 4)	… (a * b)
16	Accessibility of plan area	… (1 to 4)	… (1 to 4)	… (a * b)
Risks concerning the organisation				
17	Actors	… (1 to 4)	… (1 to 4)	… (a * b)
18	Public parties	… (1 to 4)	… (1 to 4)	… (a * b)
19	Private parties	… (1 to 4)	… (1 to 4)	… (a * b)
20	Composition	… (1 to 4)	… (1 to 4)	… (a * b)
Risks concerning policy				
21	Policy framework	… (1 to 4)	… (1 to 4)	… (a * b)
22	Preconditions	… (1 to 4)	… (1 to 4)	… (a * b)
Financial risks				
23	Investments	… (1 to 4)	… (1 to 4)	… (a * b)
24	Financing	… (1 to 4)	… (1 to 4)	… (a * b)
25	Exploitation	… (1 to 4)	… (1 to 4)	… (a * b)
External risks				
26	Media	… (1 to 4)	… (1 to 4)	… (a * b)
27	Market conditions	… (1 to 4)	… (1 to 4)	… (a * b)
Total qualification score (sum of magnitudes of all variables)				**…**

Table 4: Qualification levels of project risk magnitude.

Qualification table of level of project risk magnitude		
-	Low level of project risk magnitude	27 to 72 points
+/-	Moderate level of project risk magnitude	73 to 162 points
+	High level of project risk magnitude	163 to 432 points

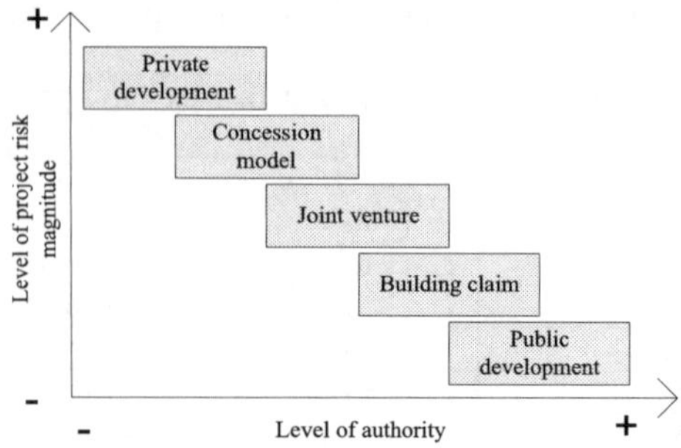

Figure 4: Levels of authority and project risks related to cooperation-forms.

Table 5: Variables composing the level of project complexity.

Level qualifying variables		**Weigh factor**
	Decision making	
1	Actors	… (0 to 5)
2	Interests	… (0 to 25)
3	Dependency	… (0 to 10)
4	Pluriformity	… (0 to 10)
5	Resistance	… (0 to 5)
	Problem / program	
6	Junction of functions	… (0 to 15)
7	Mixture of functions	… (0 to 10)
8	Realization	… (0 to 10)
	Scale	
9	Dimensions of plan area	… (0 to 10)
Total qualification score (sum of weigh factors of all variables)		**…**

Table 6: Qualification levels of project complexity.

Qualification table of project complexity level		
-	Low level of project complexity	0 to 33 points
+/-	Moderate level of project complexity	34 to 66 points
+	High level of project complexity	67 to 100 points

number of other private landowners stands for a strong municipal position. The graphical representation below (figure 6) shows this relationship and enables the governor to determine his position in the management roles of co-operation.

4.2 Combining the four questionnaires

Based on the previous paragraph, table 7 shows an overview of the possible combinations. The five cooperation-forms and corresponding governance roles are represented on the left; the four factors determining the necessity of involving actors in the process are represented above. The marks represent the principles that fit to a certain governance role.

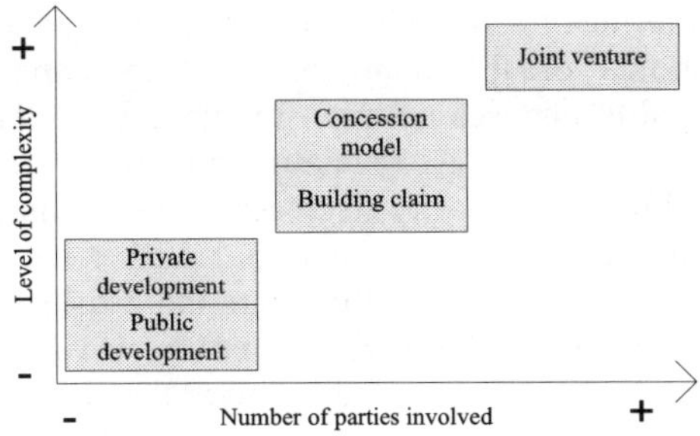

Figure 5: Levels of complexity and number of parties related to cooperation-forms.

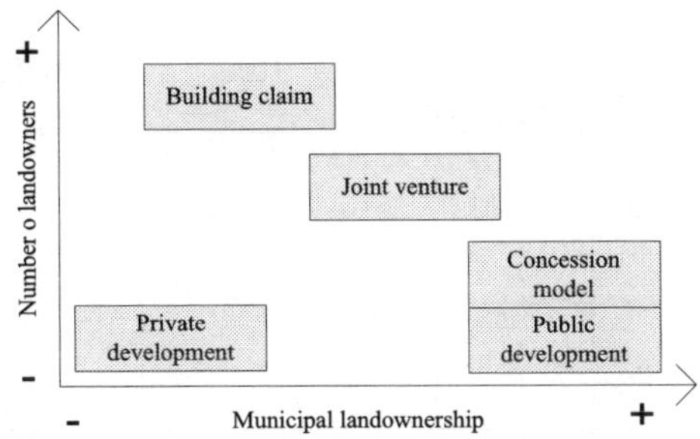

Figure 6: Levels of municipal landownership and percentage of public landowners related to cooperation-forms.

4.3 Changeability of variables

The level of changeability of the different factors is assumed to be decisive for the choice of a cooperation-form and thus of a governance role. Factors that cannot be changed are leading in this choice, and easily changeable factors can reinforce the profile of the factor. Changeability of factors is therefore a means to reach up to one of the five cooperation-forms.

Changeability is related to the strengthening of the profile of a factor. When the risk profile is very high and moderately changeable, one can choose for a cooperation-form with a medium risk profile (see figure 7). Because of the moderate level of changeability, the outcome can move 1 box to the left. When a factor can be changed easily, the outcome can move 2 boxes. The degree of changeability of the four factors is determined by the user of the management tool, on the scale (1) not (black), (2) moderately (grey) or (3) easily (white)).

In the example of figure 7, landownership is the leading factor because of the low changeability. Table 7 shows that – with this level of landownership – the cooperation forms 'joint venture' and 'building claim' are suitable. Also, the municipality can choose for a private development. Following on landownership, the risk profile is leading because of its moderate changeability. The cooperation form 'building claim' is not suitable, because of the required low risk level. To implement a joint venture, the municipality has to change the risk level of the project. The remaining factors are both easily changeable, and do not change the cooperation-form choice of the municipality. Depending on the preferred position, the municipality chooses between regulating in a private development or cooperating in a joint venture. As regulating governor, the municipality bears relatively low risks, but the authority decreases. The municipality should state clear rules in this situation, and has to monitor whether the rules are complied. As cooperating governor, the municipality bears more risks, but is better able to control the contents of the brownfield redevelopment. However, the municipality should extend her level of competences and lower the risk profile of the project when choosing to cooperate.

Table 7: Overview of governance roles with suiting profiles of the four factors.

		Capacity / competence			Risks			Complexity			Land-ownership		
		-	+/-	+	-	+/-	+	-	+/-	+	-	+/-	+
Independent governor / public development													
PPP	Cooperating governor / building claim												
PPP	Cooperating governor / joint venture												
PPP	Outsourcing governor / concession model												
Regulating governor / private development													

Capacity / competence			Risks			Complexity			Land-ownership		
-	+/-	+	-	+/-	+	-	+/-	+	-	+/-	+
x					x		x			x	

Figure 7: Example of changeability of factors.

5 Validation of the research results

The validation of the findings, their interpretation and the ways they are combined are validated by an expert panel (see [2]). The method designed was also validated. Moreover, the method was successfully applied to two cases. Minor adaptations were implemented as a result of the validations. These were mostly related to interpretation of terms.

6 Conclusions

The first conclusions concern scientific relevance of our research. To get a grip on the changing role of municipalities in brownfield redevelopment processes, we distinguished four governance roles: (1) independent governor; (2) outsourcing governor; (3) cooperating governor; and (4) regulating governor. Furthermore, we distinguish four factors – competence / capacity, risks, complexity and landownership – determining the necessity of involving actors in the process. Depending on the presence of these factors and on the mutual relation, the suitability of the several governance roles can be specified.

Secondly, to cover societal relevance, we developed a supportive management software tool enabling municipalities to determine a suiting governance role in the process of redevelopment of brownfields. The other way around a municipality could fully develop a preferred governance role by improving its performances to the levels as mentioned in the different sections of this supportive management method.

References

[1] Blokhuis and Schaefer (2007) *A sustainable approach for industrial area redevelopment in the Netherlands* – printed in: Sustainable Development and Planning III, Vol. 1. (pp. 81-93) ISBN 978-1-84564-069-9. WIT Press.

[2] Gogh, N. van (2005) *In de greep van gebiedsontwikkeling, beslisondersteunend instrument voor de invulling van de gemeentelijke regierol bij binnenstedelijke herontwikkeling* – graduation report, Eindhoven University of Technology, chair Construction Management.

[3] Graaf, R.S. de (2005) *Strategic Urban Planning – industrial area development in the Netherlands, to direct or to interact?* Thesis, University of Twente, Enschede.

[4] Korthals Altes, W. et al. (2004) *Organisatie van prestatie, regie in de stedelijke ontwikkeling* – VNG – Den Haag.

[5] Louw, E. (2000) *The production of business sites in the Netherlands* - in: Tijdschrift voor Economische en Sociale Geografie, vol 91, nr. 1, pp 85–91.

[6] Priemus, H. (2006) *Stedelijke strategieën en stedelijke regie* - In s.n. (Ed.), Strategieën voor stedelijke vernieuwing (pp. 1–8). Eindhoven University of Technology.

[7] Pröpper, I. et al. (2004) *Lokale regie uit macht of onmacht? Onderzoek naar de optimalisering van de gemeentelijke regiefunctie* – Report under authority of the Dutch Ministry of Internal Affairs - Vught, the Netherlands.

[8] Valk, A. van der (2002) *The Dutch planning experience* - in: Landscape and Urban Planning 58 (201–210) - Elsevier Science – London.

[9] Whitman, I.L. (2006) *Brownfield redevelopment by the private sector: market driven decision making* – paper presented at conference Brownfields III, Prevention, Assessment, Rehabilitation and Development of Brownfield Sites - WIT Conference – Tallinn, Estonia.

Perception of private and public sectors of the regeneration of post-industrial areas in Japan

H. Kurata[1], H. Abe[1] & N. Otsuka[2]
[1]*Graduate School of Engineering, Osaka University, Japan*
[2]*Oxford Brookes University, School of the Built Environment, UK*

Abstract

The aim of this study is to examine private and public sector perceptions of the redevelopment of post-industrial areas. It clarifies the barriers to such regeneration, and the areas of improvement currently being sought by stakeholders in Japan, where this issue has only just begun to surface. This study was conducted using a questionnaire distributed to public and private enterprises in December 2006. The results showed that among private enterprises there was widespread demand for the government to relax regulations and establish a regulatory system, while local governments were facing cost-related issues concerning the cleanup of soil contamination. In addition, since these issues relate to both urban development and environmental protection, we can see differences of opinion between construction-related and environment-related organizations, suggesting that the vertical division of government organizations may also be a hurdle to resolving these issues.
Keywords: brownfield sites, contamination, stakeholder.

1 Introduction

In order to abide by the Kyoto Protocol that has now come into force, governments must enact policies to reduce emissions of greenhouse gases. In addition, there has already been discussion of setting further reduction targets for the years after 2013, creating a pressing need for environmental regulations and energy-conservation policies. As a result, fundamental changes in our fossil fuel-dependent society and industries are believed to be inevitable. In developed countries in particular, the restructuring or relocation of industrial facilities that have heretofore supported these countries' economic growth have led to

WIT Transactions on Ecology and the Environment, Vol 107, © 2008 WIT Press
www.witpress.com, ISSN 1743-3541 (on-line)
doi:10.2495/BF080251

increasingly large areas of unused land, or land that has no prospect of being reused (hereafter "brownfields") [1, 9]. Due to this situation, what is most important now is not the development of natural land or forests, but rather the redevelopment of unused, previously developed land [10]. The appropriate use and redevelopment of such land can be expected to involve issues related to the cleanup of contamination and the improvement of living and working environments. There are many barriers to this redevelopment, except near large metropolitan centers where such land can be expected to bring generous profits [2]. Accordingly, the first goal of this paper is to examine the views of the various stakeholders involved in brownfields redevelopment.

2 Policy context and background

Research into the issue of brownfields in Japan has included a comparative study of policy frameworks to deal with the cleanup of contamination in Europe and Japan by Miyagawa and Nakayama [3, 4], and a report illustrating a number of detailed examples of brownfields policies in the United States by Kurose and Murayama [5]. In addition, Kitazawa et al. [6] and Kitazawa and Nohara [7] performed an investigation and analysis of policies on the growing number of post-industrial sites in the Tokyo Bay area. However, only recently have the problems associated with brownfields come to be recognized in Japan, and we can expect increasingly serious efforts to tackle these problems in the coming years.

Let us first review the development of laws to deal with environmental pollution in Japan. An incident involving cadmium led to two laws on water quality being passed in the 1950s, while the discovery of the Minamata disease (mercury poisoning) in the 1960s led to the establishment of the Basic Law for Environmental Pollution Control. In 1970, the discovery of hexavalent chromium in agricultural products led to the enactment of the first law on the cleanup of contaminated land, known as the Agricultural Land Soil Pollution Prevention Law. There was little interest in soil pollution thereafter, until the discovery of dioxin contamination at the waste treatment facility in Nose-cho in 1997, and the enactment of 2001 Law Concerning Special Measures Against Dioxins. Awareness of soil contamination related to post-industrial brownfields came to the fore after the Mitsubishi Estate failed to report soil and groundwater contaminations at the site of the Osaka Amenity Park in 2002. It was only in 2003 that the Soil Contamination Countermeasures Law was enacted. In 2007, the Ministry of the Environment released the Current Status of the Brownfields Issue in Japan Interim Report, which estimated the scale of potential brownfields in Japan and identified the possibility of this becoming a major social issue [8, 11].

At the same time, in the area of urban renewal, the Urban Renaissance Headquarters was established within the Cabinet Office in 2001 and the Urban Renewal Special Measures Law was passed in 2003. Nevertheless, the stated purpose of this law was "to respond to changes in socioeconomic circumstances, including digitization, internationalization, declining birthrate, ageing population, improvement of urban living conditions, and enhancement of urban services", making it primarily an economic, rather than environmental, measure that prioritized living conditions in urban areas. Although the government has since established the Headquarters for Revitalization of Central Urban Districts and the Headquarters for Regional Revitalization, and identified key areas for renewal and enacted measures to revitalize the economy, these have had almost no implications for environmental policies (sustainable development). Even so, the effects of an increase in under-used land brought on by changes in the industrial structure, similar to those experienced by other developed nations, and the enactment of the Soil Contamination Countermeasures Law in 2003, will begin to highlight the brownfield issues in Japan.

3 Research question and methodology

This paper aims to explore public and private sector initiatives in the area of brownfield redevelopment and clarify public and private perceptions of this issue. The objective is to clarify what stakeholders expect of the national government, the barriers to redevelopment and other issues in Japan, where brownfield redevelopment initiatives have yet to gain much attention.

To that end, the authors created a questionnaire examining respondents' opinions of the current status of brownfields, redevelopment methods and problem areas. The survey was carried out as outlined below.

The questionnaire was distributed to public organizations and private enterprises in December 2006 via the national postal service or through e-mail. The questionnaire contained a total of 16 questions, combining both multiple-choice questions and questions where respondents filled in their answers.

The questionnaire subjects were selected from those organizations and enterprises believed to be the primary stakeholders in brownfield redevelopment. Public-sector organizations that were targeted included the 4 relevant divisions of government organizations, 47 prefectural and city governments, and 15 government-designated cities. A total of 19 private enterprises were targeted, including general contractors, developers, financial institutions, consultants and NPOs (Non-Profit Organization). As shown in Table 1, the response rate from local authorities was the highest, scoring 50%, while the overall response rate was 46%.

Table 1: Response rate.

	Sample size	Response rate
Government	4	1 (25%)
Local Authorities	62	31 (50%)
Private enterprise	19	7 (37%)
Total	85	39 (46%)

4 Main findings from the research

The following sections address the main questions and results related to the above objectives, and provide analysis and discussion of these results.

4.1 Perception of the current status of brownfields

According to the answers to the question, "What is your opinion of the status of current post-industrial land?" shown in Fig. 1, the response of most local authorities was that the number of such sites was either increasing or had not changed (58%), while the majority of private enterprises replied that the number was decreasing (71%). Public and private respondents who said that the number was increasing listed the shifting of manufacturing centers overseas and changes in the structure of industry as causes of this increase. Among those who stated that the number of sites was decreasing, many expressed the opinion that those sites worth investing in had already been redeveloped. In other words, it seems this difference in perception has been caused because local authorities are concerned by post-industrial land within their own communities, while private enterprises see the issue on a national scale, and consider post-industrial sites to be worth using for real estate.

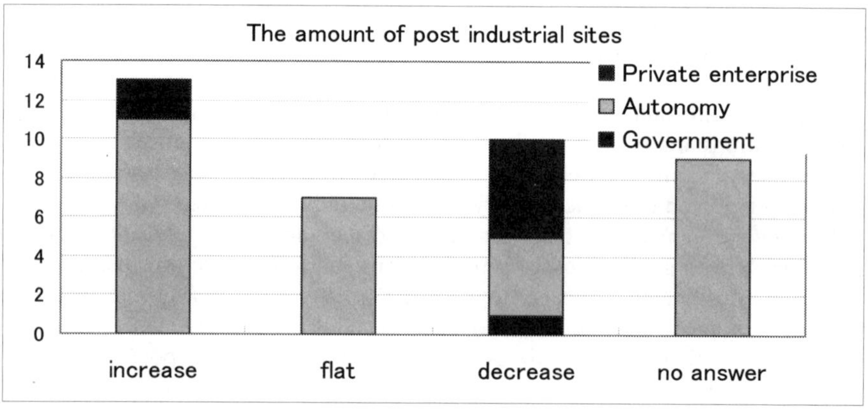

Figure 1: Answers to the question "What is your opinion of the status of current post-industrial land?".

4.2 Barriers to the redevelopment of brownfields

A sample of the responses to the question, "What are the barriers to brownfield redevelopment?" is provided below.

[Private sector]

- Regulations on the purpose of use, contamination cleanup measures, and lack of urban infrastructure

- Disorganized redevelopment procedures
- When the cleanup of soil contamination is required, there is a major issue as to whether the cost of such cleanup matches the need for land
- Risks of land, such as soil contamination, and the necessary procedures and costs needed to remove them

[Public sector]
- Private Owners have legal rights to post-industrial land
- Residents living near the site, landowners and government each have their own agendas regarding the reuse of the land
- Increasing availability of residential land in suburbs, and the reduced demand for development within downtown cores due to the transfer of public institutions

Both public and private sector respondents mentioned regulations on the purpose of use, contamination cleanup measures, and the lack of urban infrastructure. Private sector respondents mention the disorganized procedures associated with development and the high costs involved in identifying and removing soil contamination, reflecting the opinions of developers engaged in the actual land redevelopment. Public sector respondents, by contrast, tend to look at the difficulties in promoting redevelopment, such as the difficulty in identifying effective ways to reuse the land that will be supported by all stakeholders when the location is unfavorable, such as in the suburbs. Clearly, there are many barriers facing both groups, and it will be necessary for the national government to give sufficient consideration to both sides when formulating policies to resolve these issues.

4.3 Issues in contamination cleanup measures and policies

In response to the question, "Do you believe there are problems with current soil contamination cleanup measures and policies?", about 70% of the respondents answered affirmatively, as shown in Fig. 2.

A summary of the comments provided by those who stated that there were problems is provided below.

[Private sector]
- Because there are no official evaluation standards for soil contamination cleanup measures, it is relatively difficult to ensure an objective level of reassurance after cleanup has been completed
- There are few incentives to clean up contaminated soil in Japan

[Public sector]
- Land is a private asset, and, under articles 3 and 4 of the relevant law, it is the responsibility of the land owner rather than the user to survey the land. However, many land owners rent out the land without understanding the relevant regulations, and there can be trouble when the user of the land goes out of business

- Surveys specified by the Soil Contamination Countermeasures Law only apply to specific sites
- The current Soil Contamination Countermeasures Law has transitional regulations for land measuring up to 300 m^2 to be exempted from surveys related to the amount of harmful substances contained in soil, and therefore the land can be sold without identifying whether there is soil or groundwater contamination
- As there are many costs involved in cleaning up soil contamination, a support system is necessary

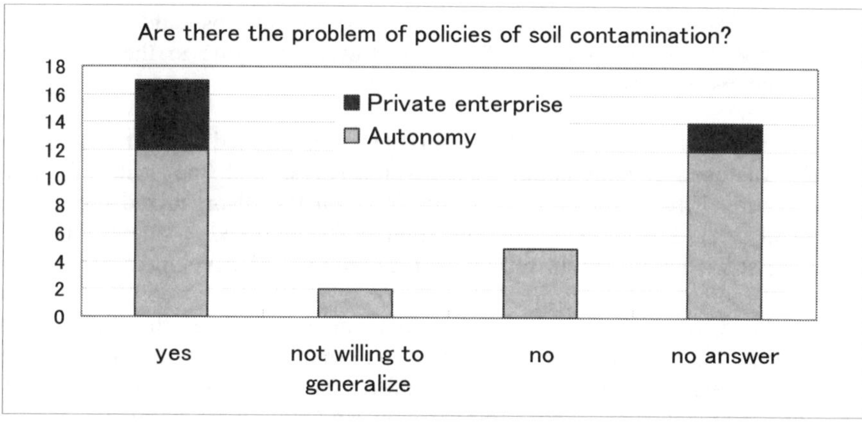

Figure 2: Answers to the question "Do you believe there are problems with current soil contamination cleanup measures and policies?".

Next, the comments provided in response to the question, "What will be required in the future?" is summarized below.

[Private sector]

- Real estate owners, users, intermediaries and others must become more knowledgeable about soil contamination, and an appropriate market must be organized
- In order to support the redevelopment of factory sites, we need flexible, forward-thinking soil contamination cleanup measures, and a local support system to consider the best method of land development
- A certain amount of public funding is required

[Public sector]

- It is extremely difficult to survey soil conditions while the land is in use, but we need a system in which such surveys are actively pursued
- There needs to be a better balance between soil contamination cleanup policies and private ownership

- There must be methods to help pay for the costs of contamination surveys and cleanup measures, as well as risk communication methods
- In order to identify areas of soil contamination as quickly as possible, there need to be legal regulations requiring surveys to be carried out whenever there is a change in the shape or use of the land, as well as regular surveys for business locations using harmful substances
- The development of low-cost and effective contamination cleanup measures and technologies is required

As shown above, private enterprises think that the current system does not reflect the reality on the ground, listing issues such as the lack of official evaluation standards, the fact that blanket regulations mean that occasionally unnecessary measures must be taken when there is a change in the purpose of use, strict measures which place the burden of risk on private enterprises, etc. For the future measures, they call for drastic revision of the Soil Contamination Countermeasures Law. In contrast, local government authorities suggest that this law lacks detail concerning surveys. They point out that for land measuring up to 300 m^2, there are transitional regulations to exempt it from surveys related to the amount of harmful substances contained in soil, and therefore the land can be sold without identifying whether or not there is soil or groundwater contamination. Others argue that, under the provision of Article 3 of the Soil Contamination Countermeasures Law, dry cleaning businesses, plating factories and other small and medium-sized businesses receive a reprieve of survey because they lack the funds to carry out such surveys and clean up contamination. As a result, soil contamination goes untreated. Furthermore, there is even a risk that the contamination could spread. Still others see a problem in the fact that surveys mandated under Article 3 of the Soil Contamination Countermeasures Law could be delayed as long as the land is in use. These respondents call for low-cost and effective survey methods and the provision of support funds. Underlying these opinions is the issue that government cleanup standards are not set for the use of the land after its redevelopment, and at present all brownfields must be completely cleaned of contaminants. In the United States, all those connected with the site are retroactively responsible for contamination; however, in Japan, only the land owner is held responsible, regardless of the responsibility for the actual contamination. Since most land owners deposit the land as collateral, fear of a decrease in the value of their real estate may lead land owners to conceal the presence of contamination in their properties.

5 Conclusions

Looking at the results of the questionnaire, we can see that there are several gaps in the perceptions of public and private sectors. Real issues seen by private sector respondents include disorganized brownfield development procedures, a lack of precise survey standards, and other barriers to daily business operations. Private enterprises value profit more than governments, and therefore they tend to focus on development of the best locations. In order to promote the development of idle land and areas of comparatively low value, private enterprises need to receive sufficient revenue from the development. In order to achieve this, the government needs to establish a framework that will provide sufficient benefits so as to make development of suburbs more attractive. In addition, there are widespread calls for a relaxation of regulations and the clear establishment of a system. In contrast, local authorities are pursuing the redevelopment of post-industrial sites for urban development or infrastructure, regardless of the scale, and yet they face difficulties securing sufficient funds to survey soil contamination and pay for the cost of cleanup. In addition, answers received from local authorities show a difference in opinions between construction-related and environment-related departments, as the questionnaire contained questions on both urban development and environmental protection. This suggests that the vertical division of government organizations is also something of a stumbling block.

In the future, we plan to focus on specific, marginal areas, and examine problems in the local brownfield development initiatives of authorities. In addition, we will perform comparative studies to determine if there are any lessons Japan can draw from cases in the UK and other developed nations.

References

[1] Sandra Alker, "The Definition of Brownfield, Journal of Environmental Planning and Management", 43(1), pp 49–69, 2000

[2] Miki Muraki, "Sustainable Development for the realization of the ideal study on urban planning: British low focused on the environmental impact of the regeneration of unused land", Journal of City Planning Institute of Japan, Issues of urban planning, No.38, pp 331–336, 2003

[3] Tomoko Miyagawa, Toru Nakayama, "Comparison of national acts on treating land contamination in Japan, The Netherlands, Germany, and The United Kingdom: Study on approaches to treat land contamination and redevelopment of brownfields Part 1", Journal of architecture, planning and environmental engineering. Transactions of AIJ (Architectural Institute of Japan), No.547, p.177, 2001

[4] Tomoko Miyagawa, Toru Nakayama, "An examination on integrated planning of treatment and reuse/redevelopment of contaminated land: Study on approaches to treat land contamination and redevelopment of brownfields Part 2", Journal of architecture, planning and environmental engineering. Transactions of AIJ, No.565, p.209, 2003

[5] Takefumi Kurose, Aki Murayama, "Strategy for Brownfield Redevelopment on Local Cities in the U.S.: Case studies of cities in New England", Summaries of technical papers of Annual Meeting Architectural Institute of Japan. F-1, Urban planning, building economics and housing problems, p.223, 2006

[6] Takeru Kitazawa, Taku Nohara, Noriko Akita, "The Framework for the Spatial Planning Process on the Sustainable Urban Regeneration in Keihin

Seaboard Area: A Study on the Sustainable Regeneration in Keihin Seaboard Area, Part1" Summaries of technical papers of Annual Meeting Architectural Institute of Japan. F-1, Urban planning, building economics and housing problems, p.675, 2005

[7] Takeru Kitazawa, Taku Nohara, "The Study for Sustainable Regeneration in the Keihin Industrial Waterfront Area: Part2 The Study for Making Spatial Planning Method by the Researches by each fields and Typical Researches", Summaries of technical papers of Annual Meeting Architectural Institute of Japan. F-1, Urban planning, building economics and housing problems, p.227, 2006

[8] Tetsuo Yasutaka, "Quantification of economical and social effect from the soil contamination and its solution", PHD paper of Yokohama National University, 2006

[9] Ministry of Land, Infrastructure, Transport and Tourism, Japan, "City centre regeneration subcommittee report", 2005

[10] Ministry of Environment, Japan, "Annual Report on the Environment in Japan", 2007

[11] Ministry of Environment, Japan, "Current Status of the Brownfields Issue in Japan, Interim Report", 2007

Author Index